Career Paths of African American Directors

Career Paths of African American Directors is a collection of in-depth conversations with African American directors.

These conversations provide an insightful overview of the interviewees' work and artistic vision and explore their personal influences, aesthetic philosophies, directorial styles, and some of the creative successes they achieved while navigating the obstacles, challenges, and biases encountered while establishing their careers in American theatre. The directors are presented with similar core questions as well as pertinent questions related to their own aesthetics, philosophy, and career. Often, these selected directors' productions are grounded in a non-European aesthetic and philosophy, and their directorial styles are refracted through the prisms of ethnicity, gender, race, and culture, thus bringing a fresh approach to their work and the art of directing.

Career Paths of African American Directors will be of interest to actors, early career and established directors, and students of Acting, Directing, and Theatre Studies.

Saundra McClain is a theatre professional with more than fifty years of experience. She has performed in plays and musicals, many of them world premieres, on and off-Broadway, and at many notable theatres including The Kennedy Center, New York Shakespeare Festival, McCarter Theatre, A Noise Within, New Federal Theatre, Spoleto Festival, Alliance Theatre, and the Negro Ensemble Company. She also created many recurring and guest-starring roles in films and on television and acted in numerous commercials. A recipient of Ovation, LA Drama Critics, and NAACP Theatre nominations, amongst other awards, Ms. McClain is a member of the Stage Directors and Choreographers Society, Screen Actors Guild-American Federation Television and Radio Artists, and Actors Equity Association.

Clinton Turner Davis is a director, playwright, dramaturge, arts consultant, educator, literary manager, board member, casting director, production supervisor, actor, dancer, singer, and puppeteer who has collaborated with world-renowned artists in the United States and abroad. A recipient of the Lloyd Richards Directing Award from the National Black Theatre Festival and numerous national and international awards, Mr. Davis is a noted interpreter of the August Wilson canon. He has mentored many young and mid-career artists and has held residencies and guest-lectured at universities in the United States and Taiwan. A member of the Negro Ensemble Company for 16 seasons, and associate professor at Colorado College for 17 years, Mr. Davis is co-founder of one of the first organizations addressing diversity and inclusion issues in the performing arts.

Career Paths of African American Directors

Pushing Boundaries

SAUNDRA MCCLAIN AND CLINTON TURNER DAVIS

NEW YORK AND LONDON

Designed cover image: © Oleksandr Nagaiets/Shutterstock.com

First published 2024
by Routledge
605 Third Avenue, New York, NY 10158

and by Routledge
4 Park Square, Milton Park, Abingdon, Oxon, OX14 4RN

Routledge is an imprint of the Taylor & Francis Group, an informa business

© 2024 Saundra McClain and Clinton Turner Davis

The right of Saundra McClain and Clinton Turner Davis to be identified as authors of this work has been asserted in accordance with sections 77 and 78 of the Copyright, Designs and Patents Act 1988.

All rights reserved. No part of this book may be reprinted or reproduced or utilised in any form or by any electronic, mechanical, or other means, now known or hereafter invented, including photocopying and recording, or in any information storage or retrieval system, without permission in writing from the publishers.

Trademark notice: Product or corporate names may be trademarks or registered trademarks, and are used only for identification and explanation without intent to infringe.

ISBN: 978-1-032-42029-5 (hbk)
ISBN: 978-1-032-42028-8 (pbk)
ISBN: 978-1-003-41073-7 (ebk)

DOI: 10.4324/9781003410737

Typeset in Dante and Avenir
by Newgen Publishing UK

Every effort has been made to contact copyright holders. Please advise the publisher of any errors or omissions, and these will be corrected in subsequent editions.

Sherry Perry, as she was affectionately called, was my brilliant friend, my first mentor, and also my own personal fairy godmother. From our first meeting, she took me under her wing and doors opened. If I was not in one of her productions, I was assisting or observing rehearsals of other productions she directed. These were master classes unto themselves. Her talent, creativity, precision, discipline, integrity, and no-nonsense demeanor left an indelible imprint on my life and career. I was humbled when her daughter, Lorraine, told me I was their favorite babysitter because of the paper puppet shows we created and performed together. Shauneille was more than family, she was like a sister to me, plain and simple. She was my guiding star who always inspired me to do more. In her book, *Pearl, A Collection of Short Stories*, she wrote "To Saundra with Love & a Future, Shauneille."

—Saundra McClain

Figure 0.1 Photo by Saundra McClain.

Shauneille Perry, my first directing mentor in professional theatre, realized we were cut from the same cloth. The paths we traversed, over different years attending Howard University, were mentored by Owen Dodson. Our love of family and similar types of theatre made us appreciate those paths even more ... Your friendship and love had a profound effect upon me. Your insistence on precision and clarity when directing was challenging to many, but you persevered. I felt the heartwarming trust you placed in me when you asked me to babysit your children or housesit when you and Don took vacations. When you expressed your love of the caladiums we planted around your beautiful home, your smiles were almost identical to my mother's, my first mentor. I cherish our times together, the stimulating conversations, memories ... Thank you is not nearly enough. But it *is* what we have.

—Clinton Turner Davis

Contents

	Acknowledgments	ix
	Foreword	xi
	Preface	xv
1	*INTENSE:* An Interview with Saundra McClain	1
2	*CENTERED:* An Interview with Oz Scott	15
3	*DREAMER:* An Interview with Sheldon Epps	38
4	*JOYFUL:* An Interview with Shirley Jo Finney	50
5	*CONTENT:* An Interview with Clinton Turner Davis	63
6	*DEDICATED:* An Interview with Chuck Smith	79
7	*CURIOUS:* An Interview with Seret Scott	91
8	*SEEKER:* An Interview with A. Dean Irby	100
9	*NURTURING:* An Interview with Michele Shay	115

10	*TENACIOUS:* An Interview with Elizabeth Van Dyke	130
11	*INQUISITIVE:* An Interview with Gregg Daniel	143
12	*PRIDE:* An Interview with Ruben Santiago-Hudson	154
13	*EMPOWERMENT:* An Interview with George C. Wolfe	172
14	*GRATEFUL:* An Interview with Ricardo Khan	178
	Final Thoughts	203
	Biographies	205
	Glossary and Works Cited	213
	Index	219

Acknowledgments

Saundra McClain, a sincere thank you to:
Mark Ramont, my teacher and advisor whose professionalism and commitment to the art form helped me further appreciate works that did not always align with my own sensibility and experiences.

Maria Cominis, your recommendation and encouragement were instrumental to writing and publishing *Career Paths of African American Directors: Pushing Boundaries*.

My professors and classmates at CSU-Fullerton for challenging me to expand my creative universe.

Fernando Pacheco, your computer wizardry and technical assistance was invaluable and made the photo-editing process a breeze.

Phyllis Belisle, my neighbor, who, when things became overwhelming, helped transcribe the interviews.

My family, especially my son, Sean, and my grandchildren, whose unconditional love and support sustain me through the good and the bad.

My dear friends, colleagues, and fellow artists for just being there.

Clinton Turner Davis, I sincerely thank:
Adrienne Lanier Seward, my North Star and inspiration, I am humbled by your friendship, incisive eye, and abiding love.

Dr. Eleanor Traylor and Vera J. Katz, your mentorship and friendship combined with incisively honest, critical eyes set countless African

American theatre artists attending Howard University on paths to success.

Janice C. Lane whom I mentored and who has become an exceptional friend and sounding board, You truly understand the implications of "Cue One. Go."

Horacena J. Taylor, as the matriarch of my artistic family, you are more than a cousin. You opened many doors in theatre to me. Our ancestors are proud.

To my family and friends, fellow collaborators and conspirators, your support has provided stability. You comprehend the implications of "Watch the Skies" when uttered by your "Spirit Brother"—a nickname I cherish forever and all my days.

Foreword

The Black Theater artist and scholar, Henry D. Miller, outlined the development of dramaturgy and critical theory specific to Afro - American cultural and political points of view across the years 1898 to 1965, in his seminal book, *Theorizing Black Theatre*, and how important this was in the creation of a recognizable and codifiable canon of plays of, and specific to, Black Theater. Miller's work, as well as other great books by artists and scholars such as Lofton Mitchell, James Hatch, Ted Shine, Margaret Walker Alexander, or William Branch, for instance, rightly focus on the playwrights whose works illuminated the lives and souls of black folk in this wilderness of North America across the twentieth century and into these still early days of the twenty-first century.

The book you will read, however, looks at another set of theater artists—the Directors—whose suggestions to the playwright or whose visions/interpretations of the playwrights' work often served to help in defining the play, for better or for worse, in the eyes of the audiences that came to the theater to see the play performed. Oh, yes, make no mistake: nuance in an actor's performance, placements of lights, the ways in which actors are instructed to move about on stage, the "business" they are given to do when other actors are speaking, the line cuts, the need for additional lines to be inserted into the script, the need for additional *scenes*—all of these moments stem from the collaborative process between the Director and the Writer and thence between the Director and the Cast.

Black Theater has been as much the province of the "vision" of Directors as it has been of the Writers (and one can also throw in the judgments of Producers, but that is grist for another book). Black playwrights have given life to their ideas, dreams, and obsessions about the conditions of the lives and souls of African people across the Diaspora, but very often their visions have stopped as soon as they have written the words, "End of Play." Their eyes are soon wandering toward the next horizon, over which the next play resides.

Black Theater has grown and expanded in America because James Hewlett decided there needed to be an African Grove Theater where black actors could perform in the segregated New York of the 1820s, black musicals were born because Will Marion Cook, Bob Cole and later Sissle and Blake, in the early twentieth century, decided to make spaces for a new kind of interpretation of black life that could encapsulate the magic and power of African-American secular music. Their success inspired more efforts further afield, in academia, where Randolph Edmonds and Anne Cooke would emerge on the campuses of predominantly black colleges and universities, determined to train theatre artists who would devote themselves to the development of dramatic art based deeply in the "lives and culture of the Negro people."

Those efforts, as well as the emergence of new talent from beyond black college campuses and from within black communities themselves, would lead to the emergence of institutions like the American Negro Theater in New York during the 1940s, from which actor-writer-director Ossie Davis strode forth, or the Harlem Writers Guild, of the 1950s, which brought forth not only playwrights Lonnie Elder and the great Lorraine Hansberry, but also writer-director Douglas Turner Ward, co-founder of the Negro Ensemble Company. Rosetta Lenoire, AMAS Repertory, Vinette Carroll, Urban Arts Corp, Val Gray Ward in Chicago, C. Bernard Jackson, the Inner-City Cultural Center in Los Angeles, John Allen, the Freedom Theater in Philadelphia, John O'Neal, the Free Southern Theater, in New Orleans; all of them individuals with strong visions for spaces where theatre of black folk, by black folk, and for black folk could be performed for *everybody*—visions for spaces where the new ideas of new generations of black theatre artists might prosper.

And that brings us to more recent times where we now see black directors on Broadway, the mainstream of mainstream American theatre—Kenny Leon, Charles Randolph Wright, and Robert O'Hara, for instance—but also off-Broadway and in the regionals around the country, where other black directors are making their presence felt. This is important, this is part of the next big push in what is no longer a "new" century. The twenty-first century is nearing its 25-year mark. It is *the* century now. And whatever the national conversations about class, race, politics and *culture* are going to be, the parameters of those conversations are going to be determined by people born after 1980.

The visions of the black stage directors in these new conversational spaces will be more expansive: heterosexual, homosexual, non-binary and queer. The conversations they will have with the writers require change or, at the very least, be different, but on another level, they will be the same as the conversations with writers in the past. Directors and writers will *talk*—about the play, about the inspiration for the play, about subtext, about *structure* and theme and meaning. And they will sit up all night, drink too much, smoke too much, talk about each other behind each other's backs, complain about each other to their lovers, over re-writes, or not enough re-writes, or too many re-writes, or any other myriad number of things that complicate, occupy, strain to the breaking point, and ultimately come to define one of the most complex, satisfying, maddening, rewarding, taxing and contentious (it is what you make it), relationships in show business: the director-writer collaborative process.

This book is a collection of reminisces, thoughts, remarks, and musings of black directors across generations who have struggled, succeeded, failed, and struggled and succeeded some more, in trying to wrangle this wild beast of a cultural phenomenon known as Black Theatre into submission. They all have different perspectives, different memories of some of the same events. What they have in common, however, is love of Theatre, love of *Black* Theatre and that insatiable need to step back into the white-hot furnace of Creative Spark and do that "Fire Dance" just one more time.

—Richard Wesley

Preface

The 1970s were a very fertile time throughout the country for African American theatre and its artists. Propelled by creative energies and passions generated by the Black Arts Movement, many future theatre directors who actively participated in the civil rights movement's sit-ins and demonstrations began seeking other outlets for creative expression. Combined with impassioned responses to the assassinations of Martin Luther King, Jr., and other civil rights leaders, African American directors began stepping into paths that would lead them to successful and often inspired careers.

Howard University in Washington, DC, New York University's Tisch School of the Arts, Columbia College in Chicago, Dillard University in New Orleans, Yale University in New Haven, Rutgers University's Mason Gross School of the Arts in Newark, and Carnegie Mellon in Pittsburgh, among others, were primary institutions providing initial training for many envisioning a future in the arts. These schools, some of which were HBCU's, had become destinations for black students enthusiastic about careers in theatre. The list of faculty members at these institutions reads as Who's Who in education and performance in American theatre.

Educators at these institutions included Lloyd Richards, Owen Dodson, Theodore Ward, Loften Mitchell, Glenda Dickerson, Vera J. Katz, Paul Carter Harrison, and Israel Hicks. They, and many others, became early mentors to the 14 African American directors included in *Career Paths of African American Directors: Pushing Boundaries*. Some of these directors began as actors, others as playwrights, or stage managers. The possibilities of sustained employment seemed limitless as these directors began taking risks in pursuit of new, often unexplored artistic realities.

In the middle of the Great Depression, Negro Theatre Units in New York, Boston, Hartford, Philadelphia, Birmingham, Los Angeles, Raleigh, Newark, and Chicago, et al., were established. These units provided a strong foundation for future theaters and institutions. Karamu House (1915) in Cleveland became the home of one of these Negro Theatre Units and survives to this day.

The companies listed below with their founding dates are some of dynamic institutions that provided and continue to provide training for black actors, playwrights, technicians, administrators, and directors. Consistently producing new African American plays was and remains a component of these institutions' missions. The directing opportunities for young African American artists grew rapidly. The exciting new that were produced by these institutions required a strong directorial eye. These black theatres created "artistic homes" for black artists long before the idea had been conceived and welcomed by established American theatres. A new era of black theatre in America was rapidly manifesting itself.

New Heritage Repertory (1964)
New Freedom ('66)
New Lafayette Theatre (')
Inner-City Cultural Center ('67)
Urban Arts Corps ('67)
Kuumba Theatre Workshop ('68)
National Black Theatre ('68)
Negro Ensemble Company ('68)
Richard Allen Center for Culture & Art ('69)
Black Arts/West ('69)
Black Spectrum Theatre ('70)
New Federal Theatre ('70)
Black Theatre Troupe ('70)
DC Black Repertory Company ('71)
Billie Holiday Theatre ('72)
Ensemble Studio Theatre ('76)

Oakland Ensemble Theatre ('76)
St. Louis Black Rep ('76)
Black Ensemble Theater ('76)
Crossroads Theatre ('78)
North Carolina Black Rep ('79)

In the late 1960s and throughout the '70s, African American theatres and artistic communities grew locally and nationally into a tightly knit, exhilarating family of "creatives." These artists and institutions supported each other as they pursued their dreams, provided "sounding boards" when disappointments transpired, exchanged personnel and technical assistance, and consistently challenged each other to grow. A tremendous sense of competition and camaraderie was apparent.

Career Paths of African American Directors: Pushing Boundaries explores many of the achievements and successes, both critical and popular, the interviewed black directors have experienced. With creative processes and productions often grounded in a non-European aesthetic or philosophy, fresh and innovative approaches to theatre are present in their work. These interviews provide insights into their influences, training, aesthetic philosophies, visions, and directorial styles.

The 14 African American directors interviewed here, have helmed numerous productions presented by American theatres from the 1970s to the present. These interviews reveal how they successfully navigated the challenges and biases encountered while expanding the contributions of black artists and their works in the American theatre. Several directors have served as artistic or resident directors at major theatres; others as educators on the faculties of colleges and universities across the country. All are "multi-hyphenates"—artists who have established careers in the arts not solely limited to directing theatre. As actors, playwrights, poets, managers, administrators, and producers, these directors have worked in every aspect of the theatre and entertainment industries.

Career Paths of African American Directors: Pushing Boundaries provides compelling context for a consequential group of artists who continually challenge and reshape American theatre.

INTENSE 1
An Interview with Saundra McClain

Clinton Turner Davis: I first met you in the Theatre De Lys where you were rehearsing *Black Girl* by J. E. Franklin. My cousin, Horacena J. Taylor, was stage managing and Shauneille Perry was the director.

Saundra McClain: That was my first off-Broadway show. Seems like another lifetime ago. If I knew then what I know now … .

Interview With Saundra McClain

> CTD: As a mother, doting grandmother, painter, actor, singer, writer, musician, *and* director somehow you have found a way to balance your passions without denying any of them.
> SMcC: Yipes! I sound like a crazy person. It's a juggling act for sure and I am never bored. I just enjoy being creative. I remember as a kid, my mother thought she was punishing me by sending me to my room. Hah, if she only knew! I could always find a way to entertain myself. Which is probably why I enjoy directing so much. I get to play all the parts in my head.
> CTD: What was your motivation to write *Pushing Boundaries*?
> SMcC: I had to select a topic for my graduate thesis. It was the early days of COVID, and most of the country was still in quarantine. I decided to create one-on-one interviews via Zoom

DOI: 10.4324/9781003410737-1

2 *INTENSE*: An Interview with Saundra McClain

Figure 1.1 Photo by Brianna K. Bryan.

with African American directors I respected and admired. Since we were all long-time friends, the conversations were candid. We discussed the challenges, biases, and obstacles they had encountered, as well as their successes, accomplishments, and disappointments. When I submitted my project book for review, Maria Cominis, my advisor, was impressed and asked me to submit a proposal to her publisher. This stopped me dead in my tracks.

CTD: Why do you say that?

SMcC: Writing a thesis as a graduate requirement was one thing; writing a book to submit for publishing was a horse of a different color.

CTD: To my knowledge, there is no book that focuses on African American directors.

SMcC: Exactly. Or reveals the accomplishments of these directors, particularly when refracted through the prisms of ethnicity, gender, race, and culture. Which is why I contacted you, Clinton. Your interview for my graduate thesis, *The Career Paths of Eight Contemporary Black Directors*, was different and unique. Your insight and individual journey in this wacky business intrigued me. I was overjoyed when you agreed to undertake this opus with me. To paraphrase the last line in *Casablanca* " ... I think that was the beginning of a beautiful friendship" or should I say "collaboration." (*We laugh.*)

CTD: When did your interest in theatre begin?

SMcC: I distinctly remember directing and choreographing my first show in the first grade for the annual school bazaar. Throughout my early childhood, I put together shows to celebrate holidays or raise money to feed stray cats. I was in a ballet before I started school and was in toe shoes at six. All the girls in my family had to learn to play piano. I played flute in my high school orchestra and in the college marching band. I was in the glee club and the drama club also. I was the go-to kid to write or direct projects to help raise social awareness for groups like the Black Student League, CORE, and sorority fundraisers. As a freshman at Temple University, my first show was *Guys and Dolls*. I played Mimi, a "Hot Box Girl." I still remember my lines! Theatre intrigued me but it was just a hobby, something to do for fun. I majored in Chemistry and was going to be a scientist. But math was not my strong suit, so Calculus and Physics cured me of that illusion quick.

CTD: When did your interest in theatre shift from being a hobby?

SMcC: I was a stand-in for the film, *The Lost Man* starring Sidney Poitier. One night in between takes, I asked the actor, Al Freeman Jr. "What do I need to do to get into this business?" He bluntly replied: "The first thing you need to do is get the hell out of Philadelphia."

CTD: Where did you go?

SMcC: New York of course. I landed a very prestigious job at NBC, working for *Johnny Carson's Tonight Show* as Asst. Talent Coordinator. Fast-forward to 1971, I overheard that auditions were being held for the off-Broadway production, *Black Girl* by J. E. Franklin. A woman sitting in the box office of the Theatre de Lys eating a tuna fish sandwich gave me a copy of the sides and told me to come back at 2 pm. When I arrived for the audition, I was surprised to discover that the woman turned out to be the director, Shauneille Perry. For some reason, I took off my shoes, went on stage, and auditioned. Ms. Perry approached the stage and asked if I had seen the show before. I said "No." Shocked, she said, "You just did the exact blocking of the scene." I got the job and that was the beginning of our long and wonderful association.

CTD: Please elaborate.

SMcC: In addition to performing off-Broadway in *Prodigal Sister* and *Celebration*, I assisted Shauneille on several productions. I directed her one-act plays, *Clinton* and *Mio*, and most of her children's plays at Henry Street Settlement and the Billie Holiday Theatre. Shauneille was my first mentor and that one friend who convinced me to return to school in '93. She was a hard taskmaster and graded me an A *minus* because she said, "You can do better." In fact, it was Shauneille who said, "You are a stronger director than you are an actor." My ego never quite knew how to take that. But she always cast me.

CTD: What was the first production you directed in New York?

SMcC: I stayed under the radar, directing productions for youth and family audiences until I directed *Dark of the Moon* with a cast of 23 actors/singers/dancers and five musicians in the Experimental Theatre at Henry Street. All the sound and musical underscoring was composed by the actors themselves. The show was magical, performing to sold-out houses, remounted, and extended twice. Jonathan Ward, who was the director of Urban Youth Theatre, hired me as a teacher and workshop leader to direct several one-acts and children's plays at Henry Street Settlement. At this time in my life, directing was a hobby ... something I did when I was "between shows" as an actor.

However, I did start to dabble into writing. The period between 1990–2005 was an intense time of exploration. I felt limited in the roles I was offered. I submitted some of my work to BMI's Musical Theatre Workshop. My first musical, *Storm Warning*, with music by Donna Lynn Burns, received development grants from the National Endowment for the Arts, and others, and was presented in the ASCAP's Musical Theatre Workshop. A workshop production, directed by George Faison, starring Tamara Tunie, Debye Burrell, and Priscilla Baskerville, was presented at the Public Theatre. My second musical, *Caribe*, with music composed by Kysia (Kathryn) Bostic was workshopped in "New Visions, New Voices" at the Kennedy Center, as well as Disney/ASCAP Musical Theatre Workshop in Los Angeles. I am adapting *Caribe* into a series of children's books and pitching it to producers as an animated film, *Peepo and the Magic Talisman*.

CTD: What is one of the early memorable experiences you had as a director?

SMcC: My most rewarding experience was a project I created and developed with the Urban Youth Theatre at Henry Street Settlement. In 1991, during the excavation of land for a Federal Government office building, workers unearthed an African burial ground. After an exhibit had been created at the memorial site, I took my students, ages nine to thirteen, to view the remains of 419 Africans and over five hundred individual artifacts. Their assignment was to choose an artifact, imagine who the original owner was, then write a scene, a monologue, or a poem which incorporated the artifact into a story. Using the students' writings and original music, we created *Don't See My Bones and Think I am Dead*, choreographed by Dyane Harvey with music arrangements by Timothy Graphenreed. The production, which was a series of vignettes woven together, was moving and well received. We remounted our production for PBS as a part of their *Africans in America* series. Even with all the attention and reviews, I still did not pursue directing as a viable career option.

CTD: Why?

SMcC: I was an established actor with several Broadway shows under my belt. I made numerous guest appearances and had recurring roles on TV, even a few film roles, and scores of commercials. As a single parent, I had to be practical. Acting paid the bills. Directing did not. The roles I was auditioning for were becoming more and more predictable and non-challenging. When I thought I had my star vehicle, I didn't. The near misses went on ad infinitum.

CTD: Your infectious sense of humor and laughter is well known to fill and warm a room. So how did you deal with these disappointments?

SMcC: As an actor, I always felt I was seeking approval, either my own or that of the audience. But as a director, I had control and was not concerned with receiving approval or validation of my artistic expression. Directing allowed me to break free of the boxes in which I had been placed. I always tease my actors that, as the director, I get to play *all* of the roles in my head.

I co-founded a multicultural theatre company, Troupe NY, Inc. TNY employed a diverse group of very talented actors. We adapted and directed classic works for schools in NY, as well as Youth and Family programs at the Kennedy Center. One of my favorites was *Death of a Salesman*. I had to cut the show to one hour to accommodate school schedules. I cast an African American, Count Stovall, as Willie Loman opposite an Asian wife, Wai Ching Ho. Their sons were mixed race. Willie's boss was white and his successful neighbor was black. Without changing the plot or the author's original intention, the actors had to adjust their characters and bring a new truth to Arthur Miller's classic. The audiences were riveted.

CTD: That's a very interesting path you were on. What school did *you* attend?

SMcC: I attended Temple University in the late '60s, moved to New York and pursued an acting career. Twenty-five years later, I attended Hunter College and graduated from Lehman College, majoring in Theatre. During the '90s, I began to accept directing jobs, but mostly in children's theatre, so I would not be seen as a "threat" to established directors in NY.

My first Equity production was *Spunk* at Two River Theatre in NJ in 2001. The artistic director, Jonathan Fox, upon the recommendation of Shauneille Perry, interviewed me for the job. I vaguely remember giving a conceptual interpretation of the play, leaning on my past experience and understanding working with George Wolfe on his previous productions, *The Colored Museum* and *Queenie Pie*. After collaborating with set designer Harry Feiner, who was then chair of the Theatre and Dance Department at Queens College, I was offered a position teaching Acting, I also created a Black Theatre Workshop course. The second semester, I directed a devised theatre piece. To enrich the play and give more student actors opportunity to perform, I brought elements and characters from both the Euripides and Giraudoux versions into my production of Sophocles' *Electra*. I borrowed Euripides' Furies to "stir the plot" as they weaved in and out of the scenes. The long monologue describing the chariot race was brought to life with choreography by Byron Easley.

I joined the SDC and began accepting directorial assignments at Two River Theatre, Playhouse on the Green, the Lark Theatre, the Cherry Lane Theatre and Kennedy Center. I also wrote nightclub acts for fellow performers and directed performance pieces, such as *Of Ebony Embers* with Akin Babatunde and *Harriet Returns* with Denise Burse Fernandez, written by Karen Jones-Meadows. Both of these plays toured for over five years.

CTD: **Shortly after, you disappeared from the New York/East Coast theatre scene. Where did you go?**

SMcC: In 2006, I gave up my Manhattan Plaza apartment and moved to California to be near my grandchildren. I figured my career would be a direct segue, but LA and NY are two different animals. As an actor, Father Time was not on my side. And in California, theatre is treated like the stepchild of the entertainment business. My New York agents at Bret Adams Ltd. helped me secure a manager, Chris Black at Opus Entertainment. Between them and my commercial agents at CESD, I have managed to keep my feet in the business.

CTD: **When did you receive your first directing job?**

SMcC: Jonathan Fox, who gave me my start at Two River Theatre, is now artistic director of Ensemble Theatre Company in Santa Barbara. He was the first to hire me. Since then, I have directed at colleges and performing arts schools all over Southern California, and for many theaters including the Colony, International City Theatre, Main Street Playhouse, A Noise Within, Sierra Madre Playhouse, and at least eight productions at ETC, including *The Fantasticks, In the Continuum, Frankie and Johnny in the Clare de Lune, Intimate Apparel,* and *Dancing Lessons*.

CTD: Why did you interrupt your career to go back to school?

SMcC: I noticed during tech rehearsals in both *Intimate Apparel* and *Dancing Lessons*, the climaxes I orchestrated did not land the way I wanted. What did I miss during my script preparation? Friends teased me about why I felt I needed an MFA so late in my career: I replied, "I don't need it, I want it!" The validation that said not only was I experienced, but also qualified. Going to college as a septuagenarian was not an easy decision. My classmates were the same age as my grandchildren. I worked twice as hard to keep up. This new generation had new ideas and concepts about life. They saw the world through a different lens.

CTD: How were your approaches to directing changed or enhanced?

SMcC: Many thanks to my professors. I no longer rely solely on my instincts and experiences. I have achieved a better understanding of the importance of script analysis and the language of collaboration. I will never have difficulty landing a climactic moment again. My classes expanded my artistic vision. I have a greater appreciation for plays by authors such as Ibsen, Brecht, Churchill, Francis Ya-Chu Cowhig, Suzan-Lori Parks, Edward Albee, or Adrienne Kennedy.

During the COVID epidemic, I was forced to direct a devised theatre piece via Zoom. Because school was closed, I came up with the idea of a series of monologues and vignettes, written by an ensemble of students in the Theatre department. I entitled it, *The Quarantine Memoirs*. Each scene chronicled the day-to-day experiences and isolation of the students in the early days of COVID. The project was so successful, the school received an extensive grant for me to develop and direct *Living Six Feet Apart*, which won seven Kennedy Center American College Theatre Festival Awards in 2021, including Best Direction. Both projects were rehearsed, directed, shot, and edited totally on Zoom. We added original music, a sound track, and stock footage to enhance the film quality. Kudos to students, Abel Marquez (AD), and Fernando Pacheco, also a student, who was my sound, video, and technical director. What we were able to accomplish under extraordinary circumstances can be viewed on my website or YouTube.

CTD: What types of works are you drawn to?

SMcC: I love musicals with a pink and purple passion. Being in charge and playing with all the elements of music, dance, and drama. Not to mention, the technical elements of sets, lights, sound, and costume. It's like conducting a symphony where the orchestral instruments get out of their seats to sing and dance. I especially enjoy directing plays by black authors from throughout the diaspora who are telling "our stories." I also find works by women playwrights most inspiring. I am drawn to universal stories that are not afraid to be honest and move me and the audience emotionally and spiritually.

Figure 1.2 *Intimate Apparel* by Lynn Nottage, Ensemble Theatre Company, 2015; Karole Foreman and A. K. Murtadha. Photo by David Bazemore.

CTD: What have been your most rewarding experiences as a director?

SMcC: People often ask me, what's my favorite production. I always say, "The one I happen to be working on now." I literally fall in love with every cast. It's difficult to let go and allow the show to live on without me on opening night. I think my all-time faves are *Don't See My Bones and Think I am Dead*, *Intimate Apparel*, *The Play That Goes Wrong* in the Garvin Theatre at Santa Barbara City College, and *Spring Awakening* at University Southern California.

CTD: How would you describe your approach to directing or your directing philosophy?

SMcC: As a director, I don't really prescribe to any particular approach or philosophy. I am totally open and allow my imagination time to dream up the world for the characters the author has created. I rarely have a preconceived idea of what a character should look like. What's important to me are the choices actors make and whether they fit the overall concept of the play.

I believe it is my duty to make sure all the elements of the play work in harmony. Casting to me is like orchestrating a symphony. The timbre of the actors' voices needs to work harmoniously with each other. I am in search of an actor's unique cultural and personal perspective. As opposed to color blind, *color conscious* casting allows the actor to dig deeper into the character's truth while still being true to the author's intent of the role.

When describing the world of the play to designers, I lean toward the sensual, the feeling I wish to evoke, more so than the specific. I imagine the world the play inhabits. I have been thoroughly surprised when the set design is totally different than what I envisioned. Before I say, "No," I listen to see where the designer is going … where their vision of the play meets mine. Collaboration is key. I tend to direct cinematically. My scene changes are staged as part of the action of the play. Unless it is for a dramatic reason, I avoid blackouts like the plague. I love levels and always have preliminary discussions with my set designer regarding entrances and exits, sightlines and does the design include a crossover. You'd be surprised how many theaters lack built-in crossovers.

I had the opportunity to direct *Bee-luther-hatchee* by Thomas Gibbons, twice: at Sierra Madre Theatre and again at CSU-Fullerton upon the requests of students who studied the play in the Theatre for Social Change class I taught the previous year. The whole concept revolved around the premise "who has the right to tell our stories." Since the story is not plot driven as much as thought provoking, the challenge was to keep the play moving. Not let the audience get ahead. A very intellectual play, it would be so easy to just let the actors get comfortable, sit down, and just talk ... boring. They need to create the world of the play, live the story, and not just tell it.

Every scene and monologue in the play was workshopped during rehearsal as if they were little plays unto themselves connected via transitions, overlaps, intermingling, coexistence, whatever. The script is the road map, but the little excursions and transitions were created and explored along the way.

I communicated to my designers that I wanted a seamless, but separate quality between the real world, circa 2000, and the memory aspect of the play, which is not actually memory but fantasized in Shelita's mind. And it is not until Act 2 that the fantasy is dropped and reality comes into focus.

I felt the more the creative team could support and make this happen, the more fascinating the production would be. Lights, sound, costumes, props, and the set all played an equal part in conveying the message. But the "Wow Factor" was the concept surrounding "cultural appropriation" ... the dilemma the characters find themselves in.

The playscript, like a film script, travels to many different locations. The scrim, influenced by the artwork of Aaron Douglas, who was the most prominent artist-illustrator of the Harlem Renaissance, separated these two worlds. And like graffiti art on the sides of building, the words and images of black authors depicted on the set represented the history of their work which has been suppressed or overlooked by mainstream society or white America. It's a subliminal message that becomes more apparent to the audience as the story progresses.

I remember driving home after rehearsal and noticing the faded colors of the mountains in the distance at dusk. They reminded me of the faded words of the black authors which had been lost through time.

CTD: Do you select your designers for productions? Have you ever sent a designer "back to the drawing board"?

SMcC: Given the opportunity, I prefer choosing my own designers. There are some designers I have worked with several times—Jared Sayeg, Dianne Graebner, Dave Mickey, Harry Feiner, J. R. Bruce, John Iacovelli, Fernando Pacheco—not only because they are good but because we have developed a creative shorthand. I can speak my mind without bruising egos. I remember *Spunk* by George C. Wolfe, based on the writings of Zora Neale Hurston. This was my first of five productions I did with set designer, Harry Feiner. It wasn't until his third proposed design for *Spunk* that I finally said, "Yes, this works for me."

His creative use of textures and levels, combined with evocative locations captured the thematic essence and the world of *Spunk*. Harry, along with lighting design by Shirley Prendergast, made *Spunk* a director's dream on which to play.

CTD: Have you ever accepted directing projects that frightened you?

SMcC: I was very leery about directing *The Play That Goes Wrong*. I had never directed anything like it previously. The plot was simple. The stage directions were extremely physical and technically dangerous if not well choreographed. I decided to accept the challenge. I requested Edgar Landa, an excellent stunt coordinator/fight director. We put safety first because the show was so physical. The only injury incurred was a splinter during tech. From first rehearsal to closing night, working with this cast and crew was a blast.

CTD: What one word would you use to describe yourself?

Figure 1.3 *Spunk* by George C. Wolfe, Two River Theatre, 2003; l. to r.: Byron Easley, Charles Wallace, Alvin Keith, Shirley Prendergast (lighting). Photo by Harry Feiner (set designer).

SMcC: Oh that's easy … Intense. People often think I am angry. I am not, I'm just very passionate about what I do.

CTD: What advice would you give to your younger self?

SMcC: Don't just aim for the moon, you might come up short. Reach for the stars! Trust your instincts. Sometimes the shortest distance between two points is the path of least resistance. Everything does not have to be a challenge. Take time to enjoy the moment you are in, the here and the now. The Past is past. If you truly live in the Present, you will help the Future take care of itself. Oh, and never give up your power or belief in yourself.

CTD: What is your definition of success?

SMcC: I take pride in my work and always strive to do my best. However, I feel there is so much more I want to do. I guess I measure my success by the continued joy I experience in my work, the quality time I spend with my family and friends, my bills getting paid on time and having enough left over each month to sock away for my grandchildren's future and my own prosperity.

CTD: What is your legacy?

SMcC: That's a loaded question, Clinton. I feel my legacy is more than just money accumulated or the intellectual property I leave behind. My legacy is the positive difference I have made in the lives of others. And the positive role model I try to be for my son, my grandchildren, the young people I mentor and all the generations that follow.

CTD: *Pushing Boundaries* is an integral and very significant part of that legacy, Saundra. By collaborating on *Pushing Boundaries: Career Paths of African American Directors* ... we have come full circle.

CENTERED   2

An Interview with Oz Scott

SMcC: Oz describes himself as calm and centered, and indeed he is—at least on the outside. Oz kept his career goals close to his vest. Until one day, a poetry project became the darling of off-Broadway.

CTD: *For Colored Girls Who Have Considered Suicide When the Rainbow Is Enuf* by Ntozake Shange moved to Broadway and ran for over two years!

SMcC: We affectionately call him his "Wiz-ness" or "Papa Bear" because he and his wonderful wife, Lynne, an artist and sculptor in her own right, keep "our theatre family" together and in touch.

Interview With Oz Scott

SMcC: Oz, how old were you when you saw your first play?

Oz Scott: OMG, you just took me way back. I was playing a professor in a third-grade play. I remember walking on stage and having my hat knocked off immediately when I came through the curtain, and my brother said, "You just kept on going." That was the beginning. But when I talk about theatre, what really inspired me—I had a teacher, Mrs. Morgenstern, who had a theatre appreciation class in my high school in

16 CENTERED: An Interview with Oz Scott

Figure 2.1 Photo by Oz Scott.

Mt. Vernon and I don't know if it was the 10th grade or 11th grade, but she took us to Broadway plays.

SMcC: **I remember you mentioning that before.**

OS: That year, I saw Christopher Plummer in *Royal Hunt of the Sun* and Hal Holbrook's *Mark Twain*. I saw the original *Man of La Mancha*. It was in a Quonset Hut-style theater, ANTA Theatre in Washington Square where the NYU library was built, and the original production on Broadway of *Marat Sade*. That same year could my mother took me to the final Broadway performance of *A Hand is on the Gate* directed by Roscoe Lee Brown with Cicely Tyson, Moses Gun, and Ellen Holly—fascinating, in which the play of poetry really took me there … was so much coming at me at one time. Then in my high school theatre group during 10th, 11th, and 12th grade, I was in *Li'l Abner* as General Bull Moose, and *The Fantasticks*. I was doing a lot of plays. When I went to college, I performed in *R.U.R.* I also directed and acted in *Dutchman*.

I did a lot of theatre when I was in college. I started at Friends World College, in Westbury, Long Island, where we would study and travel all around the world; I did six months in Mexico. I was supposed to go to Africa but transferred to Marlboro College in Vermont, which had a great theatre program.

SMcC: Wait a minute, how many colleges did you go to?

OS: Hated college but I liked the schools I went to with Friends World College; when I was in Mexico I attended Universidad de Michoacan, then I went to Marlboro College and Antioch where I graduated. I ended up at NYU.

SMcC: So why did you go to school?

OS: Stay off the street.

SMcC: No, seriously.

OS: Seriously.

SMcC: Ha-ha, how bad was the street in Mt. Vernon back in the day ... ?

OS: Mt. Vernon could be really bad. However, when I say getting off the street, I mean you go to college, or you get a job.

SMcC: In Mt. Vernon?

OS: Well, Mt. Vernon, that's a whole 'nother story. When I was at Antioch, it was a Work Study Program. When I went there the work study was "we gotta get you a job, so you're working and studying at the same time." I ended up working for this theatre company called Back Alley Theatre doing whatever they needed. Production assistant, intern type of things. I helped find one of the theaters that they moved into for a number of years.

And then I went over to The Living Stage at Arena Stage, which was an improvisational theatre company where we took to the streets. We went to daycare centers, schools, rehab facilities, prisons, and performed improvisational theatre. I worked with great actors like Teddy Wilson—you remember Teddy Wilson?—he starred in *Sanford Arms*. He was married to Anita Wilson—his wife was an actress from way back when. We had some really great actors. Louise Robinson was in that company, she's in Sweet Honey in the Rock. It was a great experience being the stage manager, especially when I had to give notes on performances—the director wouldn't come out on the road with us, so it was me. I was up there giving notes at the end of the performance, saying, "I don't know how you made that transition." "I didn't feel it." "It wasn't organic." So, I was giving notes on improvs, and I did that for two years and it helped me as a director. I was also the utility actor. We had two men and three women and when we needed a third man, I'd get out there with them. I did all the improv rehearsals with them as well as sweeping the floors, setting up, tearing down, and driving the truck with our equipment and cast in it. I was doing everything as well as acting in it. And when I say I was rehearsing with them, we did eight weeks, six-day weeks of intense improvisational workshops. One week we did overnight rehearsals. Intense. I rehearsed with everyone, but one of my other jobs was to find a place for us to go have breakfast when we finished.

One great moment was when Kirk Young and I were acting in a scene. I played his son in an improv. We were going at it. Deep into it. The other actors were afraid we were getting lost in the parts. They had to stop the scene. We both sort of snapped out of it. I always talk about how actors walk that fine line of insanity. That was definitely one of those moments.

SMcC: I like that line. "A fine line of insanity."

OS: I remember, at the O'Neill, I asked this actress to do something—this Texas girl—she took my direction, and I watched her step over that line into "insanity" and come back. Scared me to death. She turned to me and asked, "Was that what you were talking about?" I just stared at her and said, "Yeah."

I try to stay current. I was still taking acting classes as of ten years ago. One teacher was asking me, "What's the best thing that ever happened to you and what's the worst thing? Visualize that." It was right when my mother was dying ... After I'd been in about two classes doing that, I said, "Nah. Not right now. I can't do this. I don't want to go there." And I left that class.

SMcC: How did you end up in stage management?

OS: At Arena Stage—I went from the kid sweeping up not getting paid just to be there. I was in the right place at the right time. The stage manager fell out and they needed a new stage manager. "Hey kid, you want to be our stage manager?" I said yes. I was a stage manager for two years at Arena Stage. After that I came to NY as an actor and I was out there auditioning. I ended up at NYU and I even stage managed for James Earl Jones. A few years ago, I was backstage when he was playing "Big Daddy." What's the name of that play he did with Terrence Howard?

SMcC: *Cat on a Hot Tin Roof.*

OS: Yeah, *Cat on a Hot Tin Roof*. I went backstage to talk to him. Celeste Holm was there. James Earl turned to Celeste and said, "This is Oz Scott. I directed one play in my life and Oz Scott was back there telling all the actors what to do because I didn't have a clue." Soooo, since he said it, I thought it was okay to talk about it. I was always directing; I was back there reworking the actors.

While I was at NYU, Edgar White came in as Playwright-in-Residence for a semester. I stage managed a play that he did at NYU. That summer he was going to tour the streets with his play *La Gente* for Joe Papp—for the Public Theatre. He called me up to meet him at Joe's office. We walked into Joe Papp's office, and he said, "Okay, I'm going to do these plays, but I want Oz Scott as my stage manager."

SMcC: What year was that?

OS: '73. And I was still at NYU. That summer I stage managed a play for Edgar White. Each act was an hour-and-a-half long. Dennis Tate directed one act, Carla Pinza directed the second act, and I was the stage manager for this whole three-hour extravaganza. Dennis Tate would get up in the middle of rehearsal and say, "I'm going out for a smoke." And I say, "Dennis, we're in the middle of rehearsal." And he'd say, "Just keep rehearsing." "But Dennis, we're getting ready to block the big funeral procession" and he'd say, "Well, block it. I'll be back." And he went out for about half an hour to 45 minutes. Now remember I was only like 20, 21 and with a bunch of veteran actors with major "personalities." So, I was like, "Okay, guys, let's do this." When he came back I showed him what I did and he said, "Good. Let's move on." Remember Dennis Tate?

SMcC: Oh yeah.

OS: So, after that Joe just kept me there. They put me on Shakespeare in the Park's *Merry Wives of Windsor* and several plays for Edgar White. I worked for the Public all during my second year at NYU and in the summers. And then I went on to *The Black Picture Show* at Lincoln Center with Bill Gunn! One term that last year at NYU, my stage-managing class was at 6:00 pm on a Friday evening when I was stage managing at the Public. I missed class for an entire semester. Lloyd Burlingame, who was head of the Design Department, gave me an "F" because I was not coming to stage managing class. But every Saturday morning, I would go sit with this major Broadway stage manager who was our teacher and talk for two hours with him. Every Saturday. So that was my class.

SMcC: Did they change your grade?

OS: Yeah, they changed my grade. My teacher had given me an "A," but Lloyd overruled him and gave me an "F." Danielle DeMers, who was the administrator, said, "You all need to straighten this out!" She gave me a "C" and said, "Don't worry about it." So, it worked out. Though I deserved the "A."

SMcC: You went to NYU for Theatre but what was your major focus?

OS: Directing. At that point, NYU School of the Arts had a Theatre Directing Program.

SMcC: Did you have mentors?

OS: Gil Moses, Novella Nelson. It eventually ended up being Lloyd Richards. I did the O'Neill in '78; Lloyd had me coming back a second year but a month before we started, I was offered a film by Universal, so I didn't return to the O'Neill. I went off to Hollywood to do *Busting Loose*. Lloyd was a bit upset with me for leaving, so in the '80s, he didn't hire me at all. 1990 came around and I found out that Edith Oliver and Skip Mercier got on Lloyd to bring me back, so I was there for the entire '90s.

SMcC: The O'Neill Playwrights Festival, right?

OS: Yeah, at the Eugene O'Neill Playwright's Conference. Lloyd was special. One summer he gave me four plays to do. One a week. He taught me a lot. Just being around him. One critique I got … a writer who I thought had written a great first act but got scared in the second act. I got mad. Lloyd brought me into his office and said, "You are a big imposing man. When you get mad, people will get scared. Be careful." I went to the writer and apologized. Two years later, he called up and said, "Since you apologized, not saying you were right, but I found my second act." Great lesson.

As mentors go, I think in some ways Joe Papp was definitely somebody that I looked up to. When I was stage managing at the Public, I remember Gilbert Moses telling me that Joe is watching you. I said that Joe doesn't know that I exist, he said, "Joe knows you." And I said, "No, he doesn't." And he said, "Joe knows everything that happens at that theater. If you're sneaking in there and rehearsing another play, Joe knows."

SMcC: Do you prefer scripted shows or concept shows?

Figure 2.2 Oz Scott with Ntozake Shange, author of *For Colored Girls Who Have Considered Suicide/When the Rainbow Is Enuf*. Photo is courtesy of Temple University.

OS: I'm probably more of a concept person because of things like Ntozake's *For Colored Girls* ... I think my improv experience led me towards concepts. The last play that Zake and I did together was out here in LA at the Mark Taper in one of their small spaces. It didn't go over well. My concern was that Zake was getting too much into politics in her writing and away from her personal life that I thought was her writing strength, you know, like her childhood or being a young Black woman in America. She was trying to get global.

SMcC: What was the most rewarding experience you've had as a director?

OS: Oh, you know, I keep having those rewarding experiences. It's always the last thing I do. I just enjoy myself. Doing *SWAT* the past two months was enjoyable. I had a great crew—one challenge during COVID was how do you keep people six feet apart and make it look like they're up close and personal? So, for me it's always these little challenges. *For Colored Girls* ... was special. *Cheetah Girls* was great!

Busting Loose was pure concept because Richard Pryor and I improvised the entire script. When I showed up at Universal, they handed me the script and said, "Oz, rewrite it." I was 27, 28 years old and I'm like, "Okay." So, while I was rewriting, I had finished the first draft, I took a walk; when I got back to the office the line producer had grabbed the script off my desk. I had only done a first pass—he had it published and sent it upstairs. It was approved and off we went to do the film. So, my rewrites were on the day of filming with Richard. We'd just sit up there and make up stuff.

SMcC: Have you ever been on a project that frightened you, yet you took it anyway? How did you combat that fear?

OS: I think I kind of live in stress. Everything I go into I panic a little bit because I want to get it perfect. I want to make it great. So, I believe there are a lot of times I do that. When Ellis Haizlip gave me my first television break, he said, "Okay here is the World Saxophone Quartet with David Murray, Julius Hemphill, Oliver Lake, and Hamiet Bluiett. You're going to direct it." I said "Okay, let's do it!" But I was totally terrified.

Ellis gave me free rein. I mean he just sat there and let me run it. I took those reins and said "I want to do it in four sections and Ellis, I need you to do a 5-minute interview with each of them." However, when we started shooting, I realized I had four sax players playing at one time. And I had to figure out who's doing the solo and when. So I told them, "Guys, give me the order of when somebody's going to do the solo." And they replied, "Oz, man you're messing with our creativity … We don't know when. It just happens." So, I said, "Okay, when it happens, could you do something like raise your sax and then I can come to you." It was my first time dealing with cameras and I remember the crew asking, "Oz, do you want a star filter, do you want this, do you want that?" And I said, "Oh, yes. Of course. I want that, and that." I mean I had no clue what I was doing. But glad I asked for everything. When it came time to shoot, they put the star filter on and it looked cool.

SMcC: **You mentioned taking film courses when you were enrolled in the theatre program.**

OS: At NYU, I was in the Theatre Directing Program where I would take set design class, the costume class, the dance class, and an acting class along with my directing. Plus, two or three general studies classes to fill out my curriculum. I told them when I first showed up that I wanted to do film, too. And they said, "Well we don't have an agreement with other departments—we don't crossover with the Film School. But you probably could audit a film critic's class." There was the film school and there was the academic film school. They said, "Go to the academic film school and see if you can audit one of their classes." A friend of mine was an editor, Nancy Baker. One of her ex-boyfriends, Fred Aranow, was the advisor for the first-year graduate film program. Nancy said, "Call Fred." Fred said I could audit the entire first-year film program. So, I did Sound Editing, Cinematography, along with everything else I was doing in the theatre directing program. Very intense first year.

SMcC: **You audited, and didn't get credit?**

OS: No, they gave me credit. Basically, what I did was substitute those general studies classes for the film courses to get the credits I needed. At the end of the year, nobody knew what school I was in. And the film people were like, "Are you coming back next year?" and I knew I really had to make a choice. Because I was also working 14, 15, 16, 17 hours a day trying to do both. So, my cinematography teacher, Beda Botka, and my editing teacher, Ian Maitland, sat me down and said, "Get a good editor when you get out of school and a good cinematographer, you'll learn from them quick. It's going to take you a lifetime to learn actors. Stay in the Theatre Program." Which I thought was the best advice.

SMcC: Do you use the same cinematographer and same editor when you can?

OS: When I'm doing an independent project, always. But when I'm doing a television project I don't. However, when I'm a producer/director I pick the editors and cinematographers.

SMcC: When doing theatre, do you choose your own designers?

OS: Absolutely. One of my close friends was Skip Mercier, who designed the sets for most of my theatre pieces. He was at the O'Neill for thirty years as their production designer.

SMcC: How do you express your concept to your designers?

OS: We read the script; we talk. Skip will come up with his ideas. We'll come up with color palettes ... what I learned at NYU, which was helpful, was sometimes you just draw out what you see. It doesn't have to be good. But when you draw it out, if it's a costume or whatever, at least you're using the language of that designer. And then let them take it from there.

When Skip did *Fences* with me at the Asolo, I wanted a combination of realism and impressionism in our cityscape. There was reality but as it went off—the colors, the sky in the background—felt like you were in the middle of the city, but it wasn't totally realistic.

SMcC: In *For Colored Girls* why did you choose the flower as the set design?

OS: In the beginning, Ifa Bayeza, Zake's sister, designed the first backdrop at Henry Street [New Federal Theatre]. It was bodies intertwined creating a flower. When we moved it, Ming just used her original idea and created this big flower.

Betsy, Ming's wife, tells the story that Ming was terrified of doing something that soft. Ming always did these stick-type sets. Betsy assured Ming that he could do it.

SMcC: Was that Ming Cho-Lee?

OS: Yes. Joe hooked Ming up with us and I told him, "Ming, I want it soft. I want it pretty. I wanted the women to feel if they were to turn around, they would see beauty around them." Joe wanted parts of men—hats, boots—he wanted that to be the set. He wanted it oppressive. I didn't. I wanted it to be warm. And I won.

SMcC: Have you ever sent your designers back to the drawing board? OS: Oh yeah. You know that Ming tried to please Joe. And I looked at it and said, "Oh, hell no. This is not about men. I do not want men in this." So yeah. Or Skip would come up with some stuff and I'd say, "That's cool. But ... I need this."

Often, I'll just paint on the canvas they put up. For instance, when we did *Ballad of Emmett Till* at the Goodman, I thought Skip Mercier's concept was fabulous. He put up corrugated metal panels—it was big, operatic—because it went up into the sky. We had a rotating stage, and we were going to project images onto those corrugated backdrops—you know, cotton

Figure 2.3 *Ballad of Emmett Till* by Ifa Bayeza at Goodman Theatre, 2007. Photo by Liz Lauren.

fields, etc. And oh, it just wasn't doing it. And the author, Ifa Bayeza and I started talking about this painter—Roy Clark. We got his paintings and overlaid them. It was fabulous. But, when I first looked at those pictures of cotton fields and southern town in black and white, I said, "Oh God, that looks terrible."

SMcC: Have you ever received a bad review?

OS: Probably, but you have to be able to move on. I mentioned that Gilbert Moses was one of my mentors, right? The one thing I always admired about Gil was he would take chances, big, big chances! He would be either brilliant or fall flat on his face. But you don't get to brilliance unless you put yourself out there and are prepared for failure—which will happen.

There was one time when I was expecting to get blasted by the critics. I did the first play Fugard ever wrote. It was the American premier at the Manhattan Theatre Club, after Fugard was well established. Edith Oliver, said in her review, "Oz did the best he could do with the material he had to work with." I survived the critics. I dodged that bullet.

SMcC: What genre of theatre have you not done that you would like to do?

OS: I haven't done much Classical. I haven't done any Shakespeare or any Restoration. You know, I did a *CSI New York* episode and they wanted to open up with *Madame Butterfly*. I came up with this concept of cutting between *Madame Butterfly* in Lincoln Center and a subway Rave. So, I decided to really do *Madame Butterfly*. And you know, she commits hara kiri. I had her using red ribbons as the blood. I hired a real opera singer to play the role and she said, "Oz, this is fascinating." I didn't know but the opera singer I used told me the hara kiri is always behind a curtain or behind a screen. "It's never on stage and you're putting it on stage." So, I said, "Yeah, it should be." I would love to do an opera someday.

What I did was interesting. I'd seen these two young Black violinists. I gave them Maria Callas' *Madame Butterfly*, and I had the violinists play the *Madame Butterfly* on their violins, which is usually played with oboes. I felt the violins gave it a real Asian flavor. We cut back and forth between Madame Butterfly on the stage at Lincoln Center to their violins playing in the Rave on the subway. It's an interesting piece!

The guy who created *CSI*, Anthony Zuiker, came to the editing room and said, "I heard what you guys are doing." We showed him and all he could say was "You guys did this?!!" It was a great opening.

SMcC: Post-COVID, what do you see happening?

OS: I see new things happening in theatre which has been wanting to grow and change. I think people will be more into the merging of mediums. I think partly out of necessity and partly this is where it's been heading for a long time. I mean *West Side Story* was a prime example of bringing cameras into the theater. Did you see the *60 Minutes* on the new *West Side Story* on Broadway? It's online. 'cause they even take the actors up the backstairs to one of the dressing rooms that they turned into a set, with cameras, and they're projecting what they're doing into the theater.

SMcC: When did you join SDC?

OS: I was stage managing for Joe Papp at the Public Theatre; I joined when I did *For Colored Girls* in 1977 and '78 because it was going to Broadway. I'd been in Equity and then SAG for a bit. I figured that was what you do. I was 26 years old. I subsequently learned of the benefits that I derived from the SSDC (as the SDC was known at that time): protection. The union has their own lawyers. They know the ins and outs. They know the games. They have information and that information is very valuable. I learned that some of the older directors would get together at Sardi's once a week, or once every other week, and just talk.

There's only one director. You may have five producers. You may have multiple actors. But the sharing of information that directors need is invaluable. It's easy to get taken advantage of when you don't know. It was interesting when I got on the SDC Board to be around your fellow directors and artistic directors. Found out that the artistic directors were having second thoughts about SDC. As an artistic director, you've got your businessmen and the management—the money guys. They'd say, "Oh you don't need SDC. We got you. We got you." We found a lot of artistic directors, after ten or fifteen years said, "I don't have my health insurance. I don't have this and I don't have that." What's great about the SDC is the community of information. That is very important for us. Because Saundra, you know as well as I, we love our art. We love our process. We can talk that for days. We get really into our art. The business side of it disappears.

When I was on the board of a medical school, one of the things I said to them is "We need a business curriculum to go along with our medical classes." They said, "Oz, we teach doctors." "Yes. But doctors have to go out into the world to survive." We were finding so many doctors who would go bankrupt because they did not have that information. They did not have that financial business acumen that you would get from talking with somebody else. "Watch this. Watch that when you're doing it." Having SDC and DGA instills that information, allowing you to make sense of the business of directing. I find our unions extremely important.

SMcC: When did you join the board?

OS: In 1992 or '93, I got a call, "Oz, would you run for the board?" I got on the board and for four or five years was learning the ins and outs of the union. We had negotiations here and there. I think I was one of the only Black people there. Hope Clark might have been on the board for a minute with me. It's interesting in all these unions, there's a protocol, an old boys club. Now, it's becoming an old girls club. A club that, a lot of times, we're not part of. It's still going on.

I remember I was trying to help get my son get into the DGA. After about ten years of being involved with the DGA board, somebody said, "Oh, by the way, there's an exception in New York, a minority diversity exception." I said, "I've been around you guys for ten years and you are just telling me this now?" Paris Barclay was president of the DGA. When the pandemic came down, we all got together and started talking about what *we* wanted as Black people. I said, "We should talk about that exception to the rule that is in the New York space." Paris said, "What are you talking about? Oz, I don't know what you are talking about." This is after he had been president for two terms. He did some research and said, "Oh s**t, yes, there is an exception!" And who was using that exception? Who were the only people to know about that exception ... White women!

SMcC: What is that exception?

OS: In the '80s, I think a Black woman sued the Directors Guild and the studios. In the contract, there was created a "carve out." There is something called the QL—Qualifying List which allows ADs and stage managers to get those union jobs, and you have to be on the QL to get a union job in those categories. I'm not very happy about it because it blocks people. If your daddy isn't in the union, you can't get in. It's become harder for people to get their kids in. If you get hired as a PA, you need 600 days in LA to get on the Qualifying List to be an AD, or to be Unit Production Manager (UPM) ... 600 working days. That's in the DGA Rules. In between New York and LA, it's a 150 or a 120, don't know exactly, but it's less in New York.

SMcC: Is that the same with the SDC?

OS: No, with the SDC, because we are just on the creative side, directors and choreographers, as long as you have a contract you can get in. It's the same way for the DGA as well, on the creative side. It's the production side that the QL applies. AEA represents stage managers, which is the production side of theatre. In New York for DGA, if you want to be an AD, if somebody is willing to hire you as a diverse person, you can jump over the Qualifying List and get hired. But if you want to go to another place, you need a 120 or 600 days. But hey, you got a job. You're working. You're doing it. You're in.

SMcC: What changes do you feel you helped initiate in the union?

OS: The first big one, which I am extremely proud of and very much a part of, was every one of the officers of the Stage Directors Guild: the president, vice president, treasurer, secretary, everybody, all the SDC's officials were always New York based. We liked to call ourselves a National Union because it emanates from New York. Broadway is definitely the biggest moneymaker for the union. To help show that it *is* and *can* be a National Union, I was elected National Board secretary. I was the first person, not based in New York, to ever hold an office in SDC. I was secretary for six to eight years. It allowed everybody to say, "We don't have to be in New York to participate in SDC," which I thought was extremely important.

SMcC: You alerted me not to allow my membership to lapse. How did you know?

OS: We have lists. A lot of times we get board members to make phone calls to explain and talk to members. In the beginning, I did not know some of our rights. I did not know a lot of things.

A prime example was a young lady in Los Angeles, a director, who really helped fashion a play. She was the first director. She worked on it for maybe a year with the playwright. Then, the Geffen Theatre wanted to produce it with a big-name director, Taylor Hackford. The young lady got cut out—totally cut off without anything. She had nothing. She joined SDC after that and asked if we could help. However, because she was not a member before that, our hands were tied, she was on her own. With her own dime, she would have to get a lawyer and sue them to hopefully get something. Basically, she had nothing written down, no agreement, nothing. I reached out to you for almost for the same reason. Since you're always doing something, maintain your membership. Use the SDC Contract. That way, if you ever need protection, SDC has lawyers.

This is another thing SDC has been working hard on. While I was there, we finally got the Dramatists Guild to recognize that the director can be attached to a play through the playwright. It's not owned by the producer. If you have a contract with a producer, when the play moves on you have nothing. SDC has been working on creating a document between writer and director that if a director spends time working on a play, he or she should get compensation for their work if they do not continue with the project.

Thank God, *For Colored Girls* went to Broadway. I got paid that way. Most of the structure of *For Colored Girls* came from me. Absolutely every word is Ntozake Shange's. It's her play. But as director I should get some recognition for the additional work I did, because that made it what it is.

SMcC: Were you consulted on the revivals of *For Colored Girls*?

OS: No. No. No. In some ways, I should have been. At least, people should have talked to me. I was there from day one with Ntozake. We were putting it together. We were forming it. I was in her head. She was in my head. We had a vision for what *For Colored Girls* became.

The playwright owns the play.

Once I left after those five years—on Broadway, the national tour, the Australian tour—I said, "I've got to move on. I can't just sit here and say, 'Hey, I did *For Colored Girls* for the rest of my life, I gotta move on and grow.'" So, I didn't see a full production until three years ago, right before the pandemic. It was the one that was redone and taken to Broadway. I was bothered. I'm not going to say, "It wasn't what I believe it should be." It just wasn't what Ntozake and I were doing.

SMcC: But it was a different director, so …

OS: So, it was a different director. But there was an intention that Zake had. I mean, I just remember at one point, and you, Saundra have done the play, when I watched the revival after "*… Stuff*," the women started laughing at the woman who was doing the poem. I thought, "What are you doing? Where's the support? Where's the camaraderie? Where's the sisterhood?" They were literally laughing and joking, "Oh, you let him do that, ha-ha-ha-ha?" And I'm thinking, "No, no. We're past that. That was '*Graduation Night*.' Maybe?" But by that time, it was about support. When somebody said, "It's about man bashing," Zake would always say, "It ain't got nothing to do with men. It's about these women and what they allow to happen."

SMcC: What are your thoughts regarding an author's intention vs. a director's concept with this new generation reviving shows?

OS: As much as I did not like the film version of *For Colored Girls*, I think Tyler Perry was focusing on his own abuse growing up. It worked for some people. I don't mind people changing certain things. I love to see new interpretations. The way Zake and I envisioned *FCG*, it was always about fluidity. We wanted it to be fluid. As you remember, every understudy, except the Lady in Red, had their own color, their own dress. We had different colors for understudies that weren't the yellow, green, blue. We wanted every one of the Ladies to bring their own souls to it. The one thing I always wanted to impress was, this man is not a man that you hate. You may not like what he does. But if you're going to fight for somebody; if you're going to fight for this, there's got to be some love there somewhere. I felt when I saw the movie, the men were despicable. It made me wonder, what was wrong with these women, that they're fighting for despicable men.

SMcC: On how many boards do you serve?

OS: Right now, the Directors Guild, I'm an alternate on the board and Wake Forest Institute for Regenerative Medicine—a medical research lab that builds human organs.

SMcC: Why?

OS: Why am I on it? This is very important to me. We as artists are telling stories. A lot of corporations need artistic vision on their boards. In addition to monetary concerns, they need help on how to tell their stories; they need to look at things from a different point of view. If you're always looking from the business angle, or from the science angle, you're limiting your vision. Therefore, science fiction is an artistic way of looking at science. Science fiction has made scientists think, "Whoa, that is really crazy, but there's something in that."

SMcC: How did you get on a medical board?

OS: I'm with a group called the Science and Entertainment Exchange which is a part of the National Academy of Sciences. Jerry Zucker was instrumental in putting this together. When you're doing a movie, or when you're doing a play, or writing a book for film and TV, the Science and Entertainment Exchange will put you with a scientist to help you tell the story.

Jerry Zucker, working on a film about a married couple who happened to be earth scientists. The Exchange actually provided him two married earth scientists who gave him an understanding of earth science, how their participation in science affected them as people, and how it affected their relationship.

So, what the Exchange does when you're doing a science fiction project is provide technical assistance. In *Star Trek*, they put "red matter" into the core of Vulcan and blew Vulcan up. We had scientists helping when they were writing the story. The question is, we know that there's no "red matter," but why couldn't it be placed on the surface of the planet or just be in the atmosphere? We, as artists, deal with specifics. The specifics of "boy meets girl, boy loses girl, boy gets girl back." You know, basic structure. Nobody cares about that. What they care about is the specifics as to what precipitated the boy meeting the girl. The specifics about why they broke up. The specifics of how they got back together. Those are the things that are interesting.

So, what the scientists are providing for free and giving us specific reasons for what we're trying to do. They sit there and say, "Well, that's really made-up, but wow! I can see how that could happen!" It makes it more grounded in our storytelling.

I participate in this group. We do seminars. I hosted one for the Directors Guild where I was the Emcee. We had a neurobiologist, a roboticist, and others who were all talking about their science. It just gave people, oh my God, ideas! What's the quote: "Truth is stranger than fiction, but it is because fiction is obliged to stick to possibilities; truth isn't."

The scientists told us a true story about a kid who had an inoperable brain tumor. He turned to his parents and said, "I'm going to be okay. Every night, before I go to bed, I'm going to be in a starship and I'm gonna bombard the tumor. I'm gonna shoot at the tumor." He called it, "Planet Meatball." A year or two later, he came to his parents and said, "I did it" and the parents said, "What are you talking about?" They were preparing for him to die. He said, "I did it. I got rid of the it. I got rid of 'Planet Meatball.' I want to go get tested again." They said, "No." He convinced them to take him to get tested. The tumor had solidified into a harmless lump in his brain. It's little stories like that, that make you say, "Oh my God, I could write something like this."

Keith Black was talking to me. Keith is the brain surgeon. You want to get brain surgery in the world, Keith Black is that guy. He pioneered talking to you while he does brain surgery, so he can go deeper than most people to take the tumor out. If the tumor is in your speech center, and you start slurring your words, he knows he's gone as far as he can go. All these things are fascinating. These specifics when added to these stories make us say, "Whoa! I never knew that, or I never thought about that. Oh, that's crazy. That's weird, but it's true."

SMcC: Fascinating. I can visualize *Planet Meatball* as an animated science fiction, while the rest of the movie is set in reality.

OS: I participated in a number of their retreats, where they get twelve producers, writers, directors and put them together with twelve scientists. We come up with stories, ideas. We figure out how to tell a story around their science.

SMcC: How do directors get involved in programs, societies, on boards, or committees that could expand them creatively?

OS: At the DGA, we're putting together programs that expose directors to these kinds of programs. The SDC has its Foundation which is constantly creating seminars. I would like to get the National Science and Entertainment Exchange together with the theatre people. I think the theatre community could use what the Directors Guild introduced me to through the Science Exchange.

SMcC: SDC has a program called Diversity and Inclusion. How can directors become more active in our own careers?

OS: I pushed myself into all of it. Let's talk about the Directors Guild. There was not enough Black participation on many of the committees at the Directors Guild. Before BLM, I was one of a very few who participated. It's begun to turn around now. But back a few years ago everybody would turn to me. "You're on Creative Rights Committee. You're on Special Events. You're on Global Cinema. You're the African Americans Steering Committee chair." There must have been five or six committees that I was the only Black person. I would be asked, "How come you're the only Black person on these committees?" The president of the union makes those appointments. I just let the president or the chairman of the committees know I wanted to be on those committees. I don't wait to be asked. I think that's the biggest advice I have to give … "Don't wait to be asked."

I'm on those committees. I have a big voice. At times, I was the lone Black voice. I say to our brothers and sisters, "Bring other people along with you. Get other people involved, so when you're in those meetings, and they say something stupid, you have somebody there to back you up when you have to correct them."

A lot of times, they don't get it. It's more out of ignorance, than out of spitefulness. They may think they understand. But there are times, I have to correct them and say, "Uh-uh, that ain't happening." I'm always pushing to get other Black people involved. Because it does nothing but help me. Because we have to be careful that we don't become crabs in a barrel. And a lot of times, we are just that.

SMcC: What are you doing next?

OS: I just did a podcast yesterday and today. It's like an old radio show. Remember *The Shadow*—"the Shadow knows"? It's a sort of futuristic, cyber-Shadow. There are also some films I want to do.

SMcC: Do you have any in mind?

OS: Oh yes. Walter Mosely has a piece I really want to do and there are some other pieces. Richard Wesley is supposed to be doing this play that I want to work with him on … the South African reconciliation. Do you know what I'm talking about?

SMcC: No.

OS: They would put a police officer together with the person he arrested so they could talk to each other: Truth and Reconciliation Commission. It was a court like the restorative justice body assembled in South Africa after the end of

Apartheid—they put everybody in the same room to really talk it out.

SMcC: What is your definition of success?

OS: My wife. My family. Enjoying my work. Seriously. I think my definition of success is enjoying my work. Enjoying my life.

SMcC: In one word, how would you describe yourself?

OS: I wanna use the word—calm. *Centered*. Because I like my actors, my designers, my crew members to feel that calm, because that—focus—allows them to be calm. That allows them to do their job. The fact that my blood pressure might be sky high—I just don't tell anyone.

SMcC: Your father was a minister. Is that why you were not intimidated?

OS: My father was a Colonel. My wife's father was also a Colonel. Lynne would talk about how her father would invite the white officers to dinner while her mother would grumble because she didn't want to do this. But you had to play the game to get the promotion, to move ahead.

A friend of mine had a management position at Smith Barney and I told him once, "Man, you need to go and play some golf." He said, "I do my job and I do it well. I don't need to hang out with anyone from work." He called me about six months later and was really quiet. He said, "I went out for drinks with my white co-workers. While sitting there, we talked about their stock packages that came with them becoming managers. They turned to me and asked, 'How's your stock portfolio going?' I said, 'It's coming along really well.'" He went back to the office the next day and asked his boss, "What about this stock package I should've gotten when I became a manager?" This boss said, "Oh yeah, yeah, yeah we've got that for you."

He would not have known if he hadn't gone to drinks the night before that there was a lot of money sitting there for him. All he had to do was ask for it. They don't give up nothin' if you don't ask.

SMcC: How would you describe your legacy?

OS: I would say that it's doing entertainment that leaves you with a message, with a thought that's bigger than the film or the theatre piece.

SMcC: **If you had the opportunity to start over, would you approach your career differently?**

OS: I'd probably really concentrate on writing more. I just think it is its own skill set. I'm good at … editing and working with writers. But creating and writing the whole thing, I don't think I'm as good at that. And I believe in film and television as well as theatre; most times it's the writers' medium. You have to have the words—the script—to do anything.

SMcC: Any final thoughts?

OS: One thing I want to say is, when you get insulted, or you feel like people don't like you, don't quit. Remember, you're right. There are people who don't like you. People don't want you to be there. They don't care. But don't quit. Fight! Stand up for yourself. We need your voices. When you quit, we lose a voice.

I know we've all been through it. We watched our parents go through it. No, they don't want us here. They don't want you in their theaters. But, when you *do* get there, you don't pick up your marbles and go home because they were mean to you. You stay there and you fight!

SMcC: Perseverance. That's a great note to end on … .

DREAMER 3

An Interview with Sheldon Epps

SMcC: I was thoroughly surprised when Sheldon mentioned he had a lucrative acting career prior to becoming a director. My earliest recollection of Sheldon was about the time he conceived and directed the highly acclaimed musical revue, *Blues in the Night*, and the Duke Ellington musical *Play On!*, which received several Tony nominations, as well as numerous accolades regionally.

CTD: Indeed. *Blues in the Night* and *Play On!* are two significant musicals in the African American theatre canon. I've known Sheldon for many years. Actually, our professional relationship deepened when we served on the board of the Society of Stage Directors. His focus and clarity, combined with his understanding of the needs of professional directors and choreographers, was always on point.

SMcC: He was artistic director of Pasadena Playhouse for over twenty years. And became a legend in his own time.

CTD: Indeed, he did. Sheldon is one of a few artistic directors who held the position of leading a major American theatre.

SMcC: And he is now the senior artistic advisor and company director for the Ford's Theatre in Washington, DC.

CTD: Two of the mandates of this new position include bringing more artists of color into the theatre and increasing diversity throughout the institution.

Figure 3.1 Photo by Jim Cox.

Interview With Sheldon Epps

SMcC: **Has there ever been a project that frightened you, but you accepted it anyway? Why?**

Sheldon Epps: In truth, I think I am a little bit frightened every time I start to work on a new production. Fear can be a good thing in that it inspires harder and better work. I have also chosen plays or musicals to teach myself how to do them. I think that getting into the room with a playwright and working with him or her every day is the only way to learn how to approach their work.

I chose to do Ibsen, Stoppard, and even August Wilson to teach myself how to do their work; to learn how to play their very individual music. So, for me, being frightened of a project means that it is something that I should make myself do!

If it doesn't scare me a bit, then it is probably going to be too easy and ultimately not that satisfying.

SMcC: What was your most challenging production? Why?

SE: Once again, they all are—or they all should be challenging and a little intimidating. Probably the most challenging play that I directed was Stoppard's *The Real Thing*, just because it operates on so many levels and it's so tricky to put the puzzle together. I did two productions of that one, and I really did not get it right until the second time. It took growing up a bit more to really understand it.

Doing any new musical is challenging. I always say that this is like putting a giant jigsaw puzzle together, but even more difficult because you don't have a clear picture of what it is supposed to look like at the end of the process. You are creating that as you go along. On top of that, all the pieces are being "cut" in different rooms (the book scenes here, the dances there, and the arrangements over there with the musical director).

You just hope and pray that they somehow "fit" together once you do that first run-through and that hopefully it is all making sense and telling the same story! It involves a lot of faith and a lot of prayer!!

SMcC: You left an indelible mark as artistic director of Pasadena Playhouse. Did you aspire to become an artistic director of a major theatre company?

SE: No, it was really my intent to be an actor. That is what I studied at Carnegie Mellon University; I was in the Acting Option. And I worked fairly successfully (meaning, I made a living as an actor) for several years after graduation.

About seven or eight years after getting out of school, I started a small theatre company off, off, off-Broadway in NYC with several friends from Carnegie, including Norman Rene, who went on to have a very successful directing career. He was the one who pushed me towards directing, where I felt very much at home very quickly. That began my career as a freelance director.

At one point, I started to tire of the constant traveling and moving around the country and started to think then about becoming an artistic director. Conversations with Garland

Wright at the Guthrie and Jack O'Brien at the Old Globe really made me consider that as a valuable option. That led to my time with Jack at the Old Globe as associate artistic director. Four years later, I went to Pasadena Playhouse, thinking that I might stay there for five or six years. Well … twenty years later … such is life … .

SMcC: Do you think theatre as we know it will change post-COVID? If so, how?

SE: I don't know that theatre will be fundamentally changed. I hope not, as we had a good thing going. I hope that with time people will feel safe enough that we can return to being in the same room together and sharing the same air, which is what makes the theatre special (and obviously so challenging right now). I do believe that the fundamental human desire to gather and hear stories together, to breathe it in together and make the event happen will lead us back to a healthy and prosperous theatre. Hopefully sooner than later.

I do believe that all the work that people have discovered and developed in the virtual realm will survive. Not to replace theatre, but as an augmentation and a way to continue to reach audiences both old and new. It cannot be a satisfying substitute for our work in the theatre, but it can supplement what we do and feed audiences in a different way.

SMcC: What is your definition of success?

SE: Tough question … I suppose I would say that success is knowing that you gave yourself to the work fully and courageously. Working with passion, with dedication and with the fullness of your being is a great reward. If you know that in your heart and soul, then you can declare yourself a success no matter what others might say. Giving your utmost to the creative journey is more important than good reviews. Being fully "in the arena" rather than watching from the side and fighting the good fight in every big and small way means that you are a success.

And as a leader of a theatre company, inspiring great work and providing an atmosphere for others to thrive is truly satisfying and rewarding. I consider doing that as a measure of success as well.

SMcC: What do you think is your legacy?

SE: Again, hard question … but I think that I have battered down some doors that still existed for an artist of color in the theatre during my lifetime. When I began my journey at Pasadena Playhouse, there were few leaders of color at major theatres. At moments, I may have been the one … the only one. Keeping that theatre alive and thriving meant that it is possible for a Black man to do that, which has opened the doors for many others who now are serving in such positions. That along with creating genuine diversity, both onstage and off at a theater, which prior to my coming there was a real "bastion of whiteness," gives me great pride and set a standard for the life of an American theater. I hope that those things have meaning, and I'd like to be thought of as someone who fought those important battles successfully. All of that … and finding joy in the work. Which I did and which I do!!

SMcC: What made you decide to write your book, *My Own Directions: A Black Man's Journey in the American Theatre*?

SE: I was pushed into it a little by other people when I stepped down from the Playhouse in 2017. People kept saying, "You should write a book." "Have you thought about writing a book?" When enough people say that you begin to think about it. I did consider it. I realized that I did have a rather unique story to tell, being one of the only men of color to run a major theater in America especially at the time I was doing it; but also, about racial challenges I faced all along the way in my freelance career. I hope the book will be an inspiration to others who are still facing those same challenges, so that they can be overcome. I hope it would be an inspiration to others to follow their own direction as I have followed my own. You don't allow yourself to believe the limitations that are thrust upon you by the fear of society, by America, that you can accomplish anything you want. I hope the book is an inspiration for others to follow their own direction as I have followed my own.

CTD: Throughout the writing process, were there places that presented any challenges to you? If so, what were they and how did you resolve them?

SE: I think that all of us as directors and theatre artists, we're used to plowing ahead. We reach challenges and obstacles, but you may or may not be invested emotionally in that moment. You're solving problems as you are moving ahead. We do that in rehearsals because time is short. In leadership position in a theatre, I certainly believe that you do that. The challenge was to not just say what happened, but to say, "How did I feel about what happened? How did that affect me emotionally in that space—honestly and sincerely—in a way that I had never talked about before?" As a person of color leading a theatre, as Obama did, sometimes you had to hold your tongue. And secondly, I was moving on to whatever was next. The challenge and the opportunity were to place myself back in those situations and say what happened during that time, but how did I really feel about what happened. What did I suppress emotionally that I now want to talk about? So, it was a challenge and an opportunity.

SMcC: Your book, *My Own Direction*, is so candid. Did you have second thoughts about being so honest?

SE: If not, why write it? If I was not going to be honest, why do it at all? I did not go out to slander anybody or make them look bad or feel bad. I set out to be truthful. This is the reality of my situation as I knew it. Others may disagree. This is how I felt at the time. People can't really argue about what I know. They could argue and say they felt differently or perceived it differently ... but I didn't use names even though I did mention board members and others. It was more about the events themselves rather than the people who were involved at the time. I don't think there was anything slanderous, nor have I been accused of that.

SMcC: After reading your book and doing this interview, I feel I've finally gotten to know you better.

SE: Believe it or not, I am a very shy person. I think I've had to learn to adopt a public persona which is necessary to accomplish fund raising, greeting people at the theater and welcoming artists into the theater. But innately I am rather shy. Then, now, and always.

SMcC: However, you always seem to be at ease.

SE: I am at ease. I am at ease being shy. Perhaps, we never really got to know each very well because we didn't have any sustained periods of working together. I would hope that would happen in a longer creative process. Frankly, in writing the book and in the last few years of directing, I have made myself more personally available than I may have in the past. You may call that maturity or craziness, or whatever you want to all it. [*Sheldon laughs.*] If I am honest about it, I think I am more emotionally available.

CTD: What do you do to relax?

SE: I am a great walker. I enjoy walking. The places where I walk in Pasadena, I can have complete anonymity even around the track. Very rarely on one of those walking days am I stopped by someone asking, "Aren't' you Sheldon Epps?" Directors can have that anonymity more so than actors. By walking, I can get lost in and within my own thoughts and don't have to deal with anybody. It probably has to deal with that shyness I was talking about. I love to find times when I can be quiet. Not be asked questions and not have the answers.

CTD: What types of work are you drawn to? What are some of the elements in scripts that make you say, "This is the one!"

SE: Broadly speaking I'm drawn to great stories, I like a good, well-crafted, well-made story. I am not terribly drawn to plays that are abstract, or ephemeral. I'm not drawn to those kinds of plays where, as an audience member, you sit there, and one may think about the play itself, "Well, I'm glad *they* all know what's going on, because I'm completely lost." I like to grab on to a story as a director and a theatre-goer. I think the audience likes that too. There is a Romare Bearden quote, "All great art deals with the triumph of the human spirit." So, I am particularly drawn to great stories that deal with the triumph of the human spirit and people overcoming either very small or very big adversities either alone or in partnership with their communities, or in what I call the unexpected collaborations—two people from different worlds come together and solve issues in a vacuum. They affect both the world around them and themselves. They become different people in the process of working through some adversity.

SMcC: Do you feel that way with plays that you are interested in directing or choosing in your season as the artistic director?

SE: Both. If you look at the seasons over the twenty years I was artistic director at the Pasadena Playhouse, you will find that almost all of them are "story plays." I felt that my audience, as I do, likes a story to grab onto. That story can come from any culture, any community, any color, race, as long as there is a story to grasp onto. I like to describe it as taking a good ride. You reach a destination where people in the play are different from where they started. If people remain the same throughout, it is not interesting. I want to see dramatic change. It is exciting to watch characters, individuals change over the course of the play.

CTD: Once you've engaged designers, have you sent a designer back to the drawing board to rethink their ideas?

SE: Yes. It happens many times with some of my favorite designers with whom I have had several collaborations. For example, one of my favorite designers is John Iacovelli. A wonderful, brilliant designer. He has never presented me with a design that wasn't really beautiful. It may have been beautiful but not ambitious enough or daring enough. Or unrealistic enough. John tends to go toward realism. I tend not to. But rather something that represents the real thing. Many times, I have had to say, "John, this is beautiful, but let's go back and think how does this [the set] work if we did this? How does this work if we did that?"

SMcC: Do you start with a concept and present it to the designer?

SE: It probably depends on who the designer is. Given what I have said, I do try to choose designers who I believe are in sync with whatever vague notion I have of what I want the set to look like. Knowing that some people are Ming Cho Lee and others are Robin Wagner ... who are very, very different designers. If you want a Robin Wagner set, don't ask Ming Cho Lee to do it. My first information to the designer is choosing the designer. Choosing their aesthetic. Perhaps pushing them toward the aesthetic that I think will be right for the play. Having done that, I let them do the first pass.

CTD: With designers with whom you have worked and built a language of communication, when did that language finally click?

SE: In any good relationship you learn how to please each other. Be there for each other. Help each other. A shorthand develops, as with actors you have previously worked with. It happens with designers also. The first few times I have had to do more talking in coming up with a concept working with John Iacovelli. By the time we collaborated on *Intimate Apparel*, John delivered something based on his knowledge of what I liked. This was almost exactly the same from the first sketch to arriving onstage, without me making any comments about it. He knew how I would want to do that play and delivered that from the beginning.

CTD: What advice would you give to your younger self?

SE: There are several things I would say. One is, be patient. To quote Andre DeShields, "The quickest way to get anywhere is slowly." I think that is very profound advice. Don't be afraid to say, "I don't know." That would be a big one. Don't feel you have to be the one to have all the answers. Don't feel you have to have an answer right now. It is better to say in rehearsal or in life, "I don't know. Let me think about that. And I hope to have an answer tomorrow." Rather than give the appearance that you have an answer when you do not have one. Rely on listening as much or more than you rely on talking.

It is important to fill the space by listening to your actors, listening to the playwright, listening *for* the answers from the universe, when your initial response is "I don't know." Then, bring the answer back. There is no need to filibuster the room when you don't have to.

SMcC: **If you had the opportunity to start your career over again, is there anything you would do differently?**

SE: I don't think so. My career has moved in such a wonderfully blessed progression in doing many of, and in some ways, all the things that I have ever wanted to do. I know it is unique in our field to be able to say that. But I can honestly say that. Therefore, I have to believe that the path I was provided was the right path for me to follow. The directions of my own, that I designed, were the right directions to give me that incredibly blessed and fortuitous career.

CTD: **As senior artistic advisor at the Ford's Theatre, what do you see on the horizon?**

SE: Overall it is going well. It's a wonderful association for me. It is great to be involved artistically and creatively at the theater without carrying all the administrative burdens and responsibilities, issues, and challenges. The work is good.

The outreach to audiences is great. There is more and more diversity in every area of theatre. Ford's Theatre is challenged in getting audiences into the theater as most theaters in America are right now. That is frightening, it's nervous making. But it

Figure 3.2 C. C. H. Pounder in the title role in *Hedda Gabler* by Henrik Ibsen, Old Globe Theatre, 1995. Photo by Ken Howard.

is not the first time [for any theater] and probably won't be the last. However, that doesn't make it any easier. But it is very challenging to think of the future when sales numbers are so low even when the work is good. There are so many extraordinary challenges theaters have never faced.

CTD: Will that change with new diversity efforts?

SE: It has changed with the new diversity efforts. As with my experience with Pasadena Playhouse, reaching out to new audiences means you're reaching out to larger audiences and the potential for larger audiences. We've got to find a way to bring ticket prices down everywhere, from Broadway to regional theatre. The price of tickets is discouraging when there are so many new opportunities (through media and new technology) for audiences to stay at home.

SMcC: In your book, you stated the board was afraid you would bring too many Black shows into the community. Was it a balancing act?

SE: You know, I just had to boldly do it. And fortunately, we had no idea it would be a success. If I had boldly done it and nobody came, and those shows had not been tremendous successes, I probably would have been out of there a lot faster. But, to anybody who objected, all they had to do was look at the box office numbers which were extraordinary and so much greater than anything we had ever seen in the theater's history.

SMcC: As an audience member and from reading the reviews, all the Black shows were the most successful.

SE: They were. It was hard to argue with success. Anybody who would say to me why don't you stop doing those Black shows, I would say to them, well you go and find me that extra half a million dollars that the Black shows are bringing in. That would usually be the end of the discussion.

SMcC: Are you still writing? What new projects are on the horizon?

SE: I've been directing a lot. Like you. There is a new musical called *Personality* about Lloyd Price that I'm doing in Chicago. I directed a new play called *Miss Maude*. I directed my first movie called *Christmas Party Crashers*.

SMcC: Thank you so much Sheldon.

SE: Thank you both.

JOYFUL 4

An Interview with Shirley Jo Finney

> *"Shirley Jo spoke in dream imagery, in song pieces, in bass lines with irreverence, and in emotive illustrations of whether something moved her. She found the sonic wavelength that would resonate with an audience."*
>
> —Bernard K. Addison

CTD: I have always heard glowing reports about Shirley Jo's work.

SMcC: Our career paths ran parallel and often crisscrossed each other. Her production of *Central Avenue* at the Fountain Theatre inspired me to pursue directing as a career.

CTD: I wish I could have seen that production.

SMcC: Shirley Jo's projects addressed meaningful issues and challenged the status quo. Her work was poetic, possessing great beauty and vibrancy. She was a powerhouse and trailblazer. She demanded respect. I feel a void in our artistic community.

CTD: The news of her transition knocked the wind out of me. The ancestors have welcomed an extraordinary artist.

SMcC: This interview captures aspects of Shirley Jo's artistic journey.

DOI: 10.4324/9781003410737-4

Figure 4.1 Headshot Shirley Jo Finney, 1949–2023.

Interview With Shirley Jo Finney

SMcC: **How old were you when you saw your first play?**

SJF: The first play I ever saw was the one I created when I was nine or ten. I would write, produce, and direct small stories, cast the neighborhood kids, perform them in my garage and invite our parents. I had no clue that storytelling would be my calling until years later.

I never said, "I'm gonna be in the entertainment industry. I'm going to act." To me it just happened. I have a curiosity about things. I see a door and it's closed … the voice inside me says, "What's behind that door?" I open that door and discover the world just like in *Alice in Wonderland*.

My mother was my first mentor. She exposed me to the arts because I was such a high, high, high-energy child! I had to have constant stimulation, so she kept me busy. I did everything.

I did athletics. She took me to concerts, shows; introduced me to literature. When I would get a restriction after getting into trouble, I would ask her, "Could you drive me to the library?" I'd come home with books then stay in my room absorbing stories. Yes, my mother was the first person who exposed me to good writing. She was a teacher and my foundation.

SMcC: When did you decide to make the transition from actor to director?

SJF: I was programmed to go to college. My mother would say, "I don't care if you marry a garbage man, but you are going to get that piece of paper. You're going to get your degree." I was gonna be a teacher and major in Creative Writing/English.

As a freshman, a friend of mine said, "Jo-Jo, look, I'm in the Theatre Arts Department and they are doing a show called *In White America*. They don't have any Black women and it calls for six actors playing multiple roles. You should come over and do it." I said, "Uh, Pudd," his nickname, "I don't act." He said, "Shirley Jo, you're so full of BS! You could do this!" I said, "Ok." I went and loved it! That was about a semester before my mother found out that I had changed majors.

I did my undergraduate work at Sacramento State College. My second mentor there was Dr. Gerard Larson, the head of the Drama Department. Paul Carter Harrison introduced me to African American theatre. He exposed me to the difference between Western theatre and African American theatre and introduced me to the concept of *"Nommo,"* which has influenced my work a lot. In one production, Paul exposed me to non-linear storytelling. He gave all of the cast members, who were Black, poetry by Melvin Van Peebles. He told us, "We are going to make a story out of the poetry and create a character." There was no written script, just these pieces of poetry. That's like making something out of nothing. We created the neighborhood and the community and thus developed *Ain't Supposed to Die a Natural Death* at Sacramento State College. Melvin Van Peebles and the New York producers came and saw the finished product. I played Lilly Done the Zampoughi. When Barbara Alston and I met, I told her "I did it first!"

I graduated, continued my studies at UCLA and received my MFA. My other mentor, Ed K. Martin, was my acting instructor. He taught me how to drop down, open and tell the truth, the process I incorporate in my directing. I am known as an actor's director because I understand the language of actors.

SMcC: **For the record, what is "*Nommo*"?**

SJF: Life Force ... Spirit. It's a West African word for "Spirit." Our life force. We are all energy. One of the differences between Western theatre and African American theatre, and it permeates all our work, is Spirit. You will see three components in ritual Paul instilled in me: there is drum, dance, and song in all the works that we create. We are conjuring up spirit.

SMcC: **You and Clinton have really delved into the differences between Western and African approaches to theatre. Are you drawn to any particular genre of theatre more than others?**

SJF: People always ask me that. A story will find me. The heartbeat of the story will dictate to me ... Style. You've seen a lot of my work. I'll go for something that is totally non-linear. I guess producers say, "This is a very strange show, so give it to Shirley because she'll make something out of it." They don't have the five-act or three-act constructs.

I like the non-linear because my mind likes creating the "in-between story." That's also part of our ritual as African Americans. It's our gumbo! It's not what's said that is important. The playwright gives you the words. You know what the themes are, the intellectual blah blah blah. You know what they are and you're going to do your research. But it is the in-between ... I don't know which musician said it, it might have been Miles, "It's not the notes that are being played. It's the space between the notes, the juices, where the music is." It's the same thing. I say, "It's not the words that are being said, it is the space in-between the words where the Spirit, where the Juice lie when bearing witness with the audience."

I learned by doing, so I don't know what the rules are. Uh oh, I'll never work again. [*She laughs.*] What we do is jazz. We're instinctual. We trust. Spirit is always in our work. We trust Spirit. We trust that voice. We trust our instincts. We go from that heart, the spirit-place, before we go to the head.

SMcC: Do you have an agent or do you negotiate your own contracts?

SJF: On and off when I was doing television. Because you couldn't do anything without going through that door.

SMcC: So, you directed TV?

SJF: Yeah, I did some episodes of *Moesha*. Then I did two short films. And one short film in a National Film Festival.

SMcC: Have you ever worked with a writer to develop a new work?

SJF: All the time. In school I did it and then again in 1980. Teddy Wilson the actor, wrote a lot of poetry. Teddy had a heart attack and said to me in the hospital. "If I live through this, I want to do a show and I want you to direct me in it." I said, "Yeah, Ok." I took his poetry and created a solo show. But it was a solo show augmented with five actors. It became an a cappella piece called *Impressions of a Loud Reader.* I was teaching acting at Southwest City College at that time. We developed it there, used the students and performed it there.

I started going to different people saying I have a show. But no one thought I was serious because I was just another frustrated actor, and I was a Negro. I got really frustrated. I was sitting down in my living room one evening venting, when someone said, "Shirley Jo, stop whining. I have a photography studio. You need a space to do this off campus and I close it at 5." So, it became a Judy Garland/Mickey Rooney space: "Let's put on a show!" So that's what we did.

This is kind of important in my trajectory and in my calling because I ended up not only putting the work together and developing the work, but I also directed it and produced it with my own money. People gasped! I always tell folks, "You don't have to wait for people to give you something. You can do it yourself."

We got reviewed—*The LA Times*, the whole thing—that year. We were in the top ten list of shows. Then Bill Bushnell, and those people I had gone to before, started coming to the theater. They called me "auspicious" because I had a little company. Diane White and Bill Bushnell, who had the LA Actors Theatre at that time, invited me to come to their theater and become a part of that company. They had writers and directors and did new works. When I got there, I was paired with Jeff Stetson where I developed *The Meeting*. We had a full production, and I was the first director. So then, you know how the drum goes: writers, new works, developing and directing new works … .

SMcC: What was the most rewarding experience you ever had as a director?

SJF: The opera I did about *Winnie Mandela*. Winnie Mandela is an icon. She helped change and transform a nation. She did it fearlessly. In her country, she was the first African nurse. She broke barriers. She was an activist long before she met Nelson. She was her own person.

SMcC: Did her downfall occur when she executed that child?

SJF: Allegedly. It's interesting. We showed it in the opera. She attended Opening Night. She was a revolutionary and she was an activist. When we were marketing the piece, they either loved her or felt she was an adulterous, murderous bitch. When they talked about Winnie, they were hesitant. I remember saying to them, "Well, don't even deal with that. Since we know that's the reality. Why don't we say, 'Love her or hate her but you must come hear her, because it is an opera.'" They used it in the marketing. Now, I don't know the truth about what happened, but what I do know … and you know … it was war.

SMcC: Has there ever been a project that frightened you?

SJF: *Winnie*. I was the only foreigner. They wanted all South Africans. They didn't want any foreigners. Since it was a multimedia piece, they needed somebody who was proficient in both. I think that's probably why I am doing so well with Zoom. I treat Zoom like it's television. It is! I guess my name kept coming up when Mfundi Vundla, the producer, came here looking for an African American woman director. L. Scott Caldwell introduced me to him, and then we went from there.

What frightened me, and I made sure in my contract, they only had in the budget two times for me to go there. One time to cast and then to do the show. I said, "I cannot do this woman's story unless I am able to understand the culture." So, one of the times I went there, I went everywhere. I even went where she and Nelson lived and stayed there. I got to be around the people and travel to every place she traveled. I knew I was a foreigner. How am I going to come to South Africa, direct a biographical show about Winnie Mandela, and not have a feel for the deep history of that country?

Now, here's another thing: I never did opera! So, I treated it as if it was a play. Everybody was like, "What's she doing?" Usually in opera, the chorus are the last people you see after everything else is done. Of course, it's "You people, you stand over here and you people stand over there" and so forth. I said, "Oh no, no, no! We must have a table read." I had the chorus all in one room and the featured vocalists, which was unheard of, we were in another room. This was actually very interesting, because I was teaching the chorus, who were about 20 to 25, the history their parents had lived through. To go into a foreign country that was really political ... tribal, and experience the questioning and the querying because I'm an American ... that was interesting. Not to mention, it was a 1,900-seat theater. I had forty musicians from the Durbin Symphony in the pit, ten principal singers, and thirty members of the chorus. It was the biggest show I've ever done. And that was quite frightening!

CTD: How did you overcome those fears?

SJF: I stopped looking at the enormity and historical significance of the project and I approached it as just another production. I treated it as any other show.

SMcC: How do you prepare as a director?

SJF: I'll say this, school should teach history like we prepare to do a show because of all the research that we have to do. The social, the cultural, the political, the musical time period. Whatever show you do, you must do that kind of research.

JOYFUL: An Interview with Shirley Jo Finney 57

Figure 4.2 *The Brothers Size* by Tarell Alvin McCraney, Fountain Theatre, 2014; l. to r.: Gilbert Glenn Brown and Matthew Hancock. Photo by Ed Krieger.

You have to find out what the heartbeat is. Doing that, I became an expert on jazz because a lot of the shows I did were set in the '30s and '40s. Just imagine if history was taught like that. Think how much people would retain about the story. I start with that and then the history. One important component, I must have, I have to find the piece of music!

SMcC: *(Laughing)* **I'm sorry ... were we born on the same day? I use soundtracks. I play them to keep me in the zone.**

SJF: Drum, Dance and Song! It's part of our ritual. We have the heartbeat. If I am in the audience and I get to rocking back and forth, they're in the pocket. The *Nommo*. Oh yeah, the music is there. You are in the pocket.

SMcC: Where do you get most of your inspiration?

SJF: The story. People inspire me. I like breaking down character, finding and creating the portrait, helping the actor create the portrait of that human being. There's nothing for me like it in the world. It's orgasmic.

SMcC: Do you choose most of your designers?

SJF: It all depends. Sometimes they say you can bring in a designer; sometimes you have to use theirs because of the budget. When I was at the Goodman, I couldn't bring in any designers, I had to use someone from that region.

SMcC: How do you convey your vision?

SJF: Sometimes with visuals. I don't have a formal director's book, but when I'm talking to set designers or lighting designers, I may find an image, or I'll have a piece of music that will inspire us all to create. I like working with designers who work emotionally. I love Victor En Yu Tan! If you ever get a chance to work with Victor, do! All those elements have a visceral effect on the audience: music, lights, the color palette is important because colors mean things. Colors emanate energy that affects people viscerally.

I remember one time I was doing Katherine McGee Anderson's piece, *Oak and Ivy* at Crossroads. Which I loved! "Myrna Colley Lee stepped on *dem* Costumes!!!"

Also, things come to me in dreams, Saundra. I trust that. I trust my visions coming to me. When I got *Oak and Ivy*, I thought, "Where is this coming from?" I dreamt about an octagon. I woke up and told my set designer, Peter Harrison, "I had this dream. I saw an octagon. What if we create this octagon as our playing space?" He said, "Ooh Shirley Jo, I like that idea!" I said, "Yeah, let's do that." From a dream about an octagon came the playing space for Paul Lawrence Dunbar and his love affair with Alice. They could step up into this centerpiece we made, and oh, I loved it! I also had a cello player on stage in a period costume. He was a Black musician who underscored the scenes. It was all so elegant.

SMcC: Was the idea of a cello in the script?

SJF: No. No.

SMcC: Where did it come from? Because that's a wild choice!

SJF: I saw this Black man with this cello … "Oooh, wouldn't that be wonderful, elegant." I said to Rick Khan, "Can I have that?" "Yeah, you can have that. We know a cello player." I said, "Great!" Then I said to Myrna, "I see all the costumes red!" She said, "You can't have all the costumes red, Shirley Jo." I said, "But it would be so pretty with this white drape." She created this wardrobe design with ambers, and reds … the gowns!

Oh, to see Black people in period costumes. That s**t was, oh excuse my language, it was elegant! It was classy. Because it was all about the language, the poetics that informed me, Paul and his poetry saying, "Let's go classical." *Because it is classic.* That's where the stream of consciousness comes in.

SMcC: Have you ever received a bad review? What did you garner from it?

SJF: Oh yeah. It hurt. But like all of us, you want to be affirmed. Starting off, you take it personally. If they don't like your show, they don't like you. That was my psychological hang up, being less than. I would curl up in a fetal position, but not anymore, because I don't need that validation. When I first started directing, I would babysit my shows. I didn't let go after opening. I didn't give them notes or anything, but I was there. Maybe it's a little narcissistic, I don't know, or maybe they still need me to be there to give them energy from afar. This was *waaay* at the beginning.

By the time tech comes now, I'm ready to move on. But my water will break sometime between tech and opening. Because as directors, we're giving birth to a creation. Once you go into tech, you're only needed to put the icing on the cake. But that part that includes the interrelationship with actors, is the place where you're nurturing and they need you. When I know that it's over, I weep. That's my release. I don't know when it will come. Sometimes it will come during some part of tech. One time it came just before opening night. I had to let it go.

SMcC: Did you have any works in progress during the COVID epidemic?

SJF: I was an instructor, and it was wonderful. Two of my shows … *Citizen* by Claudia Rankine, originally produced at the Kirk Douglas Theatre, was brought back in the Zoom format. It really worked because people got to appreciate her poetry, her language. Stephen Sachs adapted her book and he and I developed the play together. You can catch that one on YouTube.

The other one, which the *New York Times* said, "Oh this is one of the ones that got it right." We did a remote Zoom

Figure 4.3 *Citizen* by Claudia Rankine, Fountain Theatre, 2015; l. to r.: Leith Burke, Bernard K. Addison, Lisa Pescia, Tina Lifford, Tony Maggio and Simone Missick. Photo by Ed Krieger.

production of *Emmet Till*. It went up in August and ran until September 31st *On Demand*. It rocked!!!

SMcC: Ifa Baeza's play, right?

SJF: The one that I did at the Fountain with the five-person cast.

SMcC: Girl, you "stuck your thumb in that one!" Oh, that was so good!!!

SJF: We used video, Zoom, Q-Lab and created this piece that had all of those elements: pre-recording, the stage …

SMcC: Did you do it with the same cast?

SJF: Yeah, which was good because it was already in their bodies. It's like riding a bicycle. We were all at our separate locations. The crew went into each home and created their green screens. I'm so proud of that. When I did another Zoom production at UCSB, written by Brian Otano, I worked with him to develop it. He designed it to fit the format with a group of young alcoholics and addicts that meet on Zoom before their AA meetings. One of their own comes up missing. I crafted and pre-recorded it like we were going to do a film. I also used the Zoom format. It was seamless. People said, "You mean some of this is live?" But you couldn't tell. Ooh, I'm becoming a little Zoom Queen here. Once you realize it's television, it's a film. I think that's what freaks people out. For people who are just "theatre," this time has been horrible because we are in this technology. What is this format? I call it "the mashup," where you take both mediums, combine them, and create something new—the combination of theatre and film together. Now that live theatre has come back, this mashup is not going away. With all these other streaming devices, it is product. Everybody is creating. This platform is not going away. And I'm glad.

We'll be creating mashup performances where people don't have to leave their homes. Zoom has realized they have to make their platform a little more theatre friendly. They're creating other avenues to enhance what we do. We'll still have live theatre.

Even the studios are not going to go back to the way things were. Oh, the theaters are open. But do I want to attend? Do I really want to? Even going to a movie house? I'm fine watching TV. So that's why they're enhancing this mashup. We're so entrenched being in the comfort of our own homes.

SMcC: **How do you think they are going to make money theatrically on television?**

SJF: The actors are going to get paid the way they usually get paid. However, my actors in *Emmet Till* signed a Special Contract with Screen Actors Guild instead of Actors Equity because we were remote and we were recorded.

SMcC: **What's your definition of success?**

SJF: Waking up in the morning. [*She laughs.*] In this place, in this time, in this moment from my vantage point I can see where I have come from. That is success. I have been able to do what I do, love doing it, and making a living out of it. That's successful.

SMcC: **One word: How would you describe yourself?**

SJF: Joyful.

SMcC: **If you had the opportunity to start over, would you approach your career differently?**

SJF: One thing I wouldn't do differently; I like the idea that I wasn't trained. I like those free-spirited adventures I've had.

I wish I had a mentor like I am a mentor to many people. Coming up, I had to run this race, fall down, bleed a little bit, get my own self up. No one was there to school me on how to approach the next step, climb the next rung. So yes, that's what I would do differently. My mother was a humanist, so my foundation is about humanism. We approach the world that way.

SMcC: I was trying to remember, when I first became aware of you, Shirley Jo? You played Wilma Rudolph.

SJF: I was blessed to have played *Wilma*, which was the number one movie on TV for that week. She was an iconic woman, like Winnie. But I remember you because all the folk in New York were mad at me for playing Gail in film version of *The River Niger*.

SMcC: That was you! Oh my God! [*We both laugh.*] **You're my alter-ego. You changed my life.**

SJF: Good!!!

SMcC: But I changed yours first!

SJF: Exactly.

SMcC: We are sewn at the hip and didn't even know it.

SJF: Our parallel journeys … .

SMcC: I love your website. It's quite beautiful.

SJF: If people need to find me, there's a place they can go to find me.

SMcC: How would you describe your legacy?

SJF: I think my life lived is a model for others and other women of color. If anything: My Life Lived!

SMcC: If you had the chance to start all over again, what would you tell your younger self to do?

SJF: Travel. Saundra. I have always wanted to work and live in a foreign country. There is no further explanation than that … .

CONTENT 5

An Interview with Clinton Turner Davis

SMcC: I have always admired Mr. Davis. He started off as an actor, but then sometime during the late '70s, he became that rare person in the business whom everyone thought they knew but really didn't. A man of intrigue, a man of few words, who, by virtue of his position, said little but spoke volumes. There always seemed to be something lurking just behind his smile, hidden and unseen.

Interview With Clinton Turner Davis

SMcC: **How old when you saw your first play?**
CTD: The drama ministry in Church … the Christmas and Easter pageants. I must have been five. I was able to read and speak well because I was given a line. I still remember my first line in theatre: "And on either side of him were crucified two thieves."
SMcC: **Have you always wanted to be involved in theatre?**
CTD: In theatre or some aspect of the arts. Growing up, my mother was an educator. She was also the neighborhood "organizer." She would chaperone all the neighborhood children to concerts, galleries, through all of the Smithsonian, and other museums, even taking us all to swimming lessons and getting our first library cards. I had my first library card

Figure 5.1 Photo by Clinton Turner Davis.

when I was three years old. My mother never missed an opportunity to expose us to culture. When I was about ten years old. I envisioned myself as a classical pianist. I was very good. When I realized I wanted to play jazz and my mother insisted that I continue playing classical music, I stopped playing altogether. The mistakes of youth … .

In high school, my interest shifted to medicine. I wanted to be a neurosurgeon. I attended McKinley, a magnet high school. We were taking college-level courses. I attended Hanover College in southern Indiana with the intention of becoming a doctor. In 1968 things changed. Martin Luther King, Jr.'s assassination devastated me. I told my parents I needed to come home. I was numb.

SMcC: **Why do you think it affected you like that?**
CTD: I viewed King as the hope for the country and that hope had been assassinated. As one of only twelve ethnic students on the campus of about twelve hundred, I felt so out of place.

I knew I had to finish college. If not, the draft for Vietnam loomed large. My number was close to being called. I applied and was accepted to Howard University. Sitting on the steps of the Fine Arts building I realized I was happiest when I was doing something creative, usually in theatre. I remembered all the times I had come to the campus to visit my cousin, Horacena Taylor, who was stage managing productions for the Howard Players in Spaulding Hall, then later in HU's Ira Aldridge Theatre.

SMcC: Horacena was my stage manager on *Black Girl* at the Theatre de Lys in '71.

CTD: That's where we first met … at the Theatre de Lys.

SMcC: It's now called the Lucille Lortel Theatre. But getting back to Howard … .

CTD: I met fantastic people at Howard including Professor Owen Dodson, an exceptional theatre scholar, playwright, and poet. He was a celebrated writer during the Harlem Renaissance. He became a mentor. Another mentor was Dr. Elanor Traylor, one of the great minds of theatre, the arts, and culture. Dodson and Traylor were my Dramatic Literature and Criticism professors. They are directly responsible for enhancing my love of performance that has dramaturgical support.

I remember walking into the Chair of the Department and said to James Butcher, "I'm a transfer student. I want to major in theatre. Here's my transcript. I need to get out of here in two years." He looked at me in a tone of voice that said, "Negro, please!" He was very diplomatic, "Please sit down, young man." Mr. Butcher looked at my transcript and said, "With your credits that transferred, I don't think you will be able to graduate in two years." I said, "If I can figure out a schedule to give me the number of credits I need to graduate on time, will you sign off on it?" He said, "Yes." I said, "Ok, I'll see you tomorrow." That night with the course catalog in hand, I created a schedule for my remaining two years of college. In the first semester of my junior year, I took 27 credit hours.

SMcC: Damn, Clinton!

CTD: The required maximum credits allowed were 18 hours. In the second semester, I took 30 credits. In my Senior year, I took 33 hours in both semesters. I was living in the theatre department from about 8 am until 11 pm after rehearsals.

I graduated with a triple major, *magna cum laude*, in acting, directing, and dramatic literature and criticism. After graduation, I was performing in a musical at the Black American Theatre *Jesus Christ Lawd T'day*, an African American interpretation of *Jesus Christ Superstar*, adapted and directed by Glenda Dickerson. I was playing Judas. Debbie Allen, a classmate at Howard, was the choreographer.

I traveled to New York City to visit Horacena. I wanted to attend City University in New York because they had a program in which I could pursue a Ph.D. without having received an MFA. At the time, a BFA was considered a terminal degree. I went to the Admissions Office and inquired why I hadn't heard from them. I gave them my information. Later that day I had lunch with Phylicia Rashad who had graduated the year prior and was living in the YWCA on 8th Avenue— Clark Center. We sat at Howard Johnson's counter where she said, "I'm gonna give you your first survival tip in New York City." She ordered a tuna fish sandwich on toast, french fries, and two cups of hot water with tea bags and lemon on the side. When the order arrived, she put ketchup in the hot water, making "tomato soup" and we split the sandwich and fries, pocketing the tea bags for later use. Over lunch, Phylicia informed me of auditions at the NY Shakespeare Festival.

I auditioned for the *Slaughterhouse Play* by Susan Yankowitz directed by Richard Voss and thought nothing of it. However, the following Monday I received a call from my mother. She said, "I received two phone calls today. One was that you start graduate school next Monday, and the other, was that you start rehearsals for a play at the Public Theatre on Tuesday. Aren't you in a play here in DC?" I said, "Yes, I am." She said calmly, "I think you should come home now. We need to talk." I took the Greyhound bus back to DC. When I got home my mother asked, "What are you going to do?" I said, "Since so many doors have opened so quickly and almost effortlessly,

I think I want to go to New York." My mother loaned me $50 to return to New York. I promised, "I would reimburse her with money from my first check from the Public Theatre job, Horacena said I could stay with her. I would also seek financial aid for grad school." I did have an understudy for the play. Glenda wished me success. And off I went, "New York City, tall buildings and everything!"

SMcC: What year was this?

CTD: In '71, I came to New York and started working and going to grad school. However, graduate school became very boring. My advisor, Harold Clurman, and I had a long conversation and at the end of it he said, "Things would be more challenging after the first year. So, you have a decision to make. Either stay in grad school or just get out there and start working." I told him I would leave school and start working. Youthful impatience ... .

Well, the show closed, and I was no longer in grad school. I received a call from Horacena, who was stage managing at the Negro Ensemble Company. There was an opening for a production assistant. I went to NEC and was met by Steve Carter. He ushered me into the theater. The actors and director were still at lunch. Horacena handed me a broom and told me to clean the floor. Taking that extra initiative, I also mopped and waxed it.

When rehearsals resumed, Francis Foster, Clarice Taylor, Adolph Caesar, and Moses Gunn slipped and fell on the waxed floor when they made their entrances. That was my introduction to the cast of *Sty of the Blind Pig*, by Philip Hayes Dean, Shauneille Perry, who was directing.

SMcC: Shauneille seems to be the lynchpin that connects us both.

CTD: She is one of them. Through that connection with Shauneille, I met Woody King, Jr. I staged managed several productions that Shauneille directed. I continued working as a stage manager between NEC and New Federal. I did direct a couple of productions during that time, including the New York premiere of *Divine Comedy* by Owen Dodson at New Federal Theatre—the first play I directed in New York—also,

Puppetplay by Pearl Cleage, and *Abercrombie Apocalypse* by Paul Carter Harrison at the Negro Ensemble Company. But my primary source of income was from stage managing.

SMcC: Why did you make the shift from actor to stage managing so early on in your career?

CTD: Impatience. I had been auditioning as an actor, dancer, and singer, but I was not getting cast in shows I really wanted to do. However, without any effort, I received job offers as a stage manager. That meant a consistent paycheck. I listened to the ancestors and took the road they had opened for me. I thought about returning to acting from time to time, but my focus was on directing.

I held many positions simultaneously during my tenure at NEC: assistant to Douglas Turner Ward, production supervisor, production stage manager, literary manager, dramaturg, casting director, playwrighting, and movement-for-actors instructor. I was exhausted, working 18-hour days overseeing *A Soldier's Play* national tour, the current production at Theatre Four, the production I directed at Westside Arts, the production Horacena directed at Cherry Lane Theatre, a show in rehearsal and one in development and constantly reading scripts. I gave my two-week notice.

On the way to lunch, I ran into Veronica Claypool, a *very* good friend, who was on a brief hiatus from the *Lena Horne: The Lady and Her Music* tour. Veronica informed me that the show would need a production supervisor when it continued its national tour in a few weeks. She arranged an interview with Sherman Sneed, the producer, and Lena Horne herself! I signed on as the production supervisor for the last year of the tour which included dates in the United States, Canada, and London. What an experience that was. Witnessing Ms. Horne's performance, dining with her at amazing restaurants, and having stimulating conversations every day with her, Sherman, and many other celebrities who attended the show are cherished memories. I call it my year of champagne, limousines.

After the show closed, I remained in London trying to figure out what I was going to do next. I decided when I returned to the United States, I would focus more on directing. In a very short time, I began receiving offers to direct in regional theatres.

SMcC: Did you ever formally study directing when you were getting your MFA?

CTD: I didn't get an MFA. At the time a Bachelor of Fine Arts was considered a terminal degree. I did take directing courses at Howard University with Vera J. Katz, who has taught so many well-established African American artists in theatre, television, and film. However, I think I learned as much, if not more, from working as a stage manager observing the work of and having informative and stimulating conversations with many amazing directors including Shauneille Perry, Glenda Dickerson, Douglas Turner Ward, Zelda Fichandler, and Wole Soyinka. Those were my directorial master classes where I developed the skills necessary to convey ideas to actors, designers, crew members, and producers.

SMcC: Did you have an agent?

CTD: I had an agent for a very short time. I realized that I could negotiate for myself and keep the contractual percent share I was paying them. At that time, I was doing a lot of arts consulting work—reading contracts and grants. I knew the parameters of salaries in the theatrical universe, and what theatre companies said they could pay and actually *did* pay directors. With that information, I didn't need an agent.

SMcC: How did you become involved into the funding aspects of the business?

CTD: In 1979, through the Negro Ensemble Company I applied for a fellowship offered by the National Endowment for the Arts. The focus of the fellowship was to expose recipients to arts management and funding at the federal level. I moved back to DC for that summer.

Jimmy Carter was President. A representative from his administration came to the NEA to announce a new program in which any surplus funds from each cabinet department's budget would be pooled into a new fund that would fund the arts, in addition to the monies already appropriated by Congress to the NEA and NEH. This was a *huge* sum of money.

I asked the representative, "What percentage of these monies are being allocated for ethnically specific organizations?" Without blinking, she said, "At this time, we haven't been able to identify any organizations that could handle these kinds of sums." I said, "Really? What about the Negro Ensemble Company, the Dance Theatre of Harlem, the Alvin Ailey Dance Company?" I was livid.

When I returned to the theatre program office, Daisy Voight, the press secretary for Eleanor Holmes Norton, who was then Equal Employment Opportunity Commissioner, said, "Come with me. You have created havoc in this building." Word had spread like wildfire.

SMcC: When was this?

CTD: Summer of '79. Daisy and I created a strategy and compiled a list of everyone who attended that meeting as well as "interested others." Working behind the scenes, Daisy did her thing. Calls were made, meetings held, and clarifications and apologies were provided. Ultimately, to avoid the appearance of racial disparities in funding, the program was never launched. A low-level minion from the White House did take me to lunch to try to apologize for any misinterpretations that had occurred. This was my first DC "power lunch." The restaurant was crowded with many recognizable faces from Congress, the White House and K Street. I left lunch with a heightened understanding and confirmation that *THIS* is how it all works. You *MUST* have a seat at the table!!!

When I returned to New York, after a year as the production stage manager for Arena Stage, which included taking the company to the Hong Kong Festival of the Arts, I began receiving calls from the New York State Arts Council to become a panelist for the Theatre Program, and other panels within the agency. I also began serving on other state arts councils and the NEA, and at the time was an Obie Awards judge, a Tony Awards judge, AEA councilor, and later chair of its Ethnic Minorities Committee, as well as a consultant for the Ford Foundation. I had a firm grasp on American professional theatre.

SMcC: Your recommendations were instrumental in the decisions as to which arts organizations would be allocated operational funds and which would not.

CTD: My reports were only part of an institution's or artist's overall funding application.

SMcC: Wielding that kind of power set you apart from the rest of us.

CTD: I did not view what I was doing as having an association with power. I was only being honest about what I had witnessed in a production, or noted from all those interviews with artistic and administrative leaders of major theatre companies around the country. They knew I knew the truth about theirs and other companies, so there was very little dissembling. For several years, I was frustrated by not getting more directing jobs. Often, I felt as if I had been blackballed.

SMcC: So, why do you think they blackballed you?

CTD: I was asking uncomfortable questions, seeking the real truth, not the press release versions, of an institution's practices. I guess I was rocking the boat. During this time, many arts agencies and funding organizations were revising their guidelines. Ethnic diversity and inclusion were once again essential components of the application process. Some may have thought the questions challenging, I was only asking the questions to confirm if the funding guidelines for applications were being met. This funding would be based on criteria relative to how the questions about ethnic diversity and inclusion answered, accompanied with *verifiable* proof provided. For several years I served on panels and helped to create a new language for funding application guidelines for many agencies.

SMcC: Fascinating. I just assumed you left the artistic side and went to the political side of the business.

CTD: I was looking for directing work but couldn't find it. I couldn't get an interview. So, I started arts consulting. I began to fit the pieces of this new puzzle together. I was chair of the Ethnic Minorities Committee at Actors' Equity. There had been a lot of talk about inclusion and diversity in the business but very little was being done. We began revising contract guidelines to include language in AEA contract areas to increase the hiring of its ethnic, female, and disabled members. Contractual concessions were based on a company's or producer's responses to these issues. In 1985–86, we also conducted a study of LORT theatre hiring practices. Without the aid of computers, we collected data from several seasons of every theatre that signed an Equity LORT Agreement. Major discrepancies in the employment of ethnic and disabled artists were revealed.

Members of the Ethnic Minorities Committee envisioned AEA hosting a national symposium to address issues of diversity and inclusion. Initially, AEA was not completely enthusiastic about the idea since the money in their budget was tight. I told the executive secretary of AEA, "I think we should consider filing a federal class action lawsuit against the American theatre for discrimination in violation of Title VI of the 1964 Civil Rights Act which "prohibited discrimination by recipients of federal financial assistance and authorized government agencies that disburse the funds to investigate and terminate or withhold such funding based on their findings." I then told him I have a very good friend whose cousin is one of Thurgood Marshall's law clerks. We could get a draft of a lawsuit in Thurgood's hand in less than a week.

Equity pledged the first $10,000 for the symposium. In two days, we received a Ford Foundation grant of $60,000. With the addition of various donations and in-kind services from many, we raised the money to produce the First National Symposium on Non-Traditional Casting. Along with the co-producers of that symposium, Harry Newman, and Joanna Merlin, we established The Non-Traditional Casting Project, the first organization, at that time, to address issues of diversity and inclusion in the arts on a national level, and published *Beyond Tradition: Transcripts of the First National Symposium on Non-Traditional Casting*. The organization was renamed the Alliance for Inclusion in the Arts to clarify its mission and broaden its reach.

SMcC: As a director, what type of works are you naturally drawn to

CTD: I have grown a bit weary of revivals of the Western European canon. Works from the diaspora, particularly those that have a compelling use of language and other performance elements—Music, Dance, Song, Mime, and Masking/Puppetry.

SMcC: Clinton, what you described is similar to Shirley Jo Finney's approach to theatre. Didn't she mention Paul Carter Harrison's book, *Drama of Nommo*, as a primary source of inspiration for her?

CTD: Indeed. *The Drama of Nommo*, Paul's seminal work, posits the use of style and imagery, Drum, Dance, and Song, and the Word, combined with African and African American rituals to create distinct and often provocative approaches to performance, storytelling, traditional African thought, and spirituality. Using *Nommo* as a guiding principle, the Black experience is positioned in a larger, more diverse diasporic yet specific framework.

Nommo is the Word/Force that forms the basis of all creativity, particularly works grounded in an African aesthetic or point

Figure 5.2 *Fly* by Ricardo Khan and Trey Ellis, Capital Repertory Company, 2021; l. to r.: Shane Cameris, Yao Dogbe, Calvin Thompson, Jeremiah Packer, Torsten Hillhouse, Trevor McGhie, Ryan Fuchs. Photo by Clinton Turner Davis.

of view. *Nommo* provides a foundation that sustains African cultural underpinnings in Black theatre and performance. By combining word and speech, dance and movement, music and song, with gesture in performance, diasporic connections are revitalized and provide an enhanced understanding and sustained testament to who we were, are, and are becoming.

SMcC: Can you give an example of how you applied concepts of *Nommo* in your work?

CTD: I have been researching and writing what may become a book on performance techniques grounded in the African diasporic experience. At the center of this technique is the *dundun*, the talking drum—The Word. On the first day of rehearsals, I explain to the actors how we will be "tuning the script." By using the *dundun*, we are able to address the subtleties of tonal language—its high, medium, low, and slurred or elided tones. The actors hear the subtle nuances of speech and language as the words on the page come alive quickly. Combined with other exercises I've developed, actors claim the text faster as well. Once we begin blocking and continue the integration of a character's movement, emotional placement, diction, business, etc., the entire production manifests rapidly and seamlessly.

I applied aspects of *Nommo* in a production of *Joe Turner's Come and Gone* by August Wilson I directed at the Oregon Shakespeare Festival. *Joe Turner* was the first play by an African American playwright the company produced. It broke box office records and had extended curtain calls to standing ovations every performance.

We employed the talking drum and vocal exercises I spoke of earlier to access the text. I tasked each actor to identify the Yoruba *orisha* and its corresponding number with whom their character was associated. Costumes were created using colors, patterns, and iconography specific to each *orisha*. Although at times we were subtle in our design approach, the actors were aware of and expressed an additional presence, tangible and intangible throughout the rehearsal process.

Throughout the play, the actors had to select any point where their *orisha* number could be expressed by either clapping hands, knocking on the table, shutting a door, clearing their throats, repetitive gestures, stirring a pot, etc. These sounds and pulses could be inserted where the actor chose and thought appropriate as an underscoring or additional non-verbal comment on and to the dramatic action. I quietly suggested to LeWan Alexander, who played Bynum, to accidentally let his knife fall to the floor, the beat prior to Loomis' knock on the door. When he did so, everyone in the rehearsal room exchanged startled expressions of "Did that just happen? Uh-oh!" In a subsequent rehearsal, the actress playing Bertha dropped a spoon as Seth crosses to answer the door. The sounds of the knife falling, the knock on the door, and then the spoon falling enhanced the play's rhythms by an additional three notes/beats. When Seth answered the door, revealing Loomis and Zonia, a man and child, the dramatic action intensified as it becomes centered in African American folklore regarding a knife and spoon dropping on the floor.

We had subtly called upon the *orisha*, Eshu. Conjuring had begun. The framework was in place for the dramatic action that follows. Conjuring could occur freely. The actors who were now figuratively cowrie shells were standing on the stage that have been transformed into a divining board. The wooden floors of the set had a border of a traditional Yoruba pattern and was lit to inform us where we were—in two realms simultaneously. The additional beats the actors created augmented the script's musical and polyrhythmic structure, particularly when combined with the improvisational 'Juba' (Dance and Song) that ends Act One. The same type of process is repeated in Act Two, so that by the time that Martha enters at the very end of the play, the Word she brings, combined with Loomis' rejection of it, creates a new state of being through which Loomis is now able to traverse in search of his own Song. I knew I was onto something when August Wilson turned to me on opening night with tears in his eyes and said, "That's just what I had in mind."

SMcC: Do you choose your own designers?

CTD: Sometimes I have been able to choose them, but I'm at the point now that I will trust the artistic director.

Figure 5.3 *Crumbs from the Table of Joy* by Lynn Nottage, Nevada Conservatory Theatre, 2022; l. to r.: Nyssa Newman, Deseree Whitt, Devin Charae Williams, Skylar Schook, Rege Lewis. Photo by Jordan Z. Hall (lighting designer) / photo by Clinton Turner Davis.

SMcC: **Have you ever received a bad review?**

CTD: Oh indeed. Yes, several.

SMcC: **Do you remember them?**

CTD: Yes, some of them. I deal with them by donning my Dramatic Literature and Criticism hat. I re-read the review to see if they *really* understand what the play is about, my vision of it, and whether or not we achieved it. Bad reviews often happen when white critics misunderstand a Black or ethnic play because they are filtering it through European sensibilities. That is very frustrating.

SMcC: **I would love to hear about this residency you're doing in Taipei.**

CTD: One piece I am developing is *Fault Lines*, which examines the ancient African presence in China/Taiwan, and the contemporary significance of that early African presence there. Another piece I'm adapting is *Kiều*, a work for actors, dancers, singers, and puppeteers. It is based on an epic Vietnamese poem, *The Tale of Kiều* by Du Nguyễn.

SMcC: How did you come across that?

CTD: It fell off the shelf and landed at my feet at the University Bookstore which used to be on 14th Street and Fifth Avenue. I was captured by the love story, the characters, the imagery, the metaphors, and its sweeping scale.

SMcC: Do you have any other works in progress?

CTD: I am writing an opera libretto, *Immodest Acts*, about Sister Bernadetta Carlini that is freely based on a fascinating historical novel by Judith C. Brown. In the 1600s in a convent in Pescia, Italy, she started experiencing visions and stigmata. The Vatican sent representatives to observe and interrogate Sister Bernadetta as part of the process to become a saint. During the interview, it was alleged that she had had a lesbian relationship with one of the novitiates in the convent. The results of the Church's investigations bring many things into question including the nature of and responsibilities demanded of Faith. In addition to Brown's novel, the primary source materials are in libraries in Pescia and the Vatican Library in Rome. I'm brushing up on my Italian and Latin, then, off to Italy I go to continue research.

SMcC: What would you tell your younger self if you were just beginning your career?

CTD: I'd tell myself don't be so shy. Start directing sooner. Be more aggressive in seeking work as a director. My artistic voice has always been present; however, I kept it muffled for many years in fear of criticism, lack of understanding, and the possibility of paternal displeasure—my father all too frequently said to me, "Why don't you come home and get a good job in the government." I'd tell myself to travel and work more internationally to strengthen artistic connections throughout the diaspora. Plant more trees, physically and artistically.

SMcC: How do you define success?

CTD: I would define success as having all the bills paid while still having time to maintain and strengthen working relationships, friendships, and associations. To achieve what I experienced for the very first time in Taiwan, working with the Taiyuan Puppet Theatre—total artistic freedom. *That* is success.

SMcC: In one word, how would you describe yourself?

CTD: Content. At this point in my life, I am content. I am also artistically hungry.

SMcC: How would you describe your legacy?

CTD: I would say a major part of my legacy is that I was instrumental in making a difference in the American theatre and the arts by stimulating discussions of and implementing ideas, programs, and language to achieve diversity and inclusion. Another aspect of my legacy is that I trained and mentored many young artists: actors, playwrights, designers, administrators, and consultants. I continue to be an excellent educator. Honesty and my good name are at the center of all I do.

DEDICATED 6

An Interview with Chuck Smith

CTD: As a consultant to the Ford Foundation, I traveled around the country, viewing black theatres and submitting reports. I informed Ruth Mayleas, the director of the foundation's Education and Culture Program, about the Chicago Theatre Company.

Interview With Chuck Smith

CTD: Have you and Saundra ever met?
SMcC: No, we have not. It's a pleasure. I'm Saundra McClain. Clinton speaks volumes about you.
CTD: When did your interest in theatre begin? What affect did it have on you?
CS: My mother tells me she took me to see children's theatre here at the Goodman Theatre when I was a shorty. Before I went to high school, my grandmother took me to see a play here in Chicago at the Parkway Community Center. At the Center, there was a group called the Skylark Players, started by Langston Hughes. My aunt was a member of the Skylark Players in a play called *The Monkey's Paw*. I remember so well because my aunt was on stage. She was wearing her *own* robe during most of the play. I said, "That's *not* my aunt. But that *is*

Figure 6.1 Chuck Smith. Photo: Courtesy of The Goodman Theatre.

my aunt." I remember that dilemma. I went through that for years. That was the first play I remember going to *see*.

My interest in theatre came years later. I graduated from grade school in early '52, then, I went to the University of Illinois for a year before I joined the marine corps. I was in the marine corps from '57 to '63. Two enlistments. Peace time. I was in Japan getting ready to sign up for a third enlistment when I got homesick. Really homesick. I can't explain it. So, I decided to come home and get whatever was wrong with me out of my system, and then go back into the marine corps.

I came back home and worked for the post office. I was running around with two guys who were part of a community theatre group at Michael Reese Hospital. They were doing plays for the patients. These guys were in a dilemma because one of their actors had dropped out. They were in tech. The actor and I were the exact same size and they needed me because they wouldn't have to change the costumes. I wasn't going for it. But they convinced me by saying, "Chuck you can meet some really nice-looking ladies down there." I said, "Okay, we'll give it a try." To make a long story short, I walked into the theater, and I never walked out. That was in the winter of 1963. I got hooked.

SMcC: Did you study theatre in college?

CS: Oh yes. I did. After I was in this theatre group for a couple of years, I realized there was more to it than what we were doing. I went to Loop City College and studied business and theatre. They had a nice little theater down there. A brother named Sidney Daniels was my first theatre mentor. He was the assistant chair. I studied under him. Then, I went on and studied at Governors State University in the suburbs called Park Forest South. That's where I got my degree in business and theatre.

SMcC: Acting or directing?

CS: Acting. I picked up directing when I was working with a group called X-Bag—the Experimental Black Actors Guild. It was run by a brother, Clarence Taylor. He made me do everything and also taught me about stage managing. As a stage manager, I picked up on directing.

I directed a show at X-Bag called *The Daubers* by Theodore Ward. He became my third mentor. Ted Ward was a renowned playwright. He had been produced on Broadway. His play *Out Lan'*. Ted had seen me act, and I had directed one of his plays. He said, "You know, you're not going to make a living as an actor, because you're not that good. But you *are* a pretty good director. If I were you, I'd focus on directing."

In the mid-'70s, he told me, "There are no Black directors in Chicago doing professional work. You've got the field pretty much to yourself if you want it." I took that to heart and started directing. I directed my first professional show in 1978, Steve Carter's *Eden*, at the Victory Gardens Theatre. At the first preview, Theodore Ward was in the audience. He said, "Alright, now you're on your way." That was it. I've been directing ever since.

CTD: That must have been a wonderful opening. You there with Steve Carter *and* Ted Ward. Steve Carter always spoke so highly of you. You were one of his "faves."

CS: Oh wow. Such a beautiful man. Steve became one of the Victory Gardens writers in residence. I directed at least three of his plays in a row. That kicked off my directing career. Steve would come to Chicago every year. Victory Gardens would bring him in. They treated him like royalty, which he well deserved. *Eden* was the first play I directed at VG; *Nevis Mountain Dew* was the second. *Dame Lorraine* was the third. Esther Rolle came in to do that one. I didn't direct his *Pecong*.

In the '70–'71 season, I got a gig at the Goodman as an actor, understudying in a play called *The Night Thoreau Spent in Jail* by Jerome Lawrence and Robert E. Lee—the same guys who wrote *Inherit the Wind*. It was a role of a runaway slave. The brother that had the role hated it, so I went on a whole lot. I had such a wonderful time, I said to myself, "One of these days I want to work here full time." And twenty years later … in '92–'93 season I came on board.

SMcC: Have you always lived in the Midwest?

CS: I'm a Chicagoan period. I work other places, but I'm based in Chicago. Always.

SMcC: What do you think was your most challenging play as a director?

CS: The most challenging was a Lynn Nottage piece, *Whatever Happened to Vera Starks*. It was about Black actresses in the old days. In this play, there's a movie that you have to shoot and incorporate. There's a film clip interview of one of the characters that has to be incorporated in there also. There are television segments of a panel discussion where some of the characters refer to things they did on TV. And all of that's in the play. That was a hard one to put together. Very, very difficult. I don't think I ever want to do that play again.

SMcC: How much preproduction time did you have?

CS: Usually, we do a three-week rehearsal period. But they gave me four because of all the extra stuff we had to do. The very first time I was able to do it from beginning to end was the invited dress rehearsal. Lynn Nottage came for the dress rehearsal and the first week of previews. She said, "Yeah, OK, you got it."

SMcC: Have you ever received a bad review?

CS: Oh. Yeah. Several. One was a play by Lydia Diamond called *The Gift Horse*. But I have to admit, after reading the review and settling down, I kinda agreed with it.

Years ago, I had a playwriting contest of African American plays at Columbia College. It was started by Paul Carter Harrison and the chairman of the department at the time. The winner of the contest was produced at the college. I ran that contest for about twenty years. I actually had some of the plays published in *Seven Black Plays*. All of the plays in the book are the contest winners. *The Gift Horse* is one of the plays in the book.

SMcC: Why did you agree with the review after the fact?

CS: The play wasn't quite complete. I don't know if they were giving me a bad review or the play a bad review. They didn't quite understand what the play was all about. I always thought that it's the director's job to make sure that the audience understands what's going on stage, and if that's not right, it is the director's fault. The writer knows what they are talking about. I thought I did. But evidently, I didn't.

CTD: What types of work are you drawn to as a director?

CS: I am drawn to plays by African Americans, which have a story line with which I can identify. I really like a play that has a beginning, middle, and an end. I guess that's old school.

SMcC: Have you ever directed a devised or experimental play?

CS: I just did one. A piece called *Ride or Die* by Reggie Lawrence. Every day during the pandemic he would write an essay and then attach a flower to the essay. He would go out all over the city, take pictures of flowers and then write an essay about how he was feeling, about what was going on at the time, the death of George Floyd, all that stuff. He compiled the essays into a montage. Actually, we did it straight, so it was linear. We took the best essays and worked our way through them. It was pretty good. This was during COVID. The people who came to see it enjoyed it and it received pretty good reviews.

SMcC: Did you propose a concept to the designer or did the designer come to you?

CS: Reggie Lawrence has a theatre group called MPAACT. I've been working with MPAACT for many, many years. I work with their designers, whomever was available. When I work at the Goodman, I have my choice of designers. When I go outside, I'll work with whomever they suggest. If they ask me, I recommend somebody.

SMcC: How do you express your concepts to the designer?

CS: Usually, I just throw out an idea: I kind of see this. I see levels, I see stairs on the right, I see something over there. What I see is from reading the play. This is how I think we should go about it. And then, I'll let the designer go from there.

SMcC: Do you ever send designers back to the drawing board?

CS: Oh, yeah, yeah, yeah. You have to make changes sometimes. I'll say, "Maybe it will be better if we put stairs in the center, or upstairs on the left." A lot of it is compromise, because I think it's not only my show, but also their show too. I compromise whenever I can.

Figure 6.2 *Two Trains Running* by August Wilson, the Goodman Theatre, 2015; l. to r.: Anthony Irons, Terry Bellamy, and Nambi E. Kelley. Photo by Liz Lauren.

CTD: What is the most memorable experience you've had as a director?

CS: That's pretty easy, 1997. I directed a production of *Ma Rainey's Black Bottom*. We have a nice long preview period at the Goodman. We do about ten previews. August Wilson came in for the very first preview and worked with me polishing the play. The play set box office records, which didn't hurt my standing here. I'd only been here about five years. And bingo! A box office record with an August Wilson play was pretty big stuff.

CTD: What was the nature of that collaboration with August Wilson?

CS: Basically, we worked on certain moments in the play. He gave me tips on what was going on to embellish moments, especially moments in the band room with the brothers. During a lot of their conversations, he said, "Maybe it would be better if he stood up and said that rather than sitting down." I always say, "August Wilson was my assistant director." [*We all laugh.*] Everything he said worked.

SMcC: What is your position at the Goodman?

CS: I am the resident director here. I've been here thirty years now. All of those years I have been working under Robert Falls. I'm also on the board of directors. I was on the search committee when Bob decided to leave, and we brought in Susan Booth from the Alliance Theatre in Atlanta. Susan left here to go to Atlanta. I knew Susan when she was here. So, she's sort of the perfect fit.

CTD: I was hoping they'd make you the artistic director.

CS: I was asked if I was interested. I said, "No. I'm really not interested." Mainly, because of my age? I'll be 85 in a couple of months. I'm ready to start hanging things up. I've got associations with Nashville, Tennessee, and with a group in Sarasota, Florida. It won't be too long before I'm moving out of Chicago. I *do* go to Sarasota and direct a play every winter. These old bones ain't like they used to be, you know. Chicago winters are tough. I get out of here whenever I get a chance in the wintertime.

Figure 6.3 *Pullman Porter Blues* by Cheryl L. West, the Goodman Theatre, 2013; l. to r.: E. Faye Butler, Larry Marshall, Chic Street Man, Senuwell L. Smith, and Tosin Morohunfola. Photo by Liz Lauren.

SMcC: How do you prepare as director?

CS: If I don't like the play, I won't direct it. But I begin by reading the play over and over again, and then formulating ideas about the characters. If I can understand the characters and see the characters ... Oh yeah, this is so-and-so's type. I *know* this guy. This is my uncle. I know that dude. That kind of stuff. That's how I prepare. Nothing sophisticated at all. I just try to identify with the individuals who're there.

CTD: What is your process collaborating with playwrights on new works?

CS: When I had the contest at Columbia College, I collaborated with the author. The plays had never been done professionally. For twenty years I worked with African American writers on new work. They would come in to help casting and then we would bring them back in for previews. Then shape and reshape from there.

I directed most of the contest winners. But I brought in a lot of local directors to direct also. I would be in on the concept meetings and made sure that everything was the way the writer wanted. I wanted the writer to be happy more than anything. It's the writer's play, so you have to go with the writer.

SMcC: At the Goodman, are you relegated to directing plays by African American authors, or are you considered for the whole spectrum?

CS: The whole spectrum. We've got dramaturgs and literary managers who are designated to work with writers ... rarely do the artistic director, or me, or any other individual in what we call the "Artist Collective." The Goodman is a director-driven theatre. We have directors of all genres. If there is a problem, they're there. Very seldom, do *they* say, "Chuck could you come in and help us out here?" That usually doesn't happen at the Goodman.

I've done a David Mamet at the Goodman. He's not a Black writer. I've done three productions of *A Christmas Carol*. Years ago, when I first came on board, directing *A Christmas Carol* was a rite of passage, then you could move on up. I did it for about three seasons, then I did a small play in the old Goodman studio. Even though the Goodman had done all of August Wilson at that time, I decided to pitch *Ma Rainey's Black Bottom* and I got that.

SMcC: What is your legacy?

CS: Probably that more people would recognize my book, *Seven Black Plays*, with a foreword by August Wilson. A lot of people come up to me and say we studied your book in class. When I was working on the world premiere of *Gem of the Ocean*. I was the dramaturg on that piece. That was the second time I worked with August directly. The book was getting ready to come out, and I asked if he would write the Foreword. He said, "Yes." And bingo! There it is. If people remember Chuck Smith, they will probably go there more than anything else.

SMcC: If you had the opportunity to start your career over again, is there anything you would do differently?

CS: I don't think so. I am still enjoying what I do. I've always enjoyed it. Even back in the days when I was doing it for free—back in the community theatre days.

When I was teaching at Columbia College I didn't teach directing, I taught beginning acting. I wanted to tell my students the truth. If you are not going to be serious about this, don't come up here and clutter the process. It is hard. It's a difficult task. If you are thinking about being stars and making a lot of money on television, no! This is not the place for you. I really enjoyed working with young people, and I still enjoy working with young people.

I'm getting ready [to work] on a project in Nashville that has taken a couple of years to put together. I'm going to do *Sweat* by Lynn Nottage. I'm using the Black kids from Fisk University and the white kids from Vanderbilt University in a co-production. We will open at Fisk one weekend, and then do the closing weekend at Vanderbilt. I'm really excited about that. To get those kids talking to each other and working with each other. That's the kind of stuff that floats my boat these days.

CTD: Are there any other projects you have on the horizon?

CS: *Joe Turner's Come and Gone* next season at the Goodman. And a show that we were talking about that you did, Clinton. A company in Nashville called the Kennie Playhouse, that I've worked with a couple of times, are interested. I've got to read *Pure Confidence* by Carlyle Brown and let them know if I'm interested.

SMcC: What advice would you give your younger self?

CS: Be a bit more humble. I was pretty cocky in my younger days. I thought I knew more than I knew. I realize now I got away with a lot of stuff that I probably wouldn't have. Looking at my younger self, I should have stepped back and not be so cocky.

New York has off-Broadway, Chicago has the Off-Loop, which means outside of the downtown area. I didn't know the real significance of being, according to the *Tribune*, the first Black director to do a professional show in what we call the Chicago Off-Loop. That was a pretty big deal in those days.

I also started the Chicago Theatre Company with three other theatre guys. It was the first Black theatre company in Chicago to actually start under an Equity contract. I was the artistic director when we first started in 1984. Then, in 1986,

I said, "This is too much." Artistic director is a whole other ballgame. You've got too much stuff to do if you are going to do it right. And I don't do anything unless I'm going to do it right. I think I could have been a bit more humble and got more done if I had not been so cocky.

CTD: What is your definition of success?

CS: Being happy with what you do. Period. I am very happy with what I am doing. And for the most part I'm happy with what I've done.

CTD: What do you do to relax?

CS: I don't. [*We all laugh.*] I direct plays. I direct plays in Sarasota, Florida to relax ... in the wintertime. [*He laughs.*]

CTD: Where do you see theatre going in this post-Floydian era?

CS: It is unfortunate that we had to get to the Floydian era through all these tragic events. Producers are looking for Black material. Actually, looking for it. I don't think that is going to last. I hope and I am pretty sure that the Black theatre community is wise enough to take advantage of the situation.

We know theatre is a wave. You have to ride the wave. It is going to come, and then, it is going to go. Hopefully, we take full advantage of what is here right now for us as Black thespians. Take advantage of it as much as we can. Get this stuff out there. I think a lot of it will stick. I don't think it is ever going back to where it was exclusively white. I think we are here to stay. I just hope we take full advantage of what we have right now. I am really excited and encouraged to know that there are at least six Black-owned theatre companies throughout in the country.

At the Black Theatre Festivals in 2017 and 2019, prior to the pandemic, I invited all those individuals that I knew who owned theatre companies to breakfast. I said "You guys should know each other." I had no agenda. I just wanted them to meet. Now they are talking about co-productions which is wonderful. I think that is something that will bear some fruit in the long run for African American theatre. I love theatre, but I *love* African American theatre. I want to make sure that we thrive. That's what I want to see.

CTD: What productions are you directing at Indiana Rep?

CS: Charles Smith's *The Reclamation of Madison Hemming*, and *Golden Leaf Ragtime Blues*, which recently premiered at Shakespeare & Company, will be featured at Chicago's American Blues Theatre over the next two seasons, both under my direction, in their new theater currently under construction.

CTD: What one word would best describe you?

CS: Dedicated.

CURIOUS 7

An Interview with Seret Scott

SMcC: Seret Scott makes me think of a quote from *Alice in Wonderland:* "curiouser and curiouser." A brilliant actor. Her haunting performance and dramatic range in *My Sister My Sister* by Ray Aranha were dizzying.

CTD: Seret and I attended McKinley High School. We were reunited when I cast Seret in *Puppetplay* by Pearl Cleage at the Negro Ensemble Company. Seret and Phylicia Rashad played alter egos of the same character.

Interview With Seret Scott

SMcC: What was the first play you ever saw?

Seret Scott: As I remember, that would be at Howard University. I think the play was *Jamaica*, a musical. I must have been six or seven. At that time, Howard University and a couple other places were the only places we could go because everything was segregated. Howard had some of the best work going.

SMcC: Have you always wanted to be involved in the theatre?

SS: Always, because I was going to those places two or three times a week since I was a child. I remember that lined paper was an inch deep, because my lettering was so big, I would write and direct plays that were four or five minutes long for

Figure 7.1 Photo by Seret Scott.

my mom, dad, and my sister. I made the costumes *and* I had an intermission! I had heard that's what you were supposed to do, so the play would run about two minutes, then we would have intermission.

SMcC: What was your first professional show as an actor?

SS: I danced for years before I got into acting. Actually, I had two master classes with Martha Graham.

When I was in high school, I was studying dance and I joined the Washington Light Opera Company. I was the only Black out of like fifty people. We did two musicals. One was called … oh I can't remember now, but it was like *The King and I*. I soloed and we toured Richmond and Baltimore. It was a huge company. It had real live opera singers. I was between 14 and 15. I was going to be a dancer.

SMcC: What was the first professional show you did in New York?

SS: *Slave Ship*.

SMcC: **Whoa! You keep hitting me with surprises.**

SS: I was in the Free Southern Theatre and *Slave Ship's* first production was there. Producers from the Brooklyn Academy of Music came down, saw the show, and decided to produce it in New York. Our Free Southern budget was quite small. In New York City, we had extraordinary designers, extended rehearsals, script support, etc.

SMcC: **What year was that?**

SS: It was mounted in NYC a year after the Free Southern Theatre production in 1969. It was stunning. *Slave Ship* was my first Equity show and my first European tour. We went to France, Italy, and Switzerland.

SMcC: **I wonder why *Slave Ship* has never been revived.**

SS: That bad boy rocked the entire theatre world! Scenically, it was in the round. The upper and lower decks of a ship rocked and swayed. Some audiences got sea-sick watching it. We spoke "Yoruba" for the first half of the show. After capture in Africa, we were taken to the ship and thrown through a hatch from the upper level to the bottom. It was graphic, startling, and heartbreaking.

SMcC: **What made you shift into directing?**

SS: I literally had not a single thought about directing, I'm not kidding you. I was doing a play at the American Place Theatre at that time, in English and Spanish, and a black couple stopped me on the street. I thought, "They saw the show and want to talk about it." The guy says, "You're Seret Scott?" I say, "Yeah" and he says, "Would you like to direct a play?" I said, "Excuse me?" He said, "Would you like to direct a play? We are independent producers." The play was about incest in a black family. They wanted a black woman to direct it. The play was *Anna* by Charles Dumas, whom I knew. We had performed together.

After the explanation, I said, "Call Charles tonight and you tell him I was crossing the street in the rain and that I've never directed before, but if he wants me to do it, I will do it." They called me that same night to say Charles was excited about it. I doubt he was excited ... but anyway. It was a showcase production, about twelve performances, on 13th Street in a little theater in New York City that sometimes smelled like cat urine. I only sent out two or three flyers because I didn't want anybody to know about my first directing gig.

I sent one to a playwright friend whose play I performed the summer before. Her name was Nancy Fales Garret: "Look Nancy, somebody asked me to direct a play!" As fortune would have it, Nancy's play was under consideration at the Long Wharf Theatre in Connecticut. She gives the flyer to the artistic director, Arvin Brown, and says "Seret is directing now." He says, "Directing? Seret is an actor." Nancy says, "Well, she's directing now." They called me in for an interview and said, "Did you notice that all but three people in the play are 60 and older?" I said, "Yes," they said, "Would you have any qualms directing it being you're so much younger." I said, "No, no," very confidently. They said, "Why so confident?" and I said, "Because I would hire all my friends; I'm not going to hire people I don't know."

Over the years, I had played a daughter to many of the older black actors. Also, I thought, I don't have a chance of getting this job anyway, so I'm just going to answer as honestly as possible. At the end of the interview Arvin said, "We're going to make you an offer." And I'm not kidding, I started to sway, losing consciousness. What did I talk myself into? They began talking about getting the design team together early. Meanwhile, I knew nothing about set and lights ... As an actor, the only people you come in contact with are costume designers. You don't see lighting, set designers, etc., until tech. I didn't even have a name to suggest. It was my first learning experience. And it just came so quickly ... I started rehearsal at the top of '89.

I actually got physically sick the night before the first auditions. Why? Because I knew practically everybody auditioning. I imagined them seeing me and thinking "What's going on here?" Some older actors I just made offers to.

After that production, it was six to seven years of back-to-back jobs. They, white theatres, didn't know black women directors. They were hiring locally and not including many black men, much less black women. By then I was working across the country. The only black woman theatre director working nationally for several years. That was something I didn't know. A white general manager told me.

SMcC: **I thought, "Why did Seret give up her acting career?" You were at the height of your acting career!**

SS: I didn't actually give it up, but the first six or seven years, directing back-to-back, I didn't have a window for acting. I didn't' realize I hadn't been acting until about the seventh year when somebody asked me to do a reading as an actor.

SMcC: **Other than Oz Scott and Bill Duke, you seemed to be one of only a few of our peers who was directing professionally.**

SS: One thing I did realize, and I think that's one of the reasons why I stayed with directing, was that as a director I only had to be away from home for four or five weeks. But acting in a regional play was an eight-to-ten-week commitment. For family life, I found directing much more agreeable. My husband and son would often visit me in places like Philly, Boston, and DC. In Santa Fe, they came out for a week over my son's school's Easter vacation. That was wonderful.

SMcC: **Have you directed concept plays?**

SS: Yes. Often, if it was from a rehearsal process into an actual production. There were times, however, I was not able to follow through because a concept piece required two or three more weeks of development and I was already booked in another theater. But I enjoy devised work ... everyone in the room in a shared creative process.

SMcC: **Did you ever work with a writer in developing a new work?**

SS: Yes, I was at Sundance Playwright's Lab four different summers as a director. Also, the O'Neill, Pacific Playwright's, New Harmony, and a couple of others. A lot of those plays were in early or mid-stages of development and were going to be worked on for another year or so. But I've done workshops with plays that were going up right away, a final work-through before production. In those cases, I was already attached to direct the full production.

SMcC: **Do you choose your own designers?**

SS: Yes, basically I've always chosen my own designers. What happened early on, because I was unfamiliar with designers, I relied on the theatre suggesting four or five designers they'd worked with. I'd talk with them and make a choice. After a while, I would bring in who I wanted, and the theatre would go along with it, if they had the finances. It's important to note that theatres often make commitments to local or long-time design partners, promising them two to three productions in the season. They were all quite good; it just meant that we'd need time to learn how each other worked.

Early on, I didn't know the "language" to explain what I saw/ needed in the physical set, or costumes, lights, etc. I'd say, "I need three doors, one here, one here, one there." That was not at all what I needed. I was actually asking for exits to wherever, backstage, upstage, etc. By using the word "door," I was giving the set designer a visual that wasn't what I wanted. But for the designer, a door is a door ... literally. I had a lot to learn.

Figure 7.2 *Ruined* by Lynn Nottage, Denver Center Theatre Company, 2011; Kim Staunton (Mama Nadi). Photo by Michael Ganio (scenic designer).

Now, I say exactly what I need: "Two exits, one where the person can get back on stage immediately" or "I need height upstage" or "I don't want to be able to see into the wings." Designers are very savvy. You say it, and they come back with choices.

SMcC: **Have you ever sent a designer back to the drawing board?**

SS: Yes if it's too literal. I'll just say, "I don't need to have this." Once they put lighting on a set, it transforms. In my first professional job at Long Wharf, the artistic director, Arvin, said several things to me. One thing: "Don't go to black between scenes. Dim the lights, work it out fluidly, so the audience sees the world continue even in scene shifts." Some of the best advice I ever got.

SMcC: Is there a particular genre you are interested in directing?

SS: I haven't done Shakespeare, although I've been approached. They wanted me to go with my own concept, but I think it scared them to death. Greek drama, I've done a couple—*Electra*, *Trojan Women*, and was supposed to direct *Antigone*, but everything got shut down. I really like Greek drama … not sure what that says about me.

In *Trojan Women* at the Old Globe, this mask was so large, that when an actor stood next to it, the top of the actor's head was at the bottom of the mask's nose. It was stunning.

SMcC: Where do you get most of your inspiration?

SS: I don't know specifically, but I do know that I love to be and go other places. That inspires me. Also, I'm a real history buff. I enjoy thinking about where I would fit in that "former/past" world.

I think I've had a pretty interesting life. In 1970, when I went to Europe on tour, I got a broader understanding of what interested me. A lot was going on. People I knew dying from illnesses, car accidents, suicides. So, I went back to Paris and had a great time. The thought of being anywhere I wanted to be, doing what I wanted to do.

CTD: When you went back, how long were you in Paris?

SS: I was in London a couple of weeks then went to Paris from mid-November thru mid-March. I came back because of a family issue.

CTD: Did you do any theatre during your time there?

SS: I did two performances of the musical *Hair*, a popular musical everywhere at that time. The day I arrived in Paris, I went to an actress/friend's pad, Juanita. She said I could stay with her. She and some actors/singers mounted *Hair* in a tiny church that had been converted to a theater. I did two shows, and the fact that I don't sing or speak French didn't matter. I stayed with Juanita about three days and decided to go back to the rooming house near Citè University (Paris) where I'd stayed before. The rooming house was about $3.50 a night, breakfast included, but no heat from December to March. It was small, old, chilly, and wonderful. I spent most of my time with black American students who were in France doing their university semester abroad.

SMcC: One word. How would you describe yourself?

SS: Curious.

SMcC: If you had the opportunity to start over, how would you approach your career differently?

SS: I don't think I'd do anything differently. My career started in the Free Southern Theatre performing for "real" people—sharecroppers, tenant farmers, migrants, civil rights workers, the faith communities, etc., doing skits and plays for some people who didn't even have a word for "actor," or what we were doing. All that stimulated me to the point that I didn't understand commercial theatre when I got into it.

Now, the work I choose to direct has some social justice element to it. Even performing in my first Broadway show, *My Sister, My Sister*, was a play with a subject nobody discussed—mental illness and sexual abuse of a black child—and what that did, meant to that family and community. I'll tell you something interesting the producers said to me while the show was running, that there was discussion among some therapists who had seen the show. They thought I was slipping too easily into this young child's damaged mind. I thought that was what acting was supposed to be. They wanted to talk to me. *My Sister, My Sister* was pivotal for me in a lot of ways as an actor. It was my first Broadway show, followed years later by *For Colored Girls* as my second.

SMcC: **If someone were to ask you to describe your legacy, what would you say?**

SS: I am an artist because of writing, acting, and directing, an artist who worked often and enjoyed every moment of what she did in her creative life.

SMcC: **One of my fondest memories is of you eating in front of your cast during rehearsals.**

SS: I met someone in some city who said, "You're Seret Scott? I heard you eat all the time, right?" You, Saundra, always say to me "Seret, every time I see you, you're eating!" I wanted you to know that even people I don't know seem to have that opinion of me.

SMcC: **Where do you think theatre is going after COVID?**

SS: Ooooh. Something different is coming. I have no sense of what it is. I don't think traditional theatre, as we know it, will occupy the same amount of space as before. The sand has shifted ... it's out of the bottle. What is the first thing we did together? I can't remember.

SMcC: **Actually, it was one of your plays,** *Safehouse* **at the Public Theatre. I hope to direct it one day.**

SS: Oh. *Safehouse!* Wow. I get quite a few calls from universities. Some to teach and most often it's to come and talk to the students, because I guess I have some historical perspective.

SMcC: **Yeah, 'cause you're old.** [*We both laugh.*]

SS: And do you know what, that's not what I say to students. I don't say, "I'm old." I say, "Back in 1965 when I first did ... ." Students and audiences say, "That's older than my grandmother!"

[*Laughter continues.*]

SMcC: **What advice would you give your younger self?**

SS: I'd really listen to myself. I gave myself some great advice ... but didn't always take it. I've had some hiccups but no real regrets. We measure our success by doing what we enjoy doing, not by how much money we make or by comparing ourselves to someone else's career ... .

SEEKER   8

An Interview with A. Dean Irby

SMcC: The '60s was a time when the civil rights movement and the war in Vietnam intensified. Tensions around social issues, particularly when it came to women's rights, racial segregation, assassinations, the use of drugs, and the war increased along generational lines.

CTD: The possibility of being drafted of going to war had many of us looking for alternative choices. The Black Arts Movement was gaining momentum. The formation of black theatre institutions was on the rise. Increasing number of ethnic artists were seeking places to present their works and hone their crafts.

SMcC: When I met Dean he had just been discharged from the army and had an air of no nonsense about him and kept those experiences close to his vest. When asked about his past, he said, "I'm from Jamestown, New York, where Lucille Ball was born."

Interview With Dean Irby

SMcC: When did your interest in theatre begin? What was the first play you remember seeing and what effect did it have on you?

Dean Irby: Whoa! Well, if we go all the way back, my mother was the Sunday school superintendent, meaning that she was

Figure 8.1 Photo by Natalie Woolams-Torres.

in charge of all the Christmas plays and Easter pageants. I had to be *in* all of that stuff. From four years old, I was reciting things, speeches for Sunday school presentations and things like that. So, my mother was my first director.

Now the first play I remember seeing was *You Can't Take It With You* by Kaufman and Hart. It was in Jamestown, New York where I was born and raised. My sister was in it. It was done at a little community theater. There were two Black folks in it and my sister was the maid. I might have been seven or eight, but I recall how the folks on the stage were larger than life. I was a TV baby growing up. Watching TV, and then seeing those live performances ... everybody, including my sister, just seemed so huge. There was a magic about it. They were like gods. Bigger than life. I became absorbed in the magic of theatre with that show. Meeting them afterwards, I recall looking in awe at these people. There was something about being part of that live audience with live people on stage.

When I was a kid, listening to the radio, they would announce, "Now we've got Frank Sinatra singing ... ." I would think that Frank Sinatra was performing in Jamestown. I would think all those people on the radio were there in town and I was listening to them. I wanted to go see those people.

Seeing live performances had that same kind of effect on me. The irony is when I was in high school, I was in *You Can't Take it With You*, playing one of the cops. And so, my sister was a maid, I was a cop. When her son was in high school, he did *You Can't Take It With You* and he played the grandfather. So, we went from playing the maid, and the cop, to the grandfather in the same play.

SMcC: Where did you go to college? What was your major? Any significant moments ... .

ADI: I left home at 17, went to undergrad school in New Orleans—Dillard University. I was very ambitious in my freshman year, perhaps overly so. As a freshman, I was in the choir, I played varsity basketball and I was in the plays. Let me back up. I was in plays performed by the Dillard Players Guild. But my motivation for being in the guild was they had some of the finest women and they threw the best parties. My thing was how do I get into the parties and meet these women. So, I volunteered to run the lights. I knew that if I was backstage that would get me into the parties.

My very first production that year was *Tiger, Tiger Burning Bright*. I don't know if you know that play, but the guy who had the male lead became ill and there was no understudy. People kept prodding me to audition for it and I said, "No, I just want to run the lights." But I did, I auditioned, and got the part. There was something about that production ... just about everybody who enters this field, steps on the stage, and is swept up and taken over by some other force. That force has been with me from that time on. I thought, "This is kinda cool. Plus, I get to go to the parties."

SMcC: I always thought you were so quiet. I have a completely different image of you now.

ADI: I didn't do it!

SMcC: Who were some of your mentors, then and now?

ADI: Wow. Back then I don't know if I thought in terms of mentors so much. I was a political science/history major with plans of going to law school. I did not even think about acting as a career. However, I was associated with a number of folks in New Orleans, like the Free Southern Theatre which was the theatre arm of the Civil Rights Movement. Seret Scott was part of it along with Leroy Giles, Barbara Clark, and Denise Nicholas. Gil Moses and John O'Neil were the co-founders. I was associated with a lot of these folks well into my senior year. However, I was more political than artistic. I was president of Afro-Americans for Progress which promoted the inclusion of Black Studies courses in the curriculum. In the summer of '66, I went to Togo to work with Operations Crossroads Africa. We built a school and I taught English. That experience heightened my global awareness of the African Diaspora.

I had a TV show in New Orleans called *Coffee House* on the educational channel. It was a talk and entertainment show geared toward college students. Folks would come on, mostly poets, musicians, artists, and the like. I was in that circle even though my intent was to go to law school. A lot of the actors were not in college. They were people living in the city and former Dillard graduates who would come back and perform with the Dillard Players Guild. At a certain point, they decided to break off and form another company, the Dashiki Project Theatre, which ran for a good while under the leadership of Professor Ted Gilliam, as the artistic director. N. R. Davidson, Jr., who wrote *El Hajj Malik*, Carol Sutton, Adella Gautier were members of the Dashiki Project.

SMcC: When did your interest in theatre shift to something you thought you could do to make a living?

ADI: In my senior year, Michael Miller, the assistant dean at NYU School of the Arts, and Israel Hicks, who was a directing student, were on an auditioning tour for the school. Seret Scott, a student on hiatus from NYU, was working with the Free Southern Theatre in New Orleans. Michael and Israel asked her to recruit people to audition. It's February 1969, I'm still thinking law school. But I went to the audition accompanying a friend of mine, Sarah Landry who was interested in going to NYU. After her audition, they asked me if I was an actor and I said, "Yeah." They said, "Why don't you do something?" I had nothing prepared, but back then we prided ourselves in memorizing a lot of ditties like Oscar Brown Jr.'s *Signifying Monkey*, *But I Was Cool*, and pieces like that. We would recite those when we were just jiving around. Far from the classical piece they asked for, I did *Signifying Monkey* as a joke. They asked if I had anything else, and I said, "No. More of the same." Three weeks later, I get a letter from NYU offering me admission into the acting program. There had to be something they saw in me other than my audition material. I was totally blindsided.

I was going to the NYU graduate program! I said, "I can go to law school any time. Let me go and see what New York City is all about." I had prepared to come to New York towards the end of that summer to meet Lloyd Richards, who was the chair of the department. However, when I got home to Jamestown, a draft notice was waiting for me. It had been there for some time. I had to report for military service at the end of August, which was about two or three weeks away. I considered splitting to Canada. I tried to find a way to get out. But I was stuck in the Army for two years, based primarily in Fort Benning, Georgia. Although it was Vietnam era, I didn't go to Nam. They might have been worried about who I was gonna shoot. [*He laughs.*]

I kept my creative juices flowing while I was in the Army, even though my MOS, Military Occupational Specialty, was clerk typist. However, I discovered there was an Army chorus that sang at schools and for diplomats. But they played volleyball more than anything else. That sounded like my kind of gig.

SMcC: What, you sing, too?

ADI: No, I'm an actor. I can *act* like [I] can sing.

SMcC: Clinton, he's a fraud. He puts out that's he's one thing and I'm finding out all this other stuff about him.

CTD: No comment. I signed an NDA. [*We all laugh.*]

ADI: If all this stuff about the Army shows up in print, I'm denying it. When there was a production of *West Side Story* on the post, they came to the chorus, because they needed some folks to sing. As a matter of fact, one of the guys in the chorus was directing the musical. He enlisted some of us to join the production. It was kinda cool because it was a diversion from all the other military b-s. After *West Side Story*, *Blues for Mr. Charlie* by James Baldwin was proposed for the Third Army Festival of Plays. I got the role of Richard. It was great. The play came in second in the tournament. I was named best actor. That was the only award, citation, or honor I received in my two years in the Army.

While at Fort Benning, I also worked at radio station WOKS in the news department. I was also the minister of information, writing and airing press releases for CAG, Community Action Group. 1971 was a politically hot summer in Columbus, Georgia. We were very busy.

Before I was discharged from the Army, the owner of WOKS also owned a station in Birmingham, Alabama. He offered me a job in the news department there. Everybody in my family is from Alabama, except me. I was born in the North. I thought there was some symmetry in going back to family roots. As tempting as the offer was, I contacted to Lloyd Richards, whom I had not yet met. I asked if I could still get my grant to study at NYU. He said, "Come on up." That was that.

In 1971, I started in NYU School of the Arts, MFA Acting Program. Frankie Faison and Reginald Vel Johnson were in my class. Trazana Beverly, Oz Scott, Sati Jamal and Kermit Frazier were also studying there. Elain Graham, who was a year ahead, always signified, "Who is this Rap Brown lookin' dude comin' in here?" I was sportin' a fatigue jacket, a beret, beard, and sunglasses. I was revolutionary down.

I was in the acting program without ever having taken courses in acting whatsoever. What I was doing was instinctual. If you asked me, "Where I was coming from?" "I was coming from over there." I had no idea how to articulate what I was doing. Lloyd recognized that very early on in my acting. He was my first acting teacher. We did a scene from *In the Wine Time* by Ed Bullins. I had the first line in the scene. The line was three sentences long. I'd memorized the line. Lloyd asked, "Where were you coming from with *that* line?" Every answer I gave him was wrong. Lloyd went off on me for the next 45 minutes based on those three sentences. I was destroyed, totally destroyed. I went home to my basement apartment on East 15th Street and said, "I can't do this. These folks coming in here know what they're doing. I don't know what the hell I'm doing." I considered dropping out right then and there. I was in there with a whole bunch of white folks. They were doing trust exercises, and I thought, "I don't trust these folks."

I went to my basement apartment on a Friday night. I was down there wrestling with the Devil deciding if I really wanted to do this. I knew if I did, I was going to have to give up a lot of who I am. That Monday, I decided I would stick with the acting program. I was still in school when we did *The River Niger.*

SMcC: My earliest memory of you was when you joined the company. Doug took you under his wing almost immediately.

ADI: That was one of the weird things, because I had been around NEC. NYU was on Second Avenue. Everything was on Second Avenue. The Public Theatre was right around there also. All that activity was right there. One day, I was walking on Second Avenue. I heard these footsteps coming up behind me, walking very fast. I had the New York suspicion going on in my mind, so I turned around, and it was Doug. He said, "I want you to come in and read something for me." I knew nothing about *The River Niger,* but I read for him. Lo and behold … there we were. That's how it started.

CTD: That was when I first met you in front of the Orpheum Theatre where I was the house manager.

SMcC: Why did you decide to make the transition to directing?

ADI: There was something about directing that appealed to me. I talked to Bill Duke, a graduate of NYU's directing program. Bill turned me on to Fantastic Art books, which I still have. Those books started me going to museums and looking at art from a different perspective, not as static objects, but having mobility. I began to see how that mobility could translate to stage. Bill talked to me, and I went to talk to Lloyd about transferring to the directing program. I'd never directed in my life. Lloyd, in his infinite wisdom said, "Listen, why don't you attack directing through the acting program." I didn't understand why he was suggesting that, but I realized later, he was saying that you don't know s**t about acting, so why don't you stick with this program and see how that works out. Then, you'll be able to make an educated choice.

CTD: What was the first play you directed?

ADI: I had been talking to Steve Carter, who ran the Playwrighting Workshop at NEC. Doug knew I wanted to try my hand at directing. They were doing workshop productions upstairs on the third floor.

Watching Doug direct *Niger*, I gained a little knowledge about staging. But I still had questions about the craft of directing. Steve offered me Herman Johnson's *Nowhere to Run, Nowhere to Hide* to direct. That cast included Frankie Faison, Samm-Art Williams, Leon Morenzie, who were some of the biggest Negroes working in New York. I'm not talking about professional status, I'm talking about their physical sizes, that I had to put on this postage stamp-size stage. It was terrible. I had no idea how to approach it. It was scary but thrilling figuring out how to do this. Solving the problems of that production drew me to directing. And why I still do it to this day.

Problem solving is the thing that interests me the most. Looking at the play as a puzzle, how do you solve the puzzle? It was not so much the intimidation of it being my first production. That did not really bother me. Or that it was being reviewed by the *Daily News* and the *Village Voice*. However, the fact that people were going to pay money to come see what I had put on stage, that scared the s**t out of me. I took on the weight of the writers, of the actors, and the prestige of the Negro Ensemble Company. I took on all that weight to produce and put on something that was worth people paying money to come see.

CTD: Do you still carry that weight when you're directing?

ADI: Yes. Not as much, because the play is the thing. But I do still feel some intimidation, but it's become a positive driving force.

CTD: **Are there plays that have frightened or challenged you?**

ADI: Early on, yes ... But fortunately, back in those days, there was a lot going on. I was directing a new show every three weeks. I was very accustomed to having a two-week rehearsal period. When somebody had to put up a show quickly, my name would come up: "Dean Irby can do that." The first time that I had a four-week rehearsal period, I didn't know what to do with those extra two weeks. I had to figure out how to fill that time. But I slowly realized that those other productions were not fully realized or thought-through well enough. I was just tossed into it. I didn't have ample time to do any pre-production. That laid a certain kind of groundwork for me on how to approach things. That came very early on, that moment of saying, "Wow, can I do this?"

Sati Jamal had a very bad car accident and was laid up in a hospital in Teaneck, New Jersey. Before that accident, he had been contracted to direct a play at U Mass-Amherst. Charlie Brown, Terria Joseph, Eva Marii, and some actors from the DC Black Rep came up to fulfill his contract. It was a benefit for him. The play was Clay Goss' *Ornette*. It was a three-act play with a cast of nine. In each act, the dialogue was identical. The

Figure 8.2 *The Balcony* by Jean Genet, State University of New York at Purchase. Photo by Zoe Markwalter.

only thing that changed was in each act the same lines were said by different actors. Sati loved the play, but I had no idea what that play was about. No idea! Sati couldn't help me. He could hardly breathe.

I knew that even though the play was entitled *Ornette*, the play was about Charlie Parker. I inundated myself with Parker's music. Bebop, I just listened and listened. Again, I was intimidated but I said, "Maybe what this play is about is a piece of music. Like bebop. And like bebop, you establish a theme and that theme may be a recognizable melody. Then you riff on that theme, which you may not recognize at all. And then come back around to that initial melody to resolve the tune." I thought, "Well, that is a three-act play." That's how I approached it. I looked at it as a piece of bebop music. You set the theme, you go into a riff, and then bring it back around with a little somethin' extra. This was totally God. I'm telling you I wasn't conscious of what I was doing. It was instinctual. However, the biggest praise that I got … . Oh, this is the other thing. If that play was done straight up, just dialogue, it was only 27 minutes long. [*We all laugh.*]

CTD: Nine minutes per act.

ADI: We were contracted for about $3,000. I thought I can't take $3,000 from these people for a 27-minute play. So, I added a jazz quartet. When we finally performed *Ornette*, we had dancing, singing and a lot of music that lengthened the play to a respectable hour and twenty minutes.

CTD: Wasn't Paul Carter Harrison at Amherst then?

ADI: Paul was there. Ted Joans was there. A plethora of black intellectuals were teaching there, and they were all going to *be* there in the audience.

SMcC: Remember Neville's wife? Was she there then?

ADI: Aishah Rahman. They were *all* there. After the show, Clay Goss looked me in the eye, and I thought, "Oh s**t, I done f**ked up his play." But he said, "Yeah. *That's* what I wrote," as if he didn't realize it while writing. It was *that* bebop orientation he may have known subconsciously.

CTD: *Ornette* **was conceived and developed at Howard University. I think Sati directed it. I've talked to Clay about**

Ornette. **What you described *is* his original intent. In addition to jazz and artwork, what other tools do you employ when you begin working on a play?**

ADI: For some reason, I have to hear it musically. I'm not a musician. I can't read music. I know when the tune goes up and down. It's interesting that I have to hear the play musically, even if it doesn't involve music and I don't have particular tunes in mind. That's the starting point for me.

This can sometimes come back to bite you in the butt.

Richard Wesley saw the first play I directed, *Nowhere to Run, Nowhere to Hide* by Herman Johnson. I chose this piece from Herbie Hancock's *Headhunters* album to use as segues between the play's eight scenes in six different locations because I thought it was cool. It had a bouncy movement and I put it after every scene to tie everything together. I was so proud of myself. After the show, Richard said, "You know I used to like that song. Now, I never want to hear it again!"

I was a political science/history major. History has always played an important part in my life. Research, going back and seeing the beginning … .

SMcC: How do you express your concepts to designers?

Figure 8.3 *The Seven Guitars* by August Wilson, Purchase University. Photo by Zoe Markwalter.

ADI: One of the good things about working in a theatre arts program in academia, is it consists of acting majors working closely with tech design majors. One of the classes I teach in tech design is Directing for Stage Managers. which gives stage managers the language and insights into the director's process. Clinton, you'd be a good person to teach that class, because you've got that area covered.

CTD: **Well, invite me! Throw my name in the pot.**

ADI: We'll talk. That class is geared towards giving stage managers what a director might be thinking when they make certain choices. To prepare the stage managers to understand those choices directors make in rehearsal and also what actors may require. I'm a strong user of metaphors.

SMcC: **Like what? Name a few.**

ADI: I was doing *The Bacchae*, the Wole Soyinka version, set in Africa or some mythical place. I approached the play with the idea that the space we are in is a liminal space. It's like a doorway. You stand in a doorway ... you're not in the hall and you're not in the room. It's not a space where you want to be. But it's transporting you to another space, either physical, emotional, or metaphorical. I began to open them up to what that space might look like.

Within his Open Theatre, Joe Chaikin frequently spoke about working in liminal spaces. The students conceived very interesting and creative solutions of utilizing liminal space. What made that work so well for *The Bacchae* was using stadium seating in the black box theater. So that configuration served the production very well.

SMcC: **A few of the plays you've mentioned are a bit abstract. Do you prefer that genre or style?**

ADI: Not necessarily. What I also appreciate about working in academia. is the ability to direct the old war horses, by such playwrights as Williams, O'Neill, Brecht, from an African American's perspective. I recently directed *Orpheus Descending* by Tennessee Williams.

In the play, Val is a white renegade, outside the norms of southern society. Lady is this Italian immigrant married to a racist bigot, Jabe, who was responsible for her father's death.

When Val and Lady fall in love, Jabe incites the KKK to hunt him down. What if Val is black? How does that relationship intensify the drama? I came to that casting choice because of the racial makeup of the company.

Also, in the original play, the only black character, Uncle Pleasant, is part Choctaw Indian. You only see him twice. He comes in, mumbles unintelligible words and they throw him out of the store. So, I thought make Uncle Pleasant a central character who is aware of everything going on. He's the misunderstood conjure man, maybe like those homeless people out there on the street. My instinct was to get closer to Uncle Pleasant and hear exactly what he was saying. I wanted to know more about him. He opens and closes the play. We see him going through rituals. He weaves in and out of scenes, seen and sometimes not seen. He becomes the catalyst, stirring the pot, driving the dramatic action. I created those moments.

I did the same thing with *Dancing at Lughnasa*, an Irish play. Four sisters have one brother who's a priest. He's vaunted, the pride and joy of a good Irish family. He's a missionary sent to Africa to Christianize the "heathens," but he becomes absorbed in African culture. When the Church finds out, he is defrocked, looked upon as insane, and sent back to Ireland, in disgrace.

SMcC: He went native.

ADI: Yes. I decided to make that a central point. I added the traditional Irish bodhrán drumming which evolved from the tambourine. The rhythms and sound were evocative of African drumming and expanded my diasporic nature of the play.

SMcC: What do you have on the horizon?

ADI: There is a play, *Socrates,* by Tim Blake Nelson. It is an intelligent, brilliant play, dealing with the trial of Socrates. In the play, democracy is under attack. It's very timely with what's happening in Congress and throughout the country right now.

SMcC: What's your definition of success?

ADI: Professionally, success is when I collaborate with actors to create something that has not been there before. That's very satisfying. As an educator, success is seeing that light of discovery in a student's eyes. That revelation surprises them and is wonderful to witness.

CTD: How do you find balance working professionally and working in the academy? How do you relax? Do you relax?

ADI: No. I smoke a joint … [*We all laugh.*] But seriously, I have never found that balance. Israel Hicks solved that problem for himself.

CTD: How?

ADI: He recruited me to Purchase. Israel was the chair and the Dean. He was also the associate artistic director at the Denver Center of the Performing Arts. He was the first to direct all of August Wilson's plays in one theater. When he left us, he went to Rutgers and was head of the department. He also co-founded with Wren Brown the Ebony Repertory Theatre in LA. He found a way for himself to balance all of those things until the day he died. I'm still searching.

SMcC: You really enjoy academia. But how do you deal with all the restrictions and the politics of academia?

ADI: It's ugly. I co-chaired the department for over twenty years. You know that old saying, "Never have so many fought so hard for so little." Dealing with administrative minutiae was depressing, especially when you go through it year after year, facing the same obstacles. It wears you down. I haven't been the chair for four years. I rediscovered the joy of simply teaching and directing. I thought, "Damn, had I known this, I would have given up chairing a long time ago." But it would have left the department in the lurch.

I *do* enjoy the students in the studio. I can have a terrible day, dread going to work. However, once I'm in the studio and we get into it, it transforms me.

SMcC: What would you want your legacy to be?

ADI: Legacy? Finding the humanity in the art. We're in an artform that deals with human foibles, human aspirations, and human needs. How do we access that? First, we have to find that sense of humanity in ourselves.

SMcC: **If you were to describe yourself in one word, what would that word be?**

ADI: Seeker.

SMcC: **If you had the opportunity to start over again, is there anything you'd do differently.**

ADI: Go to law school … .

NURTURING 9
An Interview with Michele Shay

CTD: I first met Michele at the Negro Ensemble Company and worked with her on several productions including *Home* by Samm Art-Williams and *Daughters of the Mock* by Judi Ann Mason.

SMcC: Michele and I shared the stage on several occasions, including *Goin' Thru Changes* by Richard Wesley. I directed and performed with her in *Women of Plums* by Dolores Kendrick. With a Tony nomination for August Wilson's *The Seven Guitars* and numerous other prestigious awards, her unique brand of wisdom and insight are compelling.

Interview With Michele Shay

SMcC: **How old were you when you saw your first play?**
Michele Shay: I was in high school, and it was through Jack and Jill—*In White America* with Gloria Foster.

It was off-Broadway. We were sitting very, very close. She was doing this speech about the little girl who was integrating a school in Little Rock. I watched her do that, this grown woman become this little girl, this teenager, and she cried. I could see the tears rolling down her face. We were sitting that close. It made an indelible impression on me. I couldn't believe she was going to do it more than once. It was a matinee.

DOI: 10.4324/9781003410737-9

NURTURING: An Interview with Michele Shay

Figure 9.1 Photo and makeup by Shantha Caldwell.

I just never ever forgot it. So later when I decided to go into theatre, that was the monologue I memorized. Lou Gossett coached me for my audition. He was the first person who told me I had any kind of talent whatsoever. Later, I got to work with her doing *Coriolanus* in Shakespeare in the Park. I got to be in the same space with her because she just became the "Queen of Everything" to me in terms of her work. The fact that I got to meet her, know her, and become sort of friends took me over the moon.

CTD: She was a powerhouse.

MS: Yeah. I used to try to see whatever she was in.

SMcC: What was the most memorable experience you had in the theatre as a director?

MS: I'm going to have to answer that in two parts. This show I did, *Blue Stockings* by Jessica Swayle at NYU … when was that, 2015? It was the first play I ever did first of all that the cast was completely mixed but predominantly white. It was

Figure 9.2 *Two Trains Running* by August Wilson, Matrix Theatre, 2019, with Adolphus Ward. Photo by Tiffany Judkins.

traditionally a white story. Everything else I had directed was racially centered for the most part. It was a period piece. The issues in the story were based on the true incidents about these girls trying to get a degree at Groton College in England. The boys' colleges literally would put effigies on fire because they did not want these girls to have a degree. With all the different issues I had to confront, the impact, both emotionally and visually on the audience, I consider that play to be one of my greatest achievements.

The other was directing *Two Trains Running*. There was just a moment, trying find ways in which to illuminate the experience of the text in a way that was really special. To get the actors to do that. I was working on the moment when the main character comes in. He's gotten his money from selling his place, and finds out that Hambone has died. That moment of him changing character and opening his heart to who Hambone was after he fought him the whole time … . There was a moment in rehearsal … it didn't happen all the time in performance, but in rehearsal this transcendent experience happened. The actor got what I had been trying to get him to do the whole time. That was golden. That's what I try to achieve when I direct people experiencing a level of "soul realization." That's very hard to get and illuminate it in the text … . That didn't make no kind of sense. [*She laughs.*]

CTD: It made a lot of sense.

MS: I mean it's very difficult. The stuff you see when you are on a different side, and you are not acting. There's something you understand in the text and the circumstance that is not the traditional way that an actor will go to choose something. You're trying to get something more. When that happens, its electrifying. My whole body and Sophina Brown, the producer, and everybody who witnessed it could feel it right away. I kill myself trying to have that happen in the theatre so that it reaches people on a deep level. Their lives could change.

CTD: How did the actor respond in that moment? Did he know what was happening?

Well, I'd say yes and no. He went to the place where he allowed it to happen. He does not usually take the brakes off—the control levels off himself enough—to just let that show up for him. There's an automatic place that we go to as actors that is not necessarily as true or as authentic as a moment is requiring us to be. We have habitual ways of doing something. Actors don't always trust what the director is trying to get them to do. I find that one of the challenges of directing that's happened other times when coaching an actor through a scene in a rehearsal. They get it but they can't necessarily repeat anything in that framework. They'll go around it. But they can't exactly do it in the pocket. I think that's one of the most challenging things. How do you foster that and get out of the way of it so they can do it on their own without you? That's been something I've had to learn … to inspire something and get out of the way so that they can repeat it.

SM: How do you prepare as a director? Is there anything specific you do in terms of your research or … ?

MS: Oh God yes. Because I fell into directing.

SMcC: We all did.

MS: Fortunately, when I was in school, I chose Introduction to Directing with (ooh, I'm going to date myself) Lawrence Carra who was one of my teachers at Carnegie Mellon. His book *Fundamentals of Directing* is used at many schools as a basic text for studying directing. I began to learn about staging and purpose. I never directed anything, but I did study for one semester with him. Then I would watch everybody that I worked with. And that was it.

While we were doing *Seven Guitars* on Broadway, somebody I knew who was then chair at the University of Michigan and worked with at the Guthrie, invited me there to direct *Wedding Band* by Alice Childress. It was my first show. I was terrified. I didn't know how to talk to designers or anything, so I went to the library. I got as many pictures as I possibly could about different things. I had seen *Wedding Band* you know with …

SMcC: Ruby Dee.

MS: Yes, Ruby … the TV movie of it, I think, in 1974. I was very impressed. It started at the University of Michigan so that's why I recommended that we do *Wedding Band*. I spent a lot of time studying the period. Historically, I did as much research and got as many visual images as I possibly could for the designers.

Now, I always do Pinterest boards. I get as many visuals … I keep one Pinterest board as basic research of the time. Pictures on how people have staged things. I have a Pinterest about people, about images. All kinds of things for every single show I do.

Because visual stimulation helps me a lot. I love lighting but I have no idea how they do it. I try to do images of that. People tell me I direct cinematically. So, I depend a lot on the lighting in particular to help create the emotional subtlety of a show … to help tell the story.

And Music, Rhythms and Tempos. People's attention spans are so short that I try to keep something going on all the time. Once you're building something, it doesn't flop as you're doing scene changes. Often, I choreograph scene changes so that there is life going on to add to what's happening. It's a lot of intuition and standing in the space before communicating with the set designer. I have to be in the space even when I am blocking sometimes. I tell the actors, "I'm sorry

I have to stand and do with my body to figure out what has to happen." It's a lot of intuition.

SMcC: Is there any genre or style of theatre in which you would like to direct?

MS: Story, characterization, enchantment and overcoming circumstances are key elements to navigating the path to openness in an audience. I have done a couple of musicals, new pieces. I must say mostly I get thrown into realistic kinds of things. I've never done anything really Absurd. I think *Gloria* by Brandon Jacob Jenkins took me out of the realm of normalcy because of the nature of the subject. It had been done off-Broadway. He gave me permission to do it at NYU. That stretched me in terms of the style I created since it had to do with someone shooting up an office. I would say it was not realistic. But mostly people hire me to direct realistic and traditional works.

SMcC: Have you ever directed a concept, devised, or experimental work?

MS: I am really thrilled about a compilation we did this summer, *Echoes of Us*, that had 19 different writers. The compilation was a celebration about us as black people. We had a piece from a child who remembered being more than a human. He remembered himself before he was put in a body all the way through to a futuristic time. *Echoes of Us* was being done to help move us through the pain we have experienced especially since the pandemic and George Floyd. We did three performances in San Francisco with Anna Marie Horsford and L. Peter Callender. It was thrilling because of its impact and the experience the audience had.

Helping to curate and stage that, and what happened to the audience, is what I have been living for all these years in theatre. It's a living piece that's going to change. It was a very simple staged reading. Everything was rehearsed, with visual images behind the actors and music connecting images and actors … . It was ecstatic. The black people that attended were euphoric and felt like they were experiencing being *seen* as black people. They were changed.

One of my missions is to help create healing for us, get the pain out of ourselves ... keep the wisdom, but get the pain out of ourselves. I got a grant in 1997 to focus on studying the connection between healing and acting. I studied with people that were artists and who were healers. I've been interested in the state we fall into when we are in our highest creative state. I wanted to know if there was a systematic way to cultivate that state when you are in a performance.

That led me to study energy healing. I was acting in *Blues for an Alabama Sky* by Pearl Cleage in Denver that Israel Hicks directed. The person doing my hair was a reiki master, who would do healing sessions on me. I got, what do you call it, an attunement so I could do the same thing— put my hands on myself to do that. Then I started to say, "Well, can you use this in performance?" She gave me an idea how to try it. When I started using it in performance, people responded very differently to the impact of the character. So, I created different impulses. That started me to get more curious. I've been studying that kind of thing for a long time, wondering if there is a way you can design performances that really shift people, even physically, on a deeper level.

That's been part of my quest. Is it possible to do theatre that can generate that? Doctors say it is possible. I'm still playing around with that. It's my background research, studying emotional intelligence, being in the presence of "story" biologically and how it changes people, whether they know it or not, on a cellular level. You don't have to have the agreement of the mind in order to cause that shift to happen.

All of my work has been inspired by wanting to mitigate racism in some way or the other so that we see and experience each other differently. That's what inspired me to go into theatre in the first place.

SMcC: **I directed *Spring Awakening* at USC, and was intrigued by several cast members who said you taught them to work from a "chakra." Can you explain how working from a "chakra" is incorporated in your teaching methods?**

MS: Michael Chekhov uses it a bit when he talks about working from centers. I call it, "what's under the hood." It's how we're working. There are basically seven chakras. It's like, is the character coming from their head? Are they coming from their heart? Are they coming from their gut? Are they coming from their groin? Each of these centers in our bodies are responsible for all the functions, either what flows or what blocks. Think about electricity. There are organizing principles in our bodies. Different exercises we traditionally do in acting activate them. Qi gong, tai chi, whatever. It's the life force inside of us.

Each center has a different kind of personality. The first chakra which is at the base of our spine, it's connected to our hips, our thighs, our legs, our feet, and our backbone. Because that is a connection of action. *Viewpoints* [by Anne Bogart] deals with that somewhat too. The impulse for action is coming from that center. The impulse for security and safety and being in your body is coming from that center which is below the navel. That element is the earth element. When somebody is grounded, or just kind of very basic, that's her chakra energy.

The second chakra is between the navel and the pubic bone, and that element is water. It has fluidness to it. That's the center for our creativity and our sensuality. Then that impulse arises in you or it's blocked, it's coming from there.

The third chakra has to do with the stomach area. Joy is in one aspect of it, and fear, where the kidneys are the back of us, is the other aspect of it. As the centers move from there to the second chakra, which has a fluid sensual center, into excitement and life force energy. That's where that comes from.

The heart center ... is both for receptivity to love, personal love, love with one person, or love with the whole world. Then the character can come from that. Or you can mix those centers. But that may be getting too complicated.

The throat chakra ... has to do with the ability to speak your truth or conceal your truth. The sixth chakra is thought and intuition. That's the space between the brows and the top of the head.

The quality of the seventh chakra is stillness. This is a spiritual center, the center of knowledge, ideas, and wisdom. It's like "Aha!" or "Oh my goodness!" It also could be spaciness or playing somebody that was high. (That choice would be coming from that center.) There is no weight here. The weight starts to move in the body from here up. And then actually it can even go higher, but I basically do those seven.

It's helpful as a way in for actors to think about that. But what's helpful in teaching is a process whereby the actor can discover what is accessible to them when they encounter a blockage. There are physical exercises to help the actor open up, and become more available to feeling the intensity of whatever the impulse is.

Now what's made it sort of commonplace is the Lucid Body work. Fay Simpson, who was starting her work the same time I got my grant, was exploring it through movement. She started at Yale and is now at NYU. Working this way is becoming more accepted and notable. But when I was doing it, people didn't do it. They thought it was very "woo-woo."

CTD: How do you employ the use of chakras in your directing process?

MS: It depends upon whom I am working with. I don't do it with everybody in a normal situation. In the old days when you could really touch people, there's a warm-up to make people available to it. When I was doing *Blue Stockings*, I would warm up the whole company with this. When I was teaching at the Black Arts Institute, I would give this warm-up to all the actors. Some of the people I introduced this to professionally, still use it, like Sanaa Lathan, for example, whom I coached. And Jonathan Majors, whom I directed in *Fences* at North Carolina School of the Arts. I always did the warm-up with that company. When rehearsals are open on a simplistic level, looking at another person, you engage them on a much deeper level. There is less fear and more availability. Everything is based on breath, movement, tai chi, qi gong, and other practices. Energy gets stuck in the body. When it's moved, the system becomes more available. Part of the challenge is having the actors manage the intensity that shows up.

What I love about this way of working is that it builds a sense of trust in one's own self. This allows your system to be free to be impulsive. With complex things ... there's more to it. You go through an emotion and can step in and out of whatever state the character has to be in. I work individually with actors to teach them these techniques. But I only go as far as it looks like they can handle.

I've done all this myself and opened my own system so I could handle more and more and more. I've gotten used to the levels of intensity. I don't know about anybody else. I find as actors, we get scared of where we are asked to go. Usually in the training systems, we're being taught how to really take care of ourselves. I try to find others today to give actors ways of entering and leaving the "character-life-state" safely. That's important.

SMcC: Why did you decide to shift gears to directing?

MS: When I was in college I took one elective, Directing, for two semesters. That's how I learned the basics. I just always paid attention to what the director was doing when I was acting in a play, especially as a member of the Guthrie Theatre Company, which did many different styles of plays. I shifted gears when companies started asking me to direct.

SMcC: How did you make the transition from actor to director?

MS: I have not transitioned out of acting; however, I love the perspective. Directing gives me the whole process and the power of interpreting the story and guiding performances. I watch work, read books, study writing, gather images, do research, and manage my fears when I am being challenged with something I have not done before.

SMcC: What was the first show you directed?

MS: *Wedding Band* by Alice Childress at the University of Michigan.

SMcC: Did you study directing in college?

MS: Only class I took was at Carnegie Mellon with Lawrence Carra whose book, *Fundamentals of Play Directing*, was used in many schools.

SMcC: What was your most rewarding experience as a director?

MS: That's difficult to answer because I have favorites for different reasons. But I will name *Reparations* at the Billie Holiday Theatre by James Sheldon. I worked really hard on the development of that play with the playwright, who was Caucasian writing about race and sexual abuse of both sexes. There was drama and comedy. Audiences came back more than once to see the play. It was the first time I won an AUDELCO award for my directing.

SMcC: Has there ever been a project that frightened you, but you accepted? How did you overcome that fear?

MS: *Reparations*. It was the first time this black theatre was doing something by a white writer. There was a lot of shifting of perspectives that needed to happen even though the premise was really great. I had to develop the playwright's trust and willingness to shift. We were proud of what all of us contributed creating the script's success. It was controversial and could have been potentially disastrous.

The other was *Blue Stockings* by Jessica Swale, which was my first period piece. It required a tremendous amount of

Figure 9.3 *Reparations* by James Sheldon, Billie Holiday Theatre, 2021; l. to r.: Gys de Villiers, Lisa Arrindell, Alexandra Neil, and Kamal Bolden. Photo by Dex R. Jones.

research and complex staging. I learned to face the fear, trust myself and my team and create anyway. That, to this day, has been one of my most favorite shows. I directed it at NYU.

CTD: Who were your mentors?

MS: Fran Bennett was one of my major mentors. I worked at the Guthrie Theatre for three years with her when I first got out of school. Lloyd Richards, Israel Hicks … Hal Scott. Those were the main ones. My mentors directorially have been Michael Langham, Israel Hicks, Hal Scott, and Oz Scott. But first of all was Lloyd Richards.

SMcC: Did you work with Hal Scott?

MS: Hal and his family were very good friends of my mother. We all lived in Orange, New Jersey. My mother brought me to meet Hal. And through Hal, I met Lloyd. Hal opened the door for me to audition for the O'Neill. That started everything. I worked with them directing me at the O'Neill. Lou Gossett … if it wasn't for Lou, none of this would have happened. If he hadn't coached me in my audition. I am still in touch with him. Lou never saw me act until he saw me do Aunt Ester [*Gem of the Ocean*] in the readings at the Kennedy Center. That was the first time he ever saw me act. But if it hadn't been for him, I wouldn't have gotten into school, because I had never been in a play when I auditioned.

SMcC: What do you prefer, acting or directing?

MS: I don't know if I can answer that. I prefer to be creative. Right now, I am missing acting because I have not done it in a while. I love directing. I must be creative in whatever form that is. There are times when I feel like I need to act because my emotions back up I need to express versus to telling other people what to do. I need to do it for myself. I love what's possible. I absolutely love it … .

One of my greatest achievements was my production of *Wedding Band* at University of Michigan. Sophina Brown played Julia, the lead. She's the producer of all the August Wilson plays I directed in LA. Dominque Morisseau, and Angela Lewis were in that show. All of them have great careers.

Next thing I did was *Seven Guitars* at North Carolina School of the Arts and Rebecca Naomi Jones was in that. In *Fences*, I told you Jonathan Majors was in that. But it's just so interesting that *Wedding Band*, the first one, all of them were in it there. I created a role for Dominque. I just liked her so much. And Angela, who was short, played the little child. I have some great pictures from that show. I was told it became a famous production at University of Michigan. It was really good.

SMcC: How would you describe yourself in one word/

MS: Oh Jesus, Saundra!!! I have no idea how I would describe myself other than crazy!

SMcC: Crazy, no. I'm not going to let you do crazy. One word?

MS: Can't do one—Driven—Caring—Spiritual—I mean I'm always seeking.

SMcC: No, you can't have that because that's Dean's.

MS: Curious?

SMcC: Nope, that's Seret. You've got to come up with another one.

MS: Well, what if we *are* in the same club?

CTD: Nurturing ...

MS: Yes ... yes, I do try to nurture. Because I found out there is not enough of that going around.

CTD: If you had the opportunity to start your career all over again, is there anything you would do differently?

MS: I would pay more attention to being conscious of what to do in moments where I was being acknowledged to help build to another level.

Winning or being able to be nominated for a Tony for *Seven Guitars* was great. I had not even imagined anything like that. But how to really parlay into other things in my career. Who to talk to? What should I aspire to? I would do that differently. Positioning. I didn't realize when those things come, you really have to take advantage of the pathway that's opened for you. Things happened automatically but it wasn't by design. It wasn't by building a team of people that could build momentum (for me or my career).

I've always been somebody who if I had a dream about trying to do something, I would reach out and try to talk to that person or make a connection. Sidney Poitier was one of those people that I connected with. When I first came to LA, I would sit in Sidney's office and talk to him. I came to LA interested in producing. I wanted to be in the position to impact the whole business, providing jobs and new ideas. Sidney was a fan of my acting. He managed to see me in a play called *Split Second* in New York. He also saw me in something in LA. Sidney told me then, "People won't know what to do with you." And I didn't know what to make of that.

Now I feel I understand what he means, because I don't fall into any particular category, especially visually. Now more than ever that seems to be challenging, industry-wise. I just think it would have been helpful for me to have been more practical about things like that. How to navigate it in a way. But I've been one to have fallen into everything. It wasn't like I tried. Other than if I had a passion like the Negro Ensemble Company. I wanted to be at NEC come hell or high water. I did whatever I could to make that happen and it happened. Like I look at Saundra's career, for example. Saundra has done so many, many different kinds of things … . And she has the love and support of such a huge variety of people. How you did that I don't know, but you did.

SMcC: You see something I don't see. [*We all laugh.*] **If you had the opportunity to start over, would you approach your career differently?**

MS: No, not really. I feel I have been lucky and blessed with what I have done and where I have worked. It's just that I wish I had the energy and youth to start a career now with the wisdom I have acquired. I could have been more daring … going after and creating what I dreamed about.

Many times, I believe I was thinking ahead of my time. Because now the climate for things I thought about years ago, is ripe for them to be done today. I also no longer feel the need to prove anything to anyone … I only need to satisfy myself creatively.

CTD: What advice would you give your younger self?

MS: I don't think I had enough confidence. I mean the kind of confidence I give other young people, assuring them that they know what they are doing. I should have trusted a lot more than I did. It took me a long time before I think I knew what I was doing. It really didn't change me until I started the practice of meditation. I was very insecure about everything. It's the one thing in my teaching young people that I try to eliminate as much as possible. It interferes with moving forward a lot … that voice.

Although I think as an artist, we're always questioning … . We're always pursuing something else. I spent a long time being insecure in the beginning of my career. Part of that could have been because I was in learning environments where I was one of a few or the only black person. I just didn't get that kind of reflection back to me.

SMcC: What is your definition of success?

MS: My definition of success is evolving but the thing I care about is moving people to experience and understand one another, and what it means to be human in ways that create a spiritual sense of connection and awareness that helps transcend an isolated singular perspective.

SMcC: If someone were to ask you to describe your own legacy, how would you reply?

MS: She used drama to create compelling theatrical presentations that awakened a powerful timeless sense of majesty and greatness in human existence that illuminated the mystery of life … .

TENACIOUS 10

An Interview with Elizabeth Van Dyke

SMcC: I first saw Liz perform in the New Federal Theatre's production of *It's Showdown Time* by Don Evans.

CTD: Directed by Shauneille Perry.

SMcC: With an incredible cast: Obba Babatunde, Charlie Brown, Gloria Edwards, Lynne Whitfield, Kirk Kirksey, and Ronald "Smokey" Stephens. Liz was radiant and absolutely adorable in the ingénue role.

Interview With Elizabeth Van Dyke

CTD: When did your interest in theatre begin?

Elizabeth Van Dyke: When I was a child. My mother wanted me exposed to culture, to the world … At that time musicals, the opera, the ballet. We would have nosebleed seats.

CTD: Do you remember the first play that you ever saw?

EVD: *Camelot* and *My Fair Lady*.

CTD: What effect did seeing these productions have upon you?

EVD: They were magical. It was magic!

CTD: Where did you grow up?

EVD: Los Angeles. I was born in Oakland. I was raised in LA. Perfect classic story. I lived with my grandmother for a while until my mother got situated and then I lived with my mother.

TENACIOUS: An Interview with Elizabeth Van Dyke

Figure 10.1 Photo by Gerry Goldstein.

SMcC: When did you get involved in theatre?
EVD: I was in theatre in junior high, the glee club and the drama club. In high school, I did a compilation of plays. We put pieces together and did them. I could write. I could draw. However, I had to be in the mood to draw. I had to be in the mood to write. But I could *always* do theatre. That turned out to be my first love. After that, I would do little plays around town and in the community. I performed with the Ebony Showcase. It was always my dream to go to NYU.

CTD: Why NYU?
EVD: At that time when you went to Europe, you stopped in New York. New York was magical. NYU was a school devoted to theatre. Serious artists went to NYU School of the Arts. I got rejected. I was 17 or 18. Then I became a stewardess because I loved to travel. They asked, "Where did I want to

be based?" I said, "As close to New York as possible." So, I was based in Newark.

SMcC: What airline?

EVD: I started with United and ended up with Pan Am. One day I had off and went to the school. I said, "I want to audition for the Acting Program." They said "Well, Lloyd Richards is upstairs. Go upstairs." So, I went upstairs. They said, "Well, the school is full, but we can have you audition and put you on a wait list." I said, "OK." At some point, I must have auditioned. And lo and behold, they called me one day. I was in the school of my dreams with no money. [*She laughs.*] And that's how my journey started.

CTD: What year was this?

EVD: I ain't tellin.' [*She laughs.*]

SMcC: I know what year I saw *Ti-jean and his Brothers*, so don't even try it.

EVD: It was '71.

CTD: It seems like I've known you forever. When did we first meet?

EVD: Somewhere on the theatre scene or going after commercials. We were so young and beautiful.

CTD: What are some of the experiences that helped shape you artistically?

EVD: My mother was the most extraordinary woman I've ever known. My mother had … Vision. A vision to put me in the world and let me fly. Love me enough to let me go. I was her only child. She gave me everything I needed to achieve whatever I wanted. I said, "Momma, I want to go to the moon," she'd say, "Well, I've never been there. Let me see how I can help you." My whole journey to some degree, was shaping me artistically. My mother first paved a way for me to know culture. I went to an all-white boarding school, I remember her saying, "I want to expose you to the world. You'll learn how to be black." Boarding school was not the greatest experience for me. When I hit New York, I had a boyfriend who came to my apartment. He said, "You can't tell nobody black lives here." That struck a chord and stayed with me. So, I immersed myself in black culture, art, and literature.

At some point. I met Woodie King. I can't remember. These are fragmented memories. There are holes in them. I remember Woodie giving me a list of books. Maybe 13, 15 books, all black novels. I read all of those books. That's when I began to steep myself [in black culture] and develop an aesthetic. I think early on I was learning about the world, what I wanted to do, what I wanted to focus on. I wanted to be an actress.

Today, I know that my aesthetic is informed by the African continuum. All of those rhythms, all of those polyrhythms, all of those levels of who I am, inform the work. I know that as black people coming to this country, being displaced, the art gives us pieces of ourselves.

CTD: Who are some of your mentors?

EVD: Oh, I couldn't say that I ever thought I had mentors. Not that I didn't. That was not my form of thinking or consciousness. I'm an only child. ... You don't try to get help. You just do it. I just didn't think that way.

CTD: What were some significant moments you remember when you attended NYU?

EVD: One experience, it's vague. It's so far back ... . Kristin Linklater, my speech teacher, my voice teacher, threw a chair at me. She said, "You're like a smooth egg." Something like that I remember vaguely, but that came out of her really caring, so I got it.

Then I remember studying with André Gregory and his company one semester. I was doing *Boesman and Lena*—the monologue. He made me walk ... I don't know why I did it, but I really, really, honest to God did it. He made me go to 125th Street, carrying shopping bags, then walk from 125th Street to 2nd Avenue and 7th Street. Walk to 7th Avenue and 2nd Street! And then, start the scene as soon as I got in the room. I'll never forget that as long as I live. People in that class will never forget it. I literally did that, carrying shopping bags, and came in ... I remember that.

CTD: How did the monologue change?

EVD: I experienced that journey, carrying packages, and all that happened in that journey. Now, it's "the come from." Now, it's the subtext. Now it's, have you ever really experienced it? That was a young actor in class playing something that she had never experienced. And hadn't done a "substitution." Hadn't done an "as if." Who just started *ackin'*. But now, I actually had the experience. It's like portraying a character, experiencing a loss and you have never lost anything. I gotta do a "what if," I gotta do a, "what's that like?" Fill that gap. So, I can play it deeply and root it in truth.

SMcC: You're one of the first people I know to perform her own one-woman show about Zora Neale Hurston.

EVD: Woodie directed it. *Zora* was a one-woman show, a one-act that was done with *When the Chickens Come Home to Roost*. Phylicia did *Zora*. I directed it in 1981. Ali Woods directed *When Chickens Come Home to Roost* with Kirk Kirksey and Denzel Washington. So, the first one-person show that I acted in was *Love to All, Lorraine* about Lorraine Hansberry.

SMcC: When was that?

EVD: That was in '83, long before the one-person show genre really hit in our community.

SMcC: What kicked you into that?

EVD: Woodie King said: "Actors are for hire. Learn to activate your own work." That just resonated, a teaching moment that, "Whoa, is it not true? We're for hire?" So, to activate your own work, your destiny is in your own hands.

I was an actress. Couldn't get out of my head. I think I was lonely. I think I romanticized Lorraine Hansberry. She seemed like such an intellectual, so in her head, and lonely. That was a person, where my being in my head, could serve me. I loved her. I was enchanted with her. I started putting together the one-person show. When I finished a draft, I was told [that] to do an authorized story of her life would require rights. I could do research and use public domain information, but the rights would allow me to see private papers, photographs, and have the estate support effort. I met with the executor of her estate, her husband, Robert Nemiroff, and went through the process of getting the rights: lawyers, the estate's agent. And that's how that journey started.

SMcC: Where did you originate *Love to All, Lorraine*?

EVD: New Federal Theatre.

CTD: When did you finally decide to make the transition from acting to directing?

EVD: I don't think I have decided to make that transition. There are a couple of us. I know, Latanya [Richardson-Jackson] was one and I was another, that Woodie King wanted to give opportunities to. I've since asked him, why did he come after us to direct? This was in the '70s. Woodie says, "Because of the fervor. Because of the way you talk about art, talk about your experiences." Because of the way we went about the work. He gave me the opportunity to direct long before I had that vision for myself. So, I directed *The Mystery of Phyllis Wheatley* by Ed Bullins in the '70s.

Directing became something that would come to me. I never ever pursued it directly. Acting was my love. I loved the craft of acting. Directing would come. I would do it if somebody called and asked me.

In 2000, I was asked to do *The Old Settler* [by John Henry Redwood] at the Invisible Theatre in Tucson, Arizona. That's when I joined the SDC. Then, in 2008, my mother had a major stroke. I stopped acting. I never thought I would. But my mother needed care. She couldn't live alone. That's the moment I learned there was more to life than this theatre business. She always used to tell me there was more to life than whether I got that commercial or not.

The universe just blessed me with directing jobs, one right after another 'til this day, really. All over the country. I was able to take my mother with me for the first few years. When her condition worsened, if I took her with me, I'd have to bring a caregiver. I was able to do that.

And then, somewhere in there, Clinton and Saundra, I began to see a play from a directorial point of view. The entire play, the landscape of the play. I started thinking when I picked up a play, I was a director.

SMcC: How do you prepare as a director?

EVD: It might vary from show to show. Always reading and rereading and rereading the play. Always steeping myself in the period of the play, whatever that period may be. Even more so if it's historical, but always the times in which one lives is going to inform the work. I was asked to do *By the Way, Meet Vera Stark* by Lynn Nottage.

SMcC: Ooh, I've been wanting to do that show.

EVD: Webster University asked me to do a concept packet. I said, "What is that? I've never done that." They gave me an example of a concept packet and said, "It's your concept. How do you see the play, and some of the images? How you might see the costumes, how you might see the lights ... ?" It was a fascinating exercise. Which was really preparation on so many levels.

SMcC: How do you express your concept for a production to your designers?

EVD: I usually will articulate a vision. I always start with the set. My set is my first world. I hone into the set, then maybe the lights and the costumes. But certainly, the set. By the time I have my first production meeting, I can talk about where I'm going, about my vision, and the terrain of the set. I try to meet with the set designer before that first big production meeting. I don't like it, when we haven't had any discussion, at all. I've also used a concept packet to inform, to put my thoughts on paper, to have images. I've directed at a lot of colleges; they want images for inspiration because they are learning their craft.

SMcC: Have you ever directed a play that frightened you?

EVD: I just did a short play, called Tr@k *Grls (Pt1)* by Bleu Burrell Beckord at the Ensemble Studio Theatre, in their first all-BIPOC marathon. I was scared. This play scared me. That's why I did it. It was 35 minutes on paper of girls running: two young girls, one 14 and one 17 or 18, running track. Running, getting their laps in. I don't know if you've ever been to the Ensemble, but it has 84 seats. How do you achieve that constant motion in a small space?

SMcC: How did you overcome the fear?

EVD: I asked colleagues. "Oh my God. How do you do motion? How do you ... ?" I got a choreographer. The actors did things

I don't think I could do. When you direct, you ask all these things and actors do them. It's like, wow, could I have done that? I don't know. They never stopped moving. The choreographer helped tremendously. The critics said that they were running around the theater. It was true. They were. [*She laughs.*]

Another play that I was scared of was a *Civil War Christmas* by Paula Vogel at the University of Connecticut. Seventeen people and 62 scenes. [*She laughs.*] Set in the Civil War, it had a horse and a mule, with music and, oooh chile!

SMcC: Have you ever received a bad review? How did you deal with it?

EVD: Well, I'll tell you, a long time ago I said I wouldn't read reviews. Secretively I read some of them. If I don't, they won't be a topic of discussion. The last play I did at New Federal was *Gong Lum Legacy* by Charles L. White. You talk about preparation! Set in 1927—Chinese Americans and blacks in the Mississippi Delta. We actually went to Mississippi for three days. We went to the Chinese Museum, and some

Figure 10.2 *A Civil War Christmas* by Paula Vogel, University of Connecticut, 2018; with Forest McClendon and Tabitha Gayle (top left image). Photo by Gerry Goodstein.

little towns in the Mississippi Delta, germane to the play. We talked to people and went to the historical archives for rare photographs. We went to the Civil Rights Museum. We really did that work. We went to Mound Bayou. You could really smell the soil. It smelled different. All those little things. That was a gift of preparation. But I got bad reviews. A review is like they used to say in spirituality, "Praise or blame? It weighs the same."

SMcC: What did the critics say?

EVD: Oh, they blamed me for everything. It's okay. It's so funny. They could say, "Great ensemble. Great acting. Great." It's like that happened by itself. You didn't have a hand in that. You only had a hand in what didn't work. So, you just take it if you can take it. And move on.

CTD: What types of work are you drawn to as a director?

EVD: I created *Great Men of Gospel*. That was certainly non-linear. I love history. I love African American history. I love those stories. I was drawn to *Gong Lum Legacy*, because it was our history intersecting with Asian history at a time when

Figure 10.3 *Gong Lum's Legacy* by Charles L. White, New Federal Theatre, 2022; l. to r.: Eric Yang, DeShawn White, and Antony T. Goss. Photo by Gerry Goodstein.

Asians were being brutalized in the cities. Did you know there were Chinese in Mississippi? A big population. Those grocers and businesses, Chinese businesspeople in black communities still exist today.

That was a real case. *Gong Lum v. Rice* went all the way to the Supreme Court. Mr. Lum wanted his daughter to go to all-white schools and sued. He won locally. The state challenged him. And in 1927, the Supreme Court ruled only whites could go to all-white schools. That did not change until 1954 with *Brown v. the Board of Education*.

The Chinese at that time felt the closer they could get to whites, the further away they were from blacks who are so mistreated and oppressed. Also, in 1927, the biggest flood in the history of America displaced over 700,000 people.

SMcC: What was the genesis of the *Going to the River Festival*?

EVD: It's kind of dormant right now. It started in 1999. The late Curt Dempster and I founded it at the Ensemble Studio Theatre. A place where black women playwrights could develop their work, could have a forum. We had a festival of readings for years. We had a Solo Program, *Down by the River All by Yo'self.* We had panel discussions. In 2009, we did River Crosses Rivers, a festival of short plays … 14 short plays, literally staged them [writers such as France-Luce Benson, Lynn Nottage, Melody Cooper, Kia Cothren, Ruby Dee, J. E. Franklin, Bridgette Wimberly, Karen Cothren]. Oh, in 2011, *Post Black* by Regina Taylor. The play was cast with Micki Grant, Ruby Dee, and Carmen DeLavallade each doing a solo week. I mean … it was amazing. We did it again in 2013. And then after that, things just sort of changed. The climate of the theatre changed, the climate and my life changed. We did an annual festival of new plays until about 2017. My mother was getting more and more critical. About that time, activity stopped. It's been dormant. But a young sister who wrote *Colored Water,* Erika Dickerson-Despenza, wants to carry it on so that it lives on.

CTD: Are there any styles of theatre in which you haven't worked?

EVD: Not really. There are a lot of people coming up. Young black directors see things totally different than I do. I'm not looking for Shakespeare or a style, I'm looking at how to broaden my work so that it remains true to the play, and also expansive and creative.

Cullud Wattah is a stunning play that was at the Public Theatre, directed by Karen D. Jones. I wanted to do that play at the New Federal but at that time, before COVID, we didn't have the means to do it. I would have done it in a very traditional way. When it *was* done, they actually called it "Afro-Surrealism." I read that play. I didn't see anything that would say Afro-Surrealism. I saw the play. It was beautiful. But it didn't have the same tone or resonance that I might have brought to it. Candis [C. Jones] inspired me to think differently.

Then I saw Robert O'Hara's *A Raisin in the Sun* at the Public Theatre. I directed *A Raisin in the Sun* twice. I've been in *A Raisin in the Sun*. I wondered … am I a traditionalist? This *Raisin in the Sun* had the ghost of the Walter on the stage. Big Walter was on stage several times. Then at the end of the play, a flat comes down as if we're in the new house. Mama gives Big Walter the plant as he sits on the couch at the end. Travis comes out with a lunch pail. I'm marveling at the creativity of the new generation. Am I stuck in tradition? At the very end, in very big orange letters across this yellow facade of a house, is the word, *"Nigger."* Blackout.

This young generation is looking at a play on so many levels. There's this level of reality. But as we're sitting here, I may be thinking of something I have to do. I may be thinking of the past. I may be thinking of the future. Those are all levels of this moment that a younger director will be trying to show, calling it Afro-Surrealism, Afro-Futurism, Afro … [*Saundra laughs.*] I'm not trying to denigrate them.

I don't think about whether I'm doing Shakespeare or Chekhov or Experimental theatrr, I think more about broadening my creativity. The new generation of directors and playwrights are teaching me, challenging me. I'm continuing to learn and use that knowledge to inform my work and have my work multi-leveled in a new way.

CTD: Describe what this younger generation of directors are bringing to the table that challenges or disrupts the thinking of the traditionalist?

EVD: Even the writing? I told you I was scared about that play, *Tr@k Grls (Pt 1)*. In thirty minutes, you went to five or six different places. They could be by the pool, then you're on a mountaintop, then you're in the church, then you are in the mall. They want it literal. It's not abstract. Where they're going with our stories is … Wow, sensational.

I'm a traditionalist. I want you to *feel* the experience. If it's about *Cullud Wattah* I don't necessarily need bottles of dingy water hanging from the ceiling like art. I don't necessarily need a chalkboard with the actress marking off the days. I don't necessarily need a ritual of a prologue with a chant. I want to know what that family is going through personally. People who have never seen *A Raisin in the Sun* stood up and cheered. They loved it. I can't say I did not love it. I've tried with my whole heart and soul to be open to it and to appreciate it. Whereas Awoye Tempo's take on a play that's fifty years old or older, *Wedding Band, A Love Hate Story in Black and White* was stunning. What she put on it unearthed, informed the play and deepened the experience of the play.

CTD: Where do you see theatre going as a result of COVID, and in the post-Floydian climate of diversity and change?

EVD: July 1st, 2021, I became the producing artistic director of the New Federal Theatre. Even though everybody is lifting mandates, taking their mask ask off, working at "going back to normal" still, COVID exists. COVID is lingering and the effects are becoming known to us each and every day. There are plays that close, missed performances because somebody in the cast gets COVID. We are still seeing COVID's effect.

What has happened since George Floyd and the "I see you … " and "black theatre united"? Institutions are hiring black people to run them. Sometimes these institutions look more black than black institutions themselves. George Floyd, Brianna is really resounding. The exploration in white spaces, looking at white supremacy, at racism, going through equity, diversity, and inclusion workshops … then with Tyree Nichols … .

For black theatre, I think Woodie could probably articulate this better than anyone, the future is about continuing this rich legacy. Every generation opens the door a little, giving resources for the next Chadwick Boseman, Issa Rae, Ntozake Shange, or J. E. Franklin … .

SMcC: What is your definition for success?

EVD: Well, I have to live with myself. You know, back in the day. I had a girlfriend who wasn't married. She said, "I'm not married. I don't have any children. My life don't mean nothin'." I thought, "Wow, I can't define my life like that, because I can't say my life means nothing."

Am I successful? I have a rich life in the theatre. The theatre is one of my greatest loves. I have a life in it. I can act in it sometimes. I direct in it, sometimes. I produce in it, sometimes. I'm called on to speak with great people and have prayerfully dimensional conversations. Isn't that success? I pay my bills … .

SMcC: True. If you have the opportunity to start your career over, is there anything you would do differently?

EVD: I think I'd try to be less in my way. Less insecure. I think my journey's been fine. I don't have any regrets.

CTD: What do you do to relax?

EVD: I meditate. I pray. I've had a meditation practice for many, many years. That is probably the basis of my being in theatre. I love seeing theatre. That's relaxing.

SMcC: What advice would you give to your younger self?

EVD: Get out of your way. Don't belittle yourself. Believe in yourself.

SMcC: What inspires your work as a director?

EVD: It varies. Where does inspiration come from? Never know.

CTD: What one word would you use to describe yourself?

EVD: Tenacious … .

INQUISITIVE

An Interview with Gregg Daniel

11

> **CTD:** I don't know Gregg's work as a director. I am more familiar with Gregg as an actor.
>
> **SMcC:** Not afraid of working with actors who have strong opinions, Gregg enjoys the process and understands the intensity or frustration an actor experiences realizing a character. Gregg's company, the Lower Depth Theatre is highly respected here in Los Angeles.

Interview With Gregg Daniel

> **SMcC:** Did you begin your career as an actor?
>
> **Gregg Daniel:** I did. I didn't segue into directing until I was out of school, and I started doing regional theatre. I was all over the place for about twelve years—but I started asking questions of the directors that weren't actor questions, who would invite me to come watch them. They took me under their wing and recognized, "This kid is really interested." They exposed me to what was going on and what was their process. I'd sit there and take notes.
>
> But I didn't know if you could be a director and an *actor*. I was really confused. Literally at that time. I didn't have any templates. I didn't know any practicing actors who were also directors. I knew actors, and I knew directors. So, I wrestled

DOI: 10.4324/9781003410737-11

Figure 11.1 Photo by Diana Ragland.

with it for a long time. Finally, a voice in my head just said, "Go for it."

SMcC: When did you direct your first show?

GD: It wasn't a show, it was a scene. It was for a class. I started doing scenes from various plays: *A Raisin in the Sun,* all kinds of plays ... *Who's Afraid of Virginia Woolf?,* one of the scenes between George and Martha. And I just freakin' loved it.

My first professional play, maybe twenty years ago—*A Thimble of Smoke.* Chris Fields, the artistic director of the Echo Theater Company, which is still strong and thriving out here, was the one who produced it and invited me to direct a production of *A Thimble of Smoke* which was mounted at the 24th Street Theatre.

CTD: Why was that significant for you and your career?

GD: I guess because someone had confidence in me. Up to that time I had been known as an actor. The reading had been done at the Ojai Playwrights Conference a year or two prior. The writer has since passed on, his name was Elroyce D. Jones, an older gentleman who lived in Los Angeles. What was significant for me was that someone had the confidence in my skills as a director to actually do the production. It's one thing to be able to do a staged reading of a piece as you know, but when they invite you to do the production, there is much more money involved. With the thought that I actually understood the play and could work along with the playwright to actually direct a fully mounted production was significant for me. Because up to that point I had been very quiet about directing—that Hollywood kind of paranoia. I had it all wrong. You do what you do. You do what you do.

SMcC: Did you have mentors?

GD: Probably Stephanie Shriver. She was a brilliant director who now teaches at USC. She was the one who requested that I bring in a scene from *The Importance of Being Earnest*. She was an AD at 24th Street Theatre. She invited me to do a full production of it with an all-black cast. My wife, Veralyn Jones, was Lady Bracknell.

SMcC: Have you ever collaborated with a writer developing a new work?

GD: Oh, yes, absolutely. I remember one time I went to the Alabama Shakespeare Festival. They had an AD, a brother from out here, who had written a play in which they were interested. They brought us in for a two-week festival. It was basically a workshop to develop the play. I loved everything about it. I was hooked. It was my first time working with a relatively new playwright developing his work.

SMcC: Did you formally study directing or was it something to which you were drawn?

GD: I was drawn to it. Then I started taking classes at UCLA Extension, as well as with Ellen Stewart at La Mama. La Mama had this international director symposium one year in Italy, in Umbria. I was working with Anne Bogart.

CTD: What did you do?

GD: We had instructors from all over the globe. For me what brought me there was that I always admired Joanne Akalaitis and Anne Bogart's work. Because of "Viewpoints" and to get to work with them as a director was amazing. Anne Bogart changed up my game. I worked with Anne for a couple of weeks. She had a stage in the Italian countryside. Even now, before I direct a play, I read her book, *The Director Prepares*. I've read it like 25 to 30 times. It's a short book. But there's something about it. The wisdom and how impactful it is.

SMcC: **Have you ever accepted a project that frightened you?**

GD: Yes, most projects frighten me. I always think I'm going to fall flat on my face because I don't know what I'm doing. There's something good about approaching a project from this perspective. It makes my thinking larger. If I come in thinking, "Oh I can do this," for me that's death. I have to go in knowing this is so big, I don't know if I can do this. Then of course you do the research, you do the work, you do the rehearsals, and you make it work. But I think it's a good place for me to start.

I always think I can't do it. That's why for a while I couldn't be at opening nights. I would be there, but I couldn't sit down. I would stand in the back.

Figure 11.2 *Wedding Band* by Alice Childress, Antaeus Theatre Company, 2012; l. to r.: Gregg Daniel directing to Karole Foreman and Leo Marks. Photo by Geoffrey Wade.

SMcC: How did you overcome your fear?

GD: By doing the work. Day by day going to work, starting to work with actors, putting one foot in front of the other. Technique-wise, asking what do they want out of the scene? And who wants what? Who's the protagonist? What do they want? That's how you build the skeleton, and you find your way to the next one. I just tell myself, "Okay you signed the contract. The designer run-through is in two-and-a-half weeks, so hit it." Once you start asking the questions, you find your way through it.

SMcC: How do you prepare as a director?

GD: I do a lot of reading. Especially if it's a period piece. I will go back and pull reviews on it. Who was that critic for the *New Yorker*, the Black critic?

SMcC: Hilton Als?

GD: I think he's brilliant, his mind was so facile. I would not direct a play until I found out if he had written a review of it ... I do a voluminous amount of research on a play, but as soon as I get in the room, I throw it away because nobody wants to hear me go on and on about the facts. I just prepare. Even when I go into rehearsal, I come in with 25 ideas (how to block a scene, etc.) and I might use one because that's the one the actors like. I have to be very attentive and if the actors like that track, I stay on that track. Forget the other 24. Being over-prepared, I can always pull on them if needed. I love working with the designers; they give me great ideas.

SMcC: How do you come up with the concept for your direction?

GD: I always say, "What's the question this play is asking? What's the one central question this play wants to deal with? What's the problem this play wants to solve?" By the time I open it up to the design team, they help refine my vision.

When I did *Lady Day at Emerson's Bar and Grill,* this is a play about addiction. She was beautiful and she sang, but this is about addiction. So, let's examine this play. If I do a play that has been mounted a lot, I'll tell the designers, "Let's act like this is the first time this play's been done." Designers are very intuitive people. I start out with the set designer before I speak to costume, lights, or sound. I spend weeks with them going back and forth until we hit it. Now that I know what my physical set looks like, I can open it up to the other designers.

Designers have helped me a lot. Their collaboration has really helped me refine what I started with, change, and evolve. That's why I tend to work with the same designers. We have a shorthand.

SMcC: **What do you find most challenging when discussing your concept with designers?**

GD: Finding the kind of language that inspires them … that will excite them and bring them into my vision. I have to find the connective tissue that will ignite them. I can tell when it does. If it doesn't, I know that's on me.

I love working with Stephanie Kerley Schwartz. She's one of those designers that will go to the wall for you. I love working with someone who does more than just design, but can comment on the play in a way that's social and political. She can do that. When you find someone you have that shorthand with, you call them. That's why directors tend to work with the same people.

SMcC: **Have you ever sent a designer back to the drawing board?**

GD: I have. It doesn't happen a lot, but it has happened.

SMcC: **How are you able to convey your vision, then?**

GD: We go back to the drawing board. I have to articulate why that set design is not the play I want to do. Sometimes there are hurt feelings. But I'd rather have the hurt feelings then, than go ahead and start building when it's wrong. When they're building and you go in and change things, that's a problem. So, I'll fall on my sword and make the call early on.

SMcC: **Have you ever had a bad review?**

GD: No not bad, mediocre. There's one LA critic that has never liked my work. She didn't tear it apart; she just dismissed it. She didn't mention me or, if she did mention me, she pointed out what I could do better. Like *Gem of the Ocean*, at A Noise Within, her review was just mediocre or tepid.

SMcC: **What is your definition of success?**

GD: It's definitely moving people's hearts and minds. As a director, if I can move people's hearts and minds, then boy I've been successful.

SMcC: **What prompted you to form your own theatre company, in LA no less?**

GD: To do the kind of work we wanted to do. We were trying to get certain titles but couldn't because they were waiting on Pasadena or some other theatre. Ultimately, you don't want to wait until someone calls you. The chance to work with the actors, playwrights, and designers that I want was my prime motivation. You can only do that with a company that goes from one project to another. I resisted it for a long time because companies are a pain in the ass and there's never enough money. But in order to do the work I wanted in LA, I had to have my own springboard. Otherwise, you wait around for someone to invite you to do something you don't really want to do.

I had to start a company ... the Lower Depth Theatre Company. Now, I get to choose the actors, the titles, the designers. That's much more interesting to me than going to somebody else's house—theater—and just being a hired gun. But I do like that sometimes ... .

SMcC: **Looking back over your career, if you had the opportunity, would you do things differently?**

GD: The only thing I might have done differently would have been to come out to LA earlier. I was in my mid-thirties when I came out here, but at the same time, I would have missed twelve years of regional theatre which made me a strong actor. I would have missed working with the actors and directors I met. I often think I could have come out here earlier and gotten a series. But again, I would have missed all those experiences that helped me develop as an artist doing six, seven, eight hours a day in rehearsals. I would have missed that kind of training. I'm old enough now to realize that I probably came out here just when I should have.

SMcC: **In one word, how would you describe yourself?**

GD: Inquisitive.

SMcC: What was it like working with your wife?

GD: I love working with Veralyn. I know it's sometimes difficult for her, but I love working with her. To know how to her handle her, bring her out of her comfort zone is really challenging. And to keep the relationship going. I could go easy on her, but sometimes I need to ask her the hard question. But I have to make sure it's gentle, it's supportive.

SMcC: What effect do you think COVID has had on theatre?

GD: I can't tell you how many theatres have contacted me. Theatre companies are really questioning if they're doing diversity and inclusion.

SMcC: What changed?

GD: I think the art is going to change because of what this country has been going through the past four years, particularly since January 6. I think the kinds of things you're going to see on stage are going to be far more diverse. The artistic directors are changing. A lot of them are retiring. They're trying to look for BIPOC.

I'm working with a lot of young people. A number of them have expressed a desire to shadow me or work as an assistant. I'm happy to do that. When I'm able to bring in [an assistant], especially a BIPOC, I'm very happy to do that.

It took a man's murder on television in front of the whole world and a pandemic for them to realize they don't even have one POC on the Board! So, now they're looking in areas they never looked before. Now, they're asking the really hard questions.

SMcC: What about the theater itself?

GD: I think it's going to continue to evolve—with Zoom and shooting plays on camera. I don't see theaters getting rid of some of the virtual things they've done. I think they'll find active virtual online programming can work. Theatre companies won't abandon it. They can use actors from all over the country. Suddenly a theatre company can offer as many things to see on Zoom as they do on their stages.

SMcC: What type of work are you naturally drawn to?

GD: Well, you know the preoccupation of American drama is the family. It is just because families are that cocoon that can either damn us or free us. It can be real families or community. Those stories tend to rivet me.

SMcC: Do you like concept pieces?

GD: I do. I don't know if I'm good at doing them. I love it when other directors do them and I try to learn from them. I'm always stealing stuff. I enjoy seeing directors do work that I don't feel particularly endowed to do because it inspires me to do better.

SMcC: Do you have an agent as a director?

GD: No, I don't. It's been brought up to me several times. I get a lot of work from just "we saw your production, or we heard about your production." I'm getting offers from people who've seen my work. I haven't had to seek representation so far.

SMcC: Do you have any works in progress?

GD: There's a play that was not done last year because of the pandemic. We're doing a production at A Noise Within and we're doing something also in Denver. The one that I'm doing in Denver is a new play, *In the Upper Room* by a woman named Beaufield Barry. We workshopped it a couple of years ago at that festival and now they're going to mount it. There are several projects that are coming back and I have to make sure I have space for them because I really make most of my income as an actor. It's tricky, but you make it work.

SMcC: Why do you want to do it all, Gregg?

GD: I've been given certain gifts and as I've gotten older, I actually begin to see more possibilities. At one time, I didn't see myself as being a successful director, then as I became successful, I realized, it's limitless. It's just our thinking that is limited.

I'm trying to move to a place where you ask more from the Universe, and it will make a way for you. Don't limit yourself. Be bold and mighty forces will come to your aid.

CTD: You've done three August Wilson plays at A Noise Within. Do you plan to direct the entire cycle?

GD: They have expressed an interest in doing the cycle. Hopefully, they will do them with me. But I'm not arrogant enough to think they are going to ask me to do every one. But yes, we have discussed taking on the entire cycle. There's a professed desire and a commitment to do all ten plays. I don't know if I'll be doing all ten.

CTD: If you were speaking to your younger self, what would you tell him to do differently?

GD: Stop being afraid of what would happen if you declared yourself being as a director *and* an actor. I was really quite afraid of being identified as a director because I really thought it was going to hurt my acting career. I was really fearful, especially being in Los Angeles thirty-some-odd years, that was going to hurt me. I put a lot of pressure on myself to sort of keep the separation of Church and State. Don't let them know what you do. Just dismiss it "Oh, it's just a little thing we're doing on Santa Monica Blvd," but it really wasn't. I diminished it, so I diminished myself. I was being more concerned about their feelings and their reactions to me than being true to my own artistry. So, I would say, "Don't ever limit yourself. They're going to limit you no matter what. But don't limit yourself by saying 'I shouldn't do that because that might hurt my chances.'" If anything, it increased my chances. It increased my visibility. It increased my opportunities.

But I was young, and I was really afraid to rock the Hollywood boat. I am a much better director as an actor, and a much better actor because I direct. Much better. So that's a thoughtful question. Thanks, Clinton. In my position as an adjunct at USC School of Dramatic Arts, I tell students things I wish I had done. Because they want to climb mountains. They want to reach the peak. So, I take that off them—that burden. I try to pay it forward. I encourage them to be multi-hyphenated. I encourage them to write, to produce, to direct. A multi-hyphenated artist is the thing to be, writer-producer-actor. But back then I thought being multi-hyphenated was going to have a negative impact on my career. If I knew then what I know now.

These kids now, because they have the technology, benefit from film and writing programs. Young people have support in ways we did not have. There are so many programs now for new plays, new play development. We had it during the regional theatre days, but now every company has a second stage, or a second unit to work with playwrights developing new works.

SMcC: How would you describe your own legacy?

GD: Gregg Daniel had a lot of heart and all that implies. He would go out there and take on projects that scared him and sometimes he'd fail, but he had a lot of heart. Meaning, bringing everything he was to what he was focused on, seeing it in others, helping others. Yeah, I'd like people to think, Gregg Daniel had a lot of heart … .

PRIDE   12

An Interview with Ruben Santiago-Hudson

CTD: I first met Ruben when he auditioned for *A Soldier's Play* at the Negro Ensemble Company. I also directed him in *Conversations in Exile* by Bertolt Brecht at the New Theatre of Brooklyn.

SMcC: My earliest memory of Ruben was as an aspiring, young thespian eager to make his mark in the business. It wasn't until I got to work with him in *Seven Guitars* that I realized what a brilliant performer he was. Later, I had the privilege of directing Ruben and Keith David in a staged reading of *Fear Itself* by Eugene Lee. I knew his star was on the ascendant.

Interview With Ruben Santiago-Hudson

CTD: When did you see your first play?

Ruben Santiago-Hudson: The first professional play that really affected me was at the Studio Arena Theatre in Buffalo. I saw a production of *Aladdin*. The genie was a black man. To see all the magic was held in the hands of someone that looked like me, I must have been in the fifth or sixth grade. That play made me say, "Wow, wow, the brother holds the magic, so I can actually, have some magic." It really empowered me as a little kid to believe that we were magical people too.

CTD: After having that response, what happened?

PRIDE: An Interview with Ruben Santiago-Hudson

Figure 12.1 Photo by Mo McRae.

RS-H: I grew up in a rooming house. I had been walking around the house mimicking all the tenants at the rooming house. I had been doing plays in school since the second grade. When the next play came up, I auditioned. I just kept finding the roles, finding the challenges, and trying to find the discovery in putting my feelings inside what someone else had written. I loved it.

CTD: Where did you attend university? What significant moments helped move you toward theatre?

RS-H: Binghamton University. I was one of two black men in that department. The other one who had been the black actor in the department was not happy to see me step into his territory. I was a 17-year-old young man, full of piss and vinegar, as they would say. I had been acting, doing some wonderful touring with a group called Love Land that was at my community center, The Friendship House. We did everything. We had an African dance group, we had plays in which I was one of the directors, and one of the lead actors. We had singing groups, martial arts, all kinds of things.

We would tour to different communities all over western New York doing plays like *The First Militant Minister, It Bees That Way*. Ed Bullins' stuff, Ben Caldwell stuff. When I got to the theatre department, they were doing *Androcles and the Lion, The Shadow Box,* Ionesco's *The Chairs,* Tom Stoppard's *Jumpers*. I wanted to do Ben Caldwell and Ed Bullins. So, I had to start directing them myself.

CTD: Who were your mentors then?

RS-H: A gentleman there took me under his wing. His name was Loften Mitchell. He wrote *Bubbling Brown Sugar, Ballad for Bimshire,* and had already written *Land Beyond the River, Star of the Morning,* and *The Phonograph*. I was reading plays for Loften as he was writing. But when he took these works to New York City, Loften would take a more seasoned actor. Loften helped me a lot. I decided to leave Binghamton, two years after being there—it was no place for me. I got into a lot of fights. Whether racism on campus or just being a small-town boy dealing with big-city kids.

My roommate was a DJ and taught me how that worked. Eventually I became one of the hottest DJs in the whole Southern Tier. That only lasted so long. I got kicked off the radio station for [as they said] inciting a riot, because a sister got raped and I called for action. The FCC took my license. I didn't make the basketball team. Then, I failed in some of my classes. I got booted out of the school. I said, "I'm not going to come back. I would go to Howard if they will let me in." Loften said, "No, you're coming back here under my tutelage 'cause you won't have Loften there protecting you the way Loften protects you here." So, I came back to Binghamton. Loften eventually retired from Binghamton University and left me under the auspices of another gentleman who became my mentor, Percival Borde. He was married to one of the world's renown anthropologist/dancers named Pearl Primus.

When I got kicked out, through some maneuvering, they let me go to Buffalo State College for one semester. I worked in a play under Lorna Hill, a wonderful director and founder of Ujima Theatre in Buffalo. She was a professor at Buffalo State. She cast me and said, "Damn, where this boy come from?" We did the play, Theodore Ward's *Our Lan'* and I never looked back. I said, "I want excellence in everything I do. I want As in my classes. I wanted to do the best I can. I am going to go back to Binghamton and give it everything."

SMcC: Why did they keep kicking you out?

RS-H: I was 17 or 18 years old. I was hard. You saw me when I came to New York, Saundra. You laughed at me. I never forget, you laughed at me. That's why it took me ten times before I called you back. You laughed at me just like you're laughing now.

SMcC: Clinton, Ruben was standing on the corner of 43rd and 9th Avenue, fresh off the bus with a suitcase by his side, going on and on about all that he was going to do. I said, "Brother, you just got here." ... I ain't laughing now.

RS-H: Thank you. I was coming off the streets pretty hard. I thought I was this tough guy. Things we don't need to put in this book. I brought that mentality to school. I was fighting a lot. I needed a lot of discipline. I found the right people through the grace of God. My mother and my godmother, Mattie Overton and my mother, Nanny—Rachel Crosby. I didn't want to disappoint them so, I straightened my life up.

I came to the NEC from Detroit in May of 1983. The first place I went to was the Negro Ensemble Company. I heard there was this play called *A Soldier's Play*. They had nine, or ten brothers in it. I went there. There were three dudes sitting on the steps. I eventually found out it was Ves Weaver, Marvin [Watkins]—slim with dreadlocks, and a heavier brother, Robert Hatch. I walked to the box office and said, "Is Douglas Turner Ward here?" They said, "Who wants to know?" I said "Ruben Santiago." At that time, it was Ruben Santiago. They said, "What do you need?" I said, "I want to be in *A Soldier's Play*. I want to audition." They said, "What's your name?" I said, "Ruben Santiago." Whoever was in the box office said to me, "Ain't no Puerto Ricans in *A Soldier's Play*." I said to them, "There's going to be one now." They said, "Douglas Turner

Ward is on the road. They would not be holding auditions for some time." I said, "OK." I walked back out. The brothers were taking down the lights. I asked where the bathroom was. They said, "Right downstairs." I said, "Would you watch my portfolio?" They said, "Yeah, set it over there." I sat it down. I went to the bathroom and when I came back, my portfolio wasn't there. I said, "What happened to my portfolio? I set it right there. Don't play no games." They said, "Here it is. Let me tell you something young blood. Where are you from?" I said, "Detroit." They said, "This is New York City. You don't play around in this city. Your ass would be homeless or dead. Be careful man." I went to the Puerto Rican Traveling Theatre. They turned me down because I didn't speak Spanish. I went to the Public Theatre because I heard about Rosemarie Tischler, she was a friend of a friend. That was in May.

After putting Hudson on my name, I got an audition for *A Soldier's Play*. I was sitting in Theatre Four's lobby and Douglas Turner Ward came out to go to the bathroom. I said, "Mr. Turner Ward, I want to audition for you if you have time." Doug said, "I ... I ... Ah .... I, ahhh." I said, "I ever tell you about the time I learned how to speak Indian? Well, back in Crossroads there was a light-skinned colored man ... ." I went into Cephus Miles [from *Home* by Samm Art Williams]. Doug stopped and looked at me and said, "What's your name?" I said, "Ruben S. Hudson." He said, "Come on in here. You'll be the last audition." December 23 to be exact, I got the call to be in *A Soldier's Play*.

CTD: Inside the theater, we were packing up. Doug said, "Ahh ... Ahhh ... Let's see him now." We did. Later in the week, I called and offered you the job.

RS-H: When I hit the road it was with you and Doug. We were at the Cincinnati Playhouse. Ves Weaver was on the catwalk. He looked down at me and said, "Yo, you the Puerto Rican that was ... ." I said, "Yeah, I told you I was going to be in *A Soldier's Play*." We were in rehearsal. O. L Duke, Robert Gossett, and all the guys started appreciating me because Adolph Caesar liked me. I worked very hard. I knew I was prepared. I was very hungry. I needed to be there. I had two kids at home. I needed to get a job.

CTD: What is one of the most memorable experiences you've had in theatre as a director?

RS-H: During tech of *Gem of the Ocean*. I was sitting in the back of the theater watching them work out the City of Bones [section in the play]. August kept going out to smoke cigarettes. August came back in, leaned on the back wall of the orchestra seats, and said to me, "Man, how would you do this?" I said, "I could do it three different ways. Which one do you want to know?" He said, "The first one." I told him what I would do. He said, "Go tell the director." I said, "No, I'm not the director. But when I direct it ... ." He said, "When are you going to direct it?" I said, "When I get on the list." He said, "You're on the top of the list." We closed in February. Three months after we opened. About six months later, I got a call from the McCarter Theatre to do *Gem*. So that, as a director, was a very memorable point.

I was directing the musical *Raisin* at Battle Creek Civic Theatre in Michigan. I had an actor playing Walter Lee. I was trying to get him to do something that the play needed in the moment. I couldn't get him to do no matter how I coached him, or what information I gave him. He would say, "I can't do that." He said, "You do it. You show me." I got on stage and I did it. He walked out of the theater, and I never saw him again. So, I had to open that play as the director and actor. I said, "If I don't know how to help an actor get somewhere he needs to get, I should not be directing." So, I stopped directing and I didn't direct again for over twenty years until August told me, "You need to be directing my plays."

Now, I don't show actors what to do. I find the words to get them on that path. I'm patient—Lloyd Richards' patience. I keep giving information until the actor discovers and owns that reality.

CTD: It is interesting how actors process words as you try to get them to complete actions.

RS-H: I was talking to an actor today about what was going on in the play. He asked, "What's up with these actors who take pauses in the middle of things? Try to do some dramatic thing in the middle of lines? I don't know what they are doing." I said, "Why isn't the director handling that?" He said, "Oh, the director been gone." I said, "Why are these people directing if they are not taking care of the actors?" It's the new way of doing things. Not everybody is in tune to be fine at the craft. They want to be stars ... a lot of them. So, learning the intricacies of what it means to be a fine artist is getting pushed to the side to become a star? When you go back to the actors who I watched when I got to New York, even before, but mainly in New York ... like a Frances Foster, Moses Gunn, Roscoe Lee Brown, Rosalind Cash, Graham Brown, they had a gravitas to the work, to the craft. They were in control of the craft of acting.

CTD: What was the first production you directed?

RS-H: My comeback production was *Gem of The Ocean*, at the McCarter with Phylicia Rashad, John Amos, Russell Hornsby, Chuck Patterson, Rosalind Ruff, Raynor Scheine, Keith Randolph Smith. Wonderful, wonderful time.

CTD: As a director, what types of work are you naturally drawn to, scripted plays or devised works?

RS-H: Scripted. Mainly scripted. But I am developing several projects. I like working with writers, working with themes, and developing them. Honing them. It seems that is another part of the craft that is dissipating—the incubation of the work. Taking the work through stages. Like Lloyd gave to August. Letting him work and rework, witness, and re-witness his work, to hone it, incubate it until it was where it needed to be to be presented on the biggest stages.

These younger writers seem to get one off-Broadway review and they don't want to hear s**t from nobody. I get plays offered to me and I say, "I like this play. May I talk to the writer because I have some questions?" The agents say, "No. Do you want to direct it or not?" I say, "No. If I have no discussion, I don't need to be there. I just have questions." I'm not changing this man's or woman's play. But we need to discuss some things that are not clear to me: "I don't know what you really mean, or are trying to achieve by this. If you don't want to talk, then I don't need to be there." Because it is a discussion, a process from the beginning on to the end.

The first off-Broadway play I directed was a revival of August Wilson's *Seven Guitars* at the Signature Theatre under Jim Houghton. My next was *The First Breeze of Summer* by Leslie Lee, also at the Signature Theatre. Jim made me an associate artist there. The fabulous cast included Marva Hicks, Brenda Pressley, Harvy Blanks, the Dirden boys [Brandon and Jason]. I put both the Dirden brothers on stage, Crystal Dickinson, Keith Randolph Smith, Leslie Uggams. A wonderful production. One of my most cherished.

SMcC: What are you working on now?

RS-H: One that is coming up right away is called *Destiny of Desire*, by Karen Zacarias. It's going to the Old Globe Theatre in April and will be on Broadway in the fall. I'm doing another Latin play with John Leguizamo. He hasn't titled it yet. We're developing it together. There is also a musical, *The Ten*, based on the Ten Commandments. And then I have *Sidney*, the life of Sidney Poitier. That should take me into my retirement. [*He laughs.*] Unless someone gives me a good acting job.

CTD: Have you ever accepted directing projects that truly challenged or "frightened" you?

RS-H: I'm challenged in each one, to be quite honest. I've done several world premieres. Two of Dominique Morisseau's world premieres. She's amazing. I've developed a lot of plays. I've had no fear of any of them. Excitement? Trepidation? Yes.

The biggest challenge I had was when I was working with a writer and she decided to go buck wild on the cast. I stopped it quick. I turned my back so the cast couldn't see me and looked at her very closely and said, "You can't do that. These are our guests. I invited all these actors here, and I have to take care of them. If you have something to say, that's cool, but say it to me and let me communicate it. But don't start screaming across the desk at actors. You've got them crying." The writer said, "This is my play. I can say what I want. How I want. When I want." I said, "Not in my room. And not in a disrespectful way." She got up, got her bag. Walked out. Called her lawyer, who called the artistic director, who called me and said, "It's her play, do what she wants." I said, "Well you need to get a new director. It's her play, but it is my room. This room has to be a safe room for these actors, for all of us. She's there and we are going to honor her play. That's the way this is gonna be and if that ain't cool, get another director." He said, "If we get another director, this whole thing is going to fall apart. We're going to lose a lot of money." I said, "Well … you've got to straighten this out … . That's your job."

I went home. Had a glass of wine … . Let me think what my part is in this? What have I done, or what can I do to make it better? If I'm going to be a leader, let me figure out how to lead? I meditated. Prayed on it a little bit. I thought how my mother would say, "Find out what's your part. Take ownership of your part of it. And go see how you can make it better." So, I asked the playwright if we could have breakfast. She said, "Yes." We had breakfast. I said, "I'm sorry the way things went yesterday. I want to find out how we can make this better. I want to do better myself. I want you to do better. I want us to have a good time. I want you to have fun. It's your play. So, what can I do to help this?" The flip was going to be, "Well, let me tell you what I need." But we never got there. She said, "You are the worse person I've ever met in my life. I don't deserve you … ." I said, "I'm sorry that's the way you feel. But I'm going to complete this play." I completed it. Then on opening night everybody stood up and hugged her and clapped, screamed, and cheered, and had a parade for her. I'm sitting there like this. [*He stares silently.*]

Her lawyer said I could not talk to her, but she gave me a stack of notes every day. But we didn't talk. The artistic director had the literary person try to hand me the notes. I'd say, "Set them down right there." He would set them down on my table. I would scan them. And now that play is going all over the country. I said as long as it ain't my direction, they can do what they want. Just not my direction what that incredible group of artists had created. That was the world premiere of that play. Now that was a challenge.

Once again, I said to myself, "Maybe I should not be directing. Because I never want this headache again." I never want to have to defend my room, my actors. Literally, she had actors crying. One girl had just lost it.

I said, "Everybody take ten." I went to her and said, "Can I hug you?" Because these days you've got to ask. She said, "Please." She just fell in my arms, and I held her. I said, "It's going to be ok. I'm gonna take care of you. You'll be fine. It's fine. This is a process. I got you. Just call me anytime, 24/7. I'm accessible. Whatever you need." She did a great job. To this day she thanks me for that.

SMcC: Do you have a process, as a director, when you begin working on a play?

RS-H: Once I fall in love with the play and feel it is something I can do justice to, that I think I'm the right person for, then, I start researching everything I can about the era, the place, and the playwright. What are we doing here? And why? And for whom? For what? I start researching, finding information. That information comes from music, it comes from books, it comes from YouTube, it comes from Google, it comes from talking to people who worked with that person. I want to have as much information as I possibly can, to bursting. I can come into the room, but not with *all* the answers, because I want to discover things about the event that we are about to become a part of. That process doesn't end on the first day of rehearsal but continues to the end. I'm always seeking information and learning.

I'm getting information from the artists I'm working with, from the designers, the actors. I demand that my actors fully understand what we are doing. That we're on the same page. When I'm writing, I fix everything. I work out everything so nobody anywhere in the world can mess my play up, mess my movie up, 'cause I fixed it all. I know it all.

CTD: What inspires your work as a director?

RS-H: I want a change. This s**t's got to change. The most powerful weapon I have ain't my fists, ain't my big mouth, it ain't how many movies I've done. The most powerful weapon I have is my art. My art is going to live way beyond me. When Ruben is gone, people are going to say, "Damn he was a strange mother. But that dude man, he made a difference. He taught. He inspired."

I live with integrity. I want to make sure that I do a little bit, do my part, cause that's all a little man can do, to make a difference in all the lies they told about us. Just like in *Lackawanna Blues,* when people look at the 80-year-old black woman in Lackawanna and think she's important. And it ain't even *thinking* she's important, it's *knowing* she's important. I made a difference because that's your grandmother, that's your mama, that's this German lady's mama, that's this Irish woman's mama. And Uncle ... these salt-of-the-earth hardworking people.

I made a difference to a lot of people about who these people are. When they drive by, lock their doors, look at [them], because they are not dressed as well, or they smell like liquor and think, "Ugggh, that person is trash." They realize that's not trash, that's a treasure. In *Lackawanna Blues,* we made a difference, I know, because people walk up to me every week that I live and tell me that. That's what inspires me. I'm trying to do my part.

CTD: Do you choose your own designers or recommend designers to the Artistic Director? Have you ever asked a designer to reconsider any of their iterations?

RS-H: I always choose my designers. You can't give me a job and then give me my designers. I choose my people because I want a short language. I want people to want what we're doing to be as important to them as it is to me. I'm sending designers back to the drawing board every week. Not to totally change the concept, but to refine it.

I invited my choreographer for *Destiny's Desire* to come to meetings with the set designer. She has come to three meetings so far. She said, "I have never seen a director and a set designer have this many conversations." My conversations are three hours long. I ask, "How many square feet is that? Oh, that's about ... No. No. No. You can take a foot of that off. This gate up here? Why is it the same pattern as that Gate? I need five different patterns on the iron work. I need more cement. I need more steel. This needs to be another texture. Let me see more texture."

I've had designers actually build a wall when I did *Gem of the Ocean,* because I needed light to come through the wall and the floor to make the mast of the ship. I needed to see how the light comes through the wall and how it reflects, if it's from the side how it will look, from the front. They built one panel. They wheeled it in. Then, they wheeled in two lights. I sat there for half an hour: "Do this angle. Do that angle." I'm a different director. I'm a different cat.

I'm very particular. I had a Hollywood actor who said, "I want to work with you." I said, "Come do this reading with me." I wanted to check her out. Big star girl. We do the reading. We get one day of rehearsal. The questions and research I asked her to do *before* we came into the reading, she was like, "I got to do all that? I'm on this TV series." I said, "I don't care what you are on. If you are going to come into this reading, you need to know who this woman is. I'm going to give you five women to research. If you research three of them, you are doing your job. If you do five, you're getting two stars." But she didn't research anyone. Comes into rehearsal and didn't know who this person was. She's got her headphones on. This play takes place [in] 1930. And she's got her headphones on, listening to Mary J. Blige!

SMcC: How do you find balance between acting, writing, directing and family?

RS-H: I respect the space of each thing that I'm doing. Everything is not happening at the same time. Some things are going to take a lot longer. I've been on the musical version of *Car Wash* three years now. Do you know how long it takes to put a Broadway musical up? We've changed music directors, we've changed writers, we've changed choreographers, we've changed actors. Musicals take forever. *The Ten*, probably is going to take two years. *Sidney* probably a year and a half. *Destiny of Desire* is coming up.

I spend my day in this office, basically dividing my time up on my projects. I give *Destiny* the most amount of time right now, then I jump on *Sidney* and *The Ten*. Then, before I know it, nine hours of my day are done. Every day I get up and go do what I love. I don't do drugs. I don't hang out or go to the pub drinking beer all night. I come and do this beautiful thing called Theatre ... Art. I love it. I crawl up to the house about

5:30, 6. My wife has a good meal for me. I have a glass of wine. We talk about what life is. The life that I dreamed of as a child, I have it now.

I'll never be a rich man. To come from a rooming house in Lackawanna, where I was born … my umbilical cord was cut as my mother and I lay on the floor in November, in the winter of Buffalo, New York. And now to be sitting here saying, "I'm doing this thing I love!" I just had my office remodeled, own my own home, put all my kids through college, have an arts center built in Lackawanna with my name on it, help found a Black Arts intensive in Brooklyn where I'm teaching kids every year … . It's a blessing. I wish my momma was here to see more of it.

CTD: Are there genres, styles in theatre that you would like to direct?

RS-H: I haven't done an opera. The Metropolitan Opera and I are in talks right now. They want me to develop something there. They asked me if they could pair me with a writer. I said, "Yes. Let him write it. Let him write it and hand it to me. But if you want me to develop it … . Write it first." Write it and once I read it, I'll know where to go from there.

The other thing I haven't directed is a film. I don't need ten films. I'm not trying to go to Sundance and get an Oscar. I just want to direct *a* film. People ask me to direct TV all the time. I don't need to be a traffic cop. I love the process of theatre. I love building that family. I love the bickering. I love the debates. I love the first day of rehearsal. I love the table reads. I love the first preview. I love the opening nights. I love more than anything the process of getting there. All the in-betweens matter so much. Getting on the train, getting to rehearsal, walking in, "Good morning, everybody." Sitting down and let's talk about the ancestors; let's talk about why we're here, our purpose.

CTD: You mentioned "agent." Is your agent the same for all the things you do?

RS-H: My manager retired a few years ago; I'd been with him about 32 years. My agency is the same agency—Gersh. I like it all under one roof. Right now, where I am, they don't have to push me toward anything, mostly just answer the phone and see if it is something I really want to do. Or, if they see something that is really good for me, they make a phone call and say, "Ruben we have a client signed with us that would be great for you to work with." If they need me to go audition, I ain't beyond that. Gregory Hines used to always say, "Have you read the fine print of your job description that says you *will* audition?" I'm not coming to audition for one line in a movie. I'm not doing it. I ain't got the patience no more. I'd rather be sitting in here, in this office, or go sit on my couch or recliner and watch the Knicks.

SMcC: Do agents bring you projects as a director?

RS-H: Strangely enough, usually, it's just me traveling through the world. Leguizamo just called me: "I've got this thing, Primo. I've got this thing. Don't leave me hangin', you need to read it." Sidney Poitier's people called me about *Sidney*. People may see something I've done or hear an interview of what I've done and think that they want to deal with this headache. And then they call me 'cause they know through the headache what I'm going to do. What I'm going to do is give it everything. I was walking with my wife the other day. We were going to a play. This sister, a wonderful writer, was coming out of a restaurant. She said, "Oh my God, I've been looking for you. I've been trying to give you this play. Can I give you this play?" I said, "I'm so damn busy, and I don't know when I can do it. It's all about timing. I've got a lot of work in front of me." She said, "But you're the right person for it." I said, "Thank you. Send it to me."

CTD: What is your definition of success?

RS-H: I think my definition of success, at least in my profession, is being pleased at the work I have done and the way it has been received in the world. I would call that being successful.

CTD: What do you do to relax?

RS-H: I play my harmonica. I love sports ... mainly the New York teams. My wife knows that is where I'm going to be at a certain time of the day and fall asleep in my recliner. She reminds me I *do* have a bed here. I love my time with my family. Those moments are what I cherish most. I love when I go to Atlanta, and I see my sons there and my grandkids. I've got seven grandkids. I talk to at least one or both of my older sons a decent amount during the week. I'm always in contact with my brothers as well.

At this place in my life, I call a lot of people who I have relationships with. I talk to Eugene Lee a couple of days ago. I talked to Steve Jones last week. A lot of my main cats are gone: Bill Sims Jr., [Anthony] Chisholm. Harvy Blanks, Owiso Odera. Those guys are gone. I don't take for granted who's here. I call and say, "What's up? How are y'all doing?" Some of the conversations are two or three minutes.

A lot of the young people that I mentor check in with me all the time. And it is great. I have a group of young people who are doing very well right now in the business. They still need leadership though. They need help. They need advice. And I'm there. Like Lloyd Richards was there for me. Douglass Turner Ward. I used to call Doug. George Wolfe. Those three guys I leaned on a lot in my growth. And in some situations, George just had to say, "Slow down man. Just calm your ass down right now!"

Figure 12.2 *Jitney* by August Wilson on Broadway, 2016; l. to r.: Ruben Santiago-Hudson with Anthony Chisholm. Photo by Lia Chang.

SMcC: George told you to slow down?

RS-H: Yeah, George had to tell me … 'cause I get passionate, I get revved up. I don't like ugly. I like to speak on it. George was like, "Hold on. They can see you coming. They're going to block you. You've got to get in and do the work. They're blocking you. They're reading too much, seeing too much of what you are saying."

It's like all this stuff going on with Broadway. We're gonna name this theater … . We're gonna name that theater. Where is our work! Why are y'all so content to take the low hanging fruit. Stuff that doesn't cost them nothing.

Where is our work?! You want the name. That looks nice, but how does that impact the financial stability of our artistic community for generations? How does that empower our village, create new Broadway plays, recognize the classics, develop BIPOC Broadway designers and artists? And then, they want to argue with me: "Well the kids can see the name." My kids don't even know who they are! At least it starts the dialogue. They've got a plaque in the theater saying who that person is if you can find it. But, if you walk in that theater and see a play of Leslie Lee, Marcus Gardley, Lynn Nottage, Jose Rivera, Charles Fuller, Dominique Morisseau, Tarrell McCraney, Pearl Cleage, Quiara Hudes—my kids know who those people are that they see on that stage. They recognize family. And they're proud of that.

But, if you're going to name it, put something with it. Did it affect my community in a visceral way? They say "Ruben is impatient, Ruben is hardheaded, Ruben is a revolutionary. Ruben ain't satisfied." Ruben is pleased. Ruben is not content. Some of the Broadway stakeholders called me and said, "We hear you're upset with us"—these big organizations. I said, "Let me tell you, I'm not upset with you. I'm upset with the way things are going. I'm concerned. I'm concerned about my community. 'Cause I ain't gonna be fighting this fight forever. But, while I'm still here and fighting, I am concerned." "Well, what do you want?" "I tell you what I want, give me that theater for three years. Give my community that theater."

Broadway is not the standard of excellence. It's a location, it's real estate. And whoever can pay the rent the longest has a home. And they're hoping it's people they care and know about are those people, their friends. But that name, Broadway, is known all over the world. Not off-Broadway, not the Negro Ensemble Company, not the Public Theatre, not Shakespeare in the Park. They're not known all of the world. Broadway is. And if I could put three years of my people in that theater—writers, designers, actors, directors—for three years, we could develop a whole new cache of power. And we can take that power anywhere we wanted to. But just to put a name up there. We can't take that name nowhere. I'm proud the name's up there. But don't come calling me so you can take my picture because I'm standing out there because you've named a theater, ya know. No. I'm happy you did it. God bless you. Put three years' worth of our work up there.

CTD: **That is something I've been arguing for from day one.**

RS-H: But they cuss me. They said they ain't got no time for me. They called me and said, "Why did you write the 31-page manifesto?" I said, "I didn't even *read* the whole 31 pages. But I've read enough to know that I need to be standing behind it because it is important." Do I agree with everything, NO. Listen, if I read 31 pages, you better give me a check. If I write the 31 pages, you definitely better give me a check.

CTD: **So, it's clear, what is "31 Pages"?**

RS-H: *We See You White American Theatre.* They say, "Well, your picture is in the *New York Times.*" I say, "Well God bless them. Put me and Lynn Nottage's pictures, out of all the names on that list. One hundred and twenty thousand names, you put my picture in the *New York Times.* Why?" Someone said, "Why is your picture there." I said, "Because they think I'm important, I guess." I didn't call them and say, "You should put my picture in." Everybody calls me from all over the country, saying "Man, they out for you now, your picture in the paper." I looked on the list. They had Lin Manuel, Blair Underwood, Viola Davis on there. I have no fear. What can they do to me? For standing up for what's right? What can you do to me that you haven't already done?

SMcC: You have not changed. You're that same brother I met back in 1983 standing on the corner at 43rd and 9th Avenue. I never saw anyone with that kind of bravado.

RS-H: But I've been for the people. Do you know what gave me a lot of confidence? My mama said to me, "Baby, don't half-step, go all the way in, you're going to be one of the best. But always remember this, you can always come home." I knew I had a home. But I knew I was too proud to go home.

CTD: What advice would you give your younger self?

RS-H: Probably, don't reveal so much of my heart to everybody. I revealed it to too many people. They can step on it. And they did. They can hurt the heart. My heart's been broken so many times.

SMcC: If you had the opportunity to start your career over, would you do anything differently?

RS-H: Naw, because I wouldn't be who I am now.

SMcC: How would you describe your legacy?

RS-H: That I was a good father, a good husband, a good man with tremendous integrity. A builder. A man who didn't suffer fools. Always concerned about his community and did what he could to help that community. A man who dedicated himself to the work of making this world a better place for all of us through his art.

CTD: What word would you use to describe yourself?

RS-H: Pride... .

EMPOWERMENT 13

An Interview with George C. Wolfe

SMcC: I remember observing George Wolfe, the writer, during the rehearsal process for his jazz opera, *Queenie Pie,* and thinking to myself, "Who is this brother, perched on a table, legs crossed in a yoga position? He thought fast and he talked fast." He became artistic director of the NY Shakespeare Festival-Public Theatre. His Broadway productions of *Jelly's Last Jam* and *Bring in 'da Noise, Bring in 'da Funk* are wonderful additions to the American musical theatre canon.

George's gumbo was so popular, his New Year's Eve parties grew out of his uptown apartment and moved downtown into a giant loft. Everybody in New York theatre wanted to be there. Connections were formed. Deals were made. Talk about networking!!! Ah, those were the days!

CTD: George has donated a collection of his papers to the New York Public Library for the Performing Arts' Billy Rose Theatre Division.

Interview With George C. Wolfe

SMcC: I first met you as the creator and writer of *Queenie Pie* and *The Colored Museum*, which were in production at the same time in '86. Did you know then that you were a director at heart?

DOI: 10.4324/9781003410737-13

EMPOWERMENT: An Interview with George C. Wolfe

Figure 13.1 Photo by Carson Crow.

George C. Wolfe: Writing and directing were always hand-in-hand for me, going all the way back to high school. My cousins told me that when I was little, I would give them lines to say. In college, I started out as a design/acting major and then switched focus to acting/directing and then my last year of college, started writing. I then worked at the theater in Los Angeles called the Inner-City Cultural Center, where I taught acting and wrote and directed shows, so that when I came to New York, everyone said you can't do both. So, I focused on writing, went to NYU, and got a double MFA in Dramatic Writing/Musical Theatre. I applied for the directing program but was placed on their Wait List, a fact I point out to them anytime they ask me back to give me an award.

And then, *The Colored Museum* happened, and it established me as a writer and then came *Spunk*, which I directed and adapted, and that established me as a director. And then after that, I claimed my territory as a writer/director. So, I knew very early on what I wanted to do. I just had to go through the process of the professional landscape, figuring it out as well.

SMcC: I remember being surprised when you would meet us at the elevator to give notes.

GCW: With regards to *The Colored Museum*, and I do not say this with any degree of disrespect to Lee Richardson, but I was from the very beginning a surrogate/covert director on the production ... being very insistent and very involved in every decision on that project since Day One. Less than a year earlier I'd done a show, not *Queenie Pie*, where the director got what I had intended totally wrong, and it got clobbered and I got clobbered by the critics. I was not going to let that happen again. So, I was very aggressively involved in the shaping and crafting of *The Colored Museum*. It was a new show, a new beast, and I wanted to protect it and not let it slip into something that was clichéd or like something that was familiar.

SMcC: When did you decide to pursue a theatrical career? Who influenced you the most or was your first mentor?

GCW: It was always theatre, even when I was little. I didn't think of it as a career. I actually wanted to build an amusement park when I was eight, à la Disneyland. I still have the plans I made for it then. And when I was twelve, my mother came to NYU one summer for some advanced degree work, and I came with her and saw *Hello Dolly* with Pearl Bailey and *West Side Story* at the State Theatre and a New York Shakespeare Festival's mobile unit production of *Hamlet* with Cleavon Little, which Joe Papp directed. And so, after that, it was a done deal.

SMcC: Has there ever been a project that frightened you, but you accepted it anyway? Why? What was your most challenging production?

GCW: I prefer to only do things that frighten me. If I already know how to do something, why bother? Initially I was very daunted by *Angels in America*, mainly because it was seven hours of theatre, and I could not wrap my head around how to direct seven hours of theatre and then it came to me. You do it like everything else, one scene at a time. And that was a fun realization and ultimately a liberating one. Just dig in and do the work. And after that, fear or caution about a project became a part of its allure … . Once I say yes, get to work and to hell with everything else.

SMcC: Do you think theatre as we know it is going to change post-COVID? If so, how?

GCW: I have no idea. I truly do not.

SMcC: Did you have a mentor or mentors? Who were they?

GCW: C. Bernard "Jack" Jackson who ran the Inner-City Cultural Center, in Los Angeles, the first place which hired me after college. I gave Jack one scene I'd written and an outline I'd scribbled on an envelope, and he said, "Go do it." Peter Stone and Arthur Laurence … Arthur wrote the books for the musicals *West Side Story* and *Gypsy*, and Peter, the book for *1776*. Both were teachers of mine. Peter refused to teach a class at NYU unless I was allowed in the class, and both tried to get me hired as the book writer on Broadway musicals, neither of which were "black shows." The jobs didn't work out, but it was nice to know they had an "expansive" idea of the sort of stories I could tell, which is not always the case in the commercial theatre.

SMcC: Could you elaborate on your creative process as a writer/director?

GCW: Hire smart actors who, in the process of digging for the truth of a character or a scene, will invariably help reveal to you when a scene is working and when it is not.

SMcC: Have you ever sent a designer back to the drawing board?

GCW: I was a set designer in college, so I have an instinct about what I'm looking for. Also, working with the set designer is generally the first person you collaborate with. It's a great time to learn how to help the story breathe in a three-dimensional way.

I love working with a designer and deciding if the two of you have come up with something brilliant. Then two days later, trashing it and starting all over again. Robin Wagner, who designed *A Chorus Line* and *Dreamgirls*, and I worked with on

Jelly's Last Jam. Once said, "Collaboration is a word directors invented to make everyone feel good about obeying them."

SMcC: What types of work are you instinctively drawn to as a director?

GCW: Generally, the exact opposite of the project I've just completed. It keeps you on edge and open to discovering and using different muscles.

SMcC: Is there any style or genre of theatre you look forward to working in?

GCW: I love working on musicals because they are so damn hard. You know that by the time you are done, you will have gotten better and smarter and tougher. Also love text intense work, need it be Shakespeare or Eugene O'Neill, or August Wilson, because it's fun and challenging evolving the physical life of the project in order to help the language soar.

SMcC: You had a meteoric rise in the theatre. When did you know you were on the right track?

GCW: It didn't feel meteoric at the time. It just felt like hard intense work. But in retrospect, a lot of work came my way rather quickly. I've been blessed in that a number of people—Joe Papp, Gordon Davidson, Ricardo Khan, Lee Richardson, Margo Lion—believed in me and said, "Here's a room. Here's some money. Go play."

SMcC: How did you meet Joseph Papp?

GCW: After *The Colored Museum* was done at Crossroads Theatre, Morgan Jenness talked it up with Joe and Gail Merrifield, who was head of New Play Development. It was through Morgan I met Joe.

SMcC: You, Joanne Akalaitis, and Michael Grief were the "anointed ones" at the Public back in the '80s. Did you know then that you would eventually become artistic director?

GCW: After I did *Jelly*, my first Broadway show, and saw how fucking hard it was, i.e., the commercial landscape ... that's when I decided to become a producer as well, to help nurture other writers/artists' work. Roughly six years after Joe produced *The Colored Museum*, I got offered to become the producer of the Public.

SMcC: When you were artistic director at the Public, what seasons are memorable for you and why?

GCW: Every single one was amazing, magical, horrible, joyful, draining, wondrous, and hell.

SMcC: Looking back, is there anything you would have done differently?

GCW: Looking back, I would have taken breaks between shows/projects/jobs so that my body, brain, and spirit could replenish.

SMcC: What is your definition of success?

GCW: Success to me is forming a close collaboration with the people that you work with, making all involved to the degree that you can, feel pride and ownership of the material, and hopefully when you're done, no one has caused you to have less joy about diving into the next project.

SMcC: What do you believe is your legacy?

GCW: Hell if I know. I love to make work. I love empowering people to do their best work and to create an environment where they feel safe to discover and take risks. I like making projects that hopefully empowers the audience. That's about all one can control. It's the moment you're in, and nothing else … .

GRATEFUL 14

An Interview with Ricardo Khan

CTD: Ricardo recommended me to the artistic director of Capital Repertory Theatre in Albany, to direct *FLY* which he wrote with Trey Ellis.

SMcC: It's always an honor to be recommended by the author.

CTD: Definitely. Directing that amazing work is one of the most enjoyable experiences I've had in theatre.

Interview With Ricardo Khan

CTD: When did your interest in theatre begin?

RK: In Camden, New Jersey, which is where I grew up, there was a group that I'm sure you guys know, Jack and Jill. The mothers would take us to different things to make us more American. We would go to ski trips; we'd go to all different places. One trip, we went to Broadway to see *Hello Dolly*. We didn't really understand the full impact of it until the curtain opened and there was Pearl Bailey and Cab Calloway. Everybody looked like us. This had amazing impact on me.

SMCC: That was my first Broadway show, too. I took the train up with my mother. It was at the Saint James Theatre.

Figure 14.1 Photo by Ricardo Khan.

RK: Yes! Every time I pass the Saint James, I imagine where I was sitting. It was in the mezzanine.

SMcC: You must have been in high cotton, baby. I was up in the balcony.

RK: It probably was the balcony, Saundra. But it had an amazing impact on me; I remember early on in my life, probably the fifth or sixth grade, every year in school they would have *HMS Pinafore*, or *The Mikado*, some Gilbert and Sullivan show. They only had maybe two black people in the class, so I was always relegated to the side, never on the stage. Sometimes the chorus was on the stage too. But I was never really allowed to be up there. I grew up mainly in Quaker schools most of my life, so it was a very white culture during the day and a very black culture at night. For a kid to leave that school, relegated to the side, and then come home and pick up *A Raisin in the*

Sun and go up in my room and try to pretend I was Sidney Poitier, *that* was something.

I was born in Washington, DC, at Freedman's Hospital. My parents met at Howard University. My father came from Trinidad and my mother from Philadelphia.

CTD: What effect did seeing *Hello Dolly* have upon you?

RK: I was seeing what I thought was the best of the best, Broadway, the Great White Way. But I didn't expect *us*. We didn't have those opportunities back then. But what we *did* have was our own community. We had Howard University, we had Meharry. It was a whole different world in a pre-integrated America. We didn't look at that as anything less than. We just looked at it as this is our world.

I'll give you an example. In Camden, there was a YMCA. It was the black YMCA. Later in my years, I found out there was a white YMCA. Of course, the white YMCA was midtown. It was beautiful. It had an indoor pool. Our YMCA wasn't quite that. But it was ours. We never thought differently. Later when I realized there was another Y, I became more appreciative of that Black Y being *our* Y. A lot has happened to the betterment since then, but I miss those times.

When I look back on going to Broadway, I didn't understand that it would become more than a treat. Maybe our mothers did. And thank God that they saw that. Around that time, Louis Armstrong's big hit was *Hello Dolly*. Anytime we had that one thing, it was *the* one thing everybody talked about. It was that type of world. Any time there was a *Hello Dolly*, it had a huge impact on you that would last the rest of your life, certainly get you talking.

CTD. What additional experiences shaped your artistic development?

RK: In high school, of course, there was Vietnam. There was the Civil Rights Movement. There was the Women's Movement. In each case, we had to choose. Melvin Van Peebles would say in his prologue to *Ain't Supposed to Die a Natural Death* that it was a time when if you walked, you were making a statement. If you stood, you made a statement. If you ran, you made a statement, if you were at a baseball game and the

Star-Spangled Banner came up, do you stand or do you sit? Going through a neighborhood do you run, or do you walk? On the radio, which button do you press in the car? There's rock. There's soul. They weren't calling it R and B back then. You had to choose everything. Everything. If you were of draft age, do you go to Vietnam or do you go to Canada? Everything was like that, and I just somehow grabbed onto the theatre as an opportunity to avoid all that madness.

In high school, all I wanted to do was one musical after another. We were in *Funny Girl* and all of these shows ... and *How to Succeed in Business*. But during the summer, we would get together and do our own thing. We would do the black version of *Hello Dolly* and the black version of *My Fair Lady* and the black version of *Oliver* and *Sweet Charity*. Until I got to college, and I realized that there was a bigger dialogue than that. I very much wanted to be part of that. I didn't want theatre to be a way of building a wall around me to protect me from this mad world. Somehow, at Rutgers during the Black Power Movement and the Pan African movement, all of these things were calling me to use what I had to enter the conversation.

CTD: Had you studied voice, taken dance or acting lessons?

RK: No. We had *seen Hello Dolly* on Broadway and that was enough. I did have training in piano. We were all required to start with the piano. Then my mother would say, "OK, after that you could do whatever you want, whatever instrument you want." I stuck with piano because I absolutely loved it. I started lessons when I was six and by the time I was a teenager, I had a problem going to our parties. There would always be somebody ... Ann Foster was her name. She was an amazing pianist who would play anything we wanted to sing. It was usually Motown or the Philly sound. She could just play it. That always blew my mind. One day I asked, "How do you do that?" She said, "Ricky, get a book of chords and learn all of them." I actually went to Colony Records and got a book of 6400 chords. They're not really 6400, it's just relative. I learned them all. Then I realized I was able to play by ear with the chords. I was able to get sheet music and follow the guitar chords which meant that I stopped reading. It was bad that I did that.

Years and years later, I got a piano. I picked up *Clair de Lune* that I had stopped playing when I started playing Motown. I've been trying ever since to get through that whole thing, and I will before I die. But I have always had a love of music. My piano teacher quit when he said, "I want you to go and find something from a symphony." So, I bought *I Hear a Symphony* by Diana Ross. And he said, "Bye." That was the end of that.

SMcC: What was your major in college?

RK: Even though I had a love for music, I had a love for theatre. I also had a love for architecture. There was a community theatre group in Cherry Hill where we lived at that time. A friend of my parents was playing the lead. He was black and playing the lead in *The King and I*. Then they did *Finian's Rainbow*. He was the lead in that too. He was an architect, you see. So, I thought, well, maybe I could do both. Maybe I could be like him.

When I went to Rutgers, I was really thinking about architecture, even though I loved theatre. I also knew my parents would not allow me to major in theatre. I was thinking about Ithaca College, Carnegie Mellon.... There were a few different places I wanted to go that had both, but I thought it didn't make any sense to spend that much money if I wasn't exactly sure. So I attended Rutgers because it was a state school. It was inexpensive. I figured if I go to Rutgers for one year, I will then transfer to whatever school I wanted. But what I found was New York—35 miles away. New York! Then that's when I decided, no, I gotta stay here.

Rutgers was perfect for me. It was inexpensive and it was right there at New York. I could do whatever I wanted to do and go home when I wanted. That's why I chose Rutgers. I went from architecture to pre-med to pre-law, and other majors. I was experimenting. Remember the draft for Vietnam? I was number 35 from that draft. That meant that the moment I graduated from college, I would be drafted because they were up to 200 by then. I knew I was headed to Vietnam.

I decided I'm gonna apply to law school, because then maybe I could be part of the Jag corps and owe the Army a certain amount of time. That was my plan. My advisor in college said, "Rick, why are you trying to go to the law school, when you know what you really want is theatre?" He understood what I was trying to do about Vietnam. Somewhere in the spring of 1973, they stopped the draft. It was literally just months before my graduation. At that point I realized, I should go for what I really want.

I was still thinking about law during the summer when I was with my parents in Trinidad. We were about to come back and then I was going to start law school at Howard. But I knew I didn't want to do it. I remember talking with my father, "Dad, I know we're leaving tomorrow to go back, but I've decided to stay in Trinidad a little longer with my cousin." He said, "Okay." That's what I did.

CTD: What did you do when you returned home?

RK: When I came back, I painted houses because I love being outdoors. In the fall, the LINKS of Camden County asked me to direct *Purlie* for them. At that time, *Purlie* was the new *Hello Dolly*. And I did. It was for the kids and to raise money for Operation Bank Basket. We continued doing the show all over the place. When we got to Rutgers, my leading lady, playing Lutiebelle, was not available. Sheryl [Lee] Ralph did it. It was during that time I realized this is what I want to do. But I needed that extra time to think it through and go from there.

I was up for a job in Philadelphia, WCAU, as a production assistant at the TV station. I didn't have any experience in TV. They called me and said another person got it, I said, "OK." I hung up the phone, picked it up, and called John Bettenbender, who was the Dean of Mason Gross School of the Arts. They had wanted to start Mason Gross School of the Arts the year before, so while I was a senior, I auditioned. Knowing that I didn't get this job in Philly, I picked up the phone and said, "Can I come and be part of the first year?" He said, "Yeah." I packed my bags and the next day I was back in New Brunswick in Mason Gross School of the Arts. I was there with Avery Brooks, Lee

Richardson, and Dwight Collins. Sheryl [Lee Ralph] was there but she was still an undergrad. There were writers—William Mastrosimone, a bunch of folks.

The first year, Mason Gross didn't have all of their act together. We started to complain. They were so flexible, leaving the doors open for us to do other things and do them our way. We would go to classes all day and then go to the normal show everybody was in. MFA students were in shows, like *Romeo and Juliet*. After rehearsals, at 11 pm, we would go do our own thing at the Paul Robeson Ensemble. We would rehearse the show we were going to do until 1 am. That was my grad school experience.

I remember seeing *What the Winesellers Buy* by Ron Milner in Philadelphia. My uncle, Sonny Driver, was the first black entertainment manager in Philadelphia. This was around the time Philadelphia was the center of black music. He had a magazine called *Scoop USA*, it was all black. He was a part of that. He calls me one day, he said, "I have tickets to this thing called, *What the Winesellers Buy*. Would you like to go?" I said "Yeah." He met me there and we went in and guess who I met there? Woodie King, Ron Milner, and Dick Anthony Williams.

CTD: I was the production stage manager on *Winesellers* from the first day of rehearsal through most of the tour.

RK: Wow. Here I am at Mason Gross. I'm not getting any of this. How do I get involved? Woodie said, "Come be part of the Black Theatre Workshop." It blew my mind. I was able to convince the folks at Mason Gross to give me credit to go to Henry Street for these workshops. And that's what I did. All my life has been about needing this *and* that because one was never enough. And that's what got me through.

SMcC: What year was the Black Theatre Workshop when you were going there?

RK: It was either '74, or '75. Dick Anthony Williams was my acting teacher at Henry Street. He had replaced Gil Moses, who was my first acting teacher there. In those years, we connected with the National Black Theatre. I got to know Barbara Ann Teer. I was the stage manager of one of the shows we did, *The Middle Passage*. Avery Brooks directed it.

We took it to NBT. Walking into NBT, people were living in the building! A black theatre community. It was the most incredible thing I ever experienced in my life.

CTD: Who were some of your mentors?

RK: John Bettenbender, the Dean was head of the program and founder of Mason Gross School of the Arts. He had big visions as a director. I got my bigness in directing from him. I enjoyed that. As for mentors in the theatre itself ... Woody was absolutely a mentor. My mother and father were big mentors in my life. Also, people I've never met, like Sidney Poitier, were role models. Woodie was a big one. Bert Andrews, the photographer, was also a mentor. In grad school, we needed our photographs taken, our pictures when we started to go out on auditions. He did our first pictures.

SMcC: When did you decide to form your own theatre company?

RK: I got my MFA in acting and directing. It took me four years. Lee [Richardson] got his in acting. We graduated together and started going on auditions in New York. Lee and I were tired of the roles *we* were auditioning for.

We had both been in a CETA program, which hired artists from different disciplines. As part of that program, Lee and I were doing *Sizwe Banzi is Dead* in playgrounds and parks. Mandela was still in prison. Apartheid was still going on. These were the years of fighting and protest. This was our protest.

SMcC: What's the CETA program?

RK: The Comprehensive Employment and Training Act. It was what started many theaters at that time. The goal was to hire the hardcore unemployed and retrain them. Most actors were hardcore unemployed because "hardcore" meant unemployed for more than eight weeks, for 16 weeks. It was like the WPA Program, but in the '70s. CETA programs were all over the country.

Through this program we learned how to apply for grants and applied for money to start a black theatre. Lee and I would go to the meetings. We imagined what we would do. In a restaurant, we wrote out the mission statement on a napkin. Then found out that we got the money. That was in 1978. $225,000! With that money, we were able to hire twelve people full-time. Twelve actors. We were also able to hire full-time administrators, managers, and do all kinds of things. We had the money to actually hire who and what we needed to do our work. It was through CETA that we started Crossroads.

We didn't have to charge money for tickets. The first show we did was *First Breeze of Summer* by Leslie Lee. Lee [Richardson] also directed that one. Then I directed *Dream on Monkey Mountain* by Derek Walcott. After that we applied for another grant. As we went along, we realized that there's something in this. Black people were being paid decent money with benefits to act year-round.

SMcC: George Street Playhouse, an established *white* theatre company, was right next door. Their theater space was smaller. How did that happen?

RK: Crossroads' first space was an abandoned sewing factory on the highway right by the river. There was a big post in the middle of the stage. The windows were frosted because the owners of the factory did not want the workers to look out and be distracted. You had to walk up a long flight of stairs to enter the theater. Audience members from George Street Playhouse started to come down to Crossroads and say, "This is where it's at now." Our first subscribers were primarily Jewish. But our first group sales were mainly black. That's how we ended up half and half in terms of audiences.

At the time the city began redevelopment plans for New Brunswick. They wanted to move George Street Playhouse, which was in an old grocery store. That's where we did *Purlie* and *Raisin*. The next step was to try to develop that block as a Cultural Center. There was an old storage space there. They thought that would be good for Crossroads.

John Bettenberger by that time was a big supporter of Lee and me, and a big voice in the community. He said, "Oh no, no, no. Crossroads is not going to be in the back of anything." So, he pushed for us not to be in that building. But instead that they build a building of our own. *And* it was right next to where the YMCA was. That's how that happened. It's funny how things flip flop that way. We happen to be at the right place at the right time. People were saying, "Crossroads is doing amazing things." I think the way they put it was, "They are a jewel, but without a proper setting. Let's give them a proper setting."

CTD: Great metaphor. Throughout your career what are some memorable experiences you have had as a director?

RK: I just *had* one, *Fences* in Johannesburg. Every year my mother and father would be sure that we got down to Trinidad so that we could understand who we fully are. My father was Muslim, my mother was Episcopalian. Mother was black. My father was from Trinidad, of East Indian descent which is how I get the name "Khan." But, in Trinidad they don't look at themselves that way. You say, "Well, what are you?" They say, "I'm Trinidadian, that's who I am." They don't look at race the way we do in America. When my father first came to the states, he came to Howard University. He came on a boat. The boat got him through a storm to Florida, and then from there a train to Washington, DC. He got to Howard University and wrote back to his father, "Dad, you're not going to believe this, but most of America is black." Because all he saw was Howard University.

We grew up with the sense of us being all of these things, not just one. Not just Camden, but many. I feel that wanting to be part of the movement in South Africa, which for me started in the '80s with theatre, was always important to my being able to define myself beyond the way America wants me defined. I've always seen myself as a citizen of the world. I've always seen black people as world people. I've always totally understood why they would not want us to see that, because that's our power. Our power rests in our global roots and if we connected with them, my God, could you imagine? The connection, the power of black people around the world, if we connected from not just a cultural point of view, but a business point of view, the US, the Caribbean, Africa?

The times that directing experiences have been most profound are when they move beyond the art of it, and into a place like in South Africa, where I can see August speaking to them. I could see that in the audience. I never thought that way before. But I was doing August Wilson because there were a number of black people in South Africa saying, "We want you. We want you August Wilson." I had to help them get the rights to do it. There are theaters in South Africa who have adopted black history month in order to do African American work. This is the collaboration that they've missed.

The first show that went to South Africa after the 16-year cultural boycott during apartheid was *Sheila's Day*. *Sheila's Day* performed in Grahamstown, which was the seat where apartheid all started. To take a show, like *Sheila's Day*, to South Africa was culturally profound. Half the cast are women from the US and half the cast are women from South Africa. Bringing people together, having no idea what each would learn from the other … then finding out how amazing that was … are reasons I do what I do.

CTD: Are there additional reasons?

RK: I have never enjoyed an experience like that if it were not for artistic excellence first. The first statement in our mission is excellence. It doesn't matter what culture it is. What matters is that we are making use of our craft and we are aspiring, all of us, to artistic excellence. You achieve that by trying your best to support excellence in artists and their careers. That's what we've always done. I can list many shows I've enjoyed directing, that made a difference culturally including *Fences, Shelia's Day, FLY,* and before that *Black Eagles*.

Those are the moments that have meant the most to me as a director. We did *Black* Eagles and *FLY* before the Tuskegee Airmen were even recognized. Dr. Roscoe C. Brown was one of the original Tuskegee Airmen and also the president of Bronx Community College. He was our main advisor. He took Leslie Lee and me to a reunion of the Tuskegee Airmen. He said, "If you really want to do it right, go there." We went with our pens and paper, taking notes. The stories got bigger and bigger from people like "Dr. Death." When I think about what we were doing, knowing that they had never been given the recognition … . Then while we were doing *FLY*, the airmen received the Congressional Medal! Those are the moments that matter. Those are the moments my mother and father took me to the Potomac for, to be ready.

SMcC: Have you ever directed a play that frightened you?

RK: Have to think about that, Saundra. Why would a show frighten me? One time I was scared to death about doing a show about Langston Hughes. I had written it as an adaptation of a book that Ossie Davis wrote. Like many plays, it had a great first act and a horrible second act. The second act wasn't working, and we were in tech. Shirley Prendergast, the lighting designer said, "Look Rick, why don't you just figure it out and then let me know. I'll be waiting for you." Here we are the day before first preview and still can't figure it out. That afternoon it started to snow. It snowed harder and harder. It snowed so badly that we had to cancel the show. We had that extra day. The actors decided rather than deal with the weather, they'd stay the night in the theater. We worked through the night. I was petrified of not having a second act. So yeah, I had to call on God, and then came the snow.

CTD: Are there specific types of work to which you are drawn?

RK: I love them all. I certainly was first drawn to musicals because of the music. I got to meet people like Al Perryman, Tom Bridwell, André De Shields. These were the people I get to work with ... Tamara Tunie. We did *Don't Bother Me I Can't Cope*. Oh, my God. Micki Grant! Meeting people like that got me into musicals in those earlier years. Later, I was drawn to more cross-cultural works. Whether they were Caribbean, or South African, or plays like *Freedom Rider* in which we're trying to figure out the black and white thing in our history. But I've since been focused on directing the shows that I write, or those on which I collaborate with other writers. I directed *Fences* because John Kani asked me.

SMcC: Do you prefer collaborating with other writers when you're developing new works?

RK: I absolutely prefer to write them with other people. I don't call myself a playwright really. I'm a collaborator and I love working with other writers to create the work, to find it. I think what I know as a director leads me to develop roles like the Tap Griot in *FLY*. The character doesn't use words but tap dances to tell an important part of the story. I enjoyed working with Trey Ellis to find out what that is.

With *Freedom Rider*, I started writing it myself. I drew up the characters. I drew up the structure. I did all of that until I realized I know writers like that. I said, "Wow this Jewish character I'm trying to write, reminds me of Murray Horwitz. A female character from Detroit wants to be a freedom rider. She reminds me of Kathleen McGee Anderson." Another, by Nicole Salter, is a guy from Howard University. He reminded me of a writer I knew in Kansas City, Nathan Jackson.

SMcC: Have you collaborated on any other plays?

RK: *Freedom Rider* was the collaboration of me and these other four writers. It took us a few years to develop this piece. After that, I did *Letters from Freedom Summer*, which takes place in 1964. I collaborated with Denise Nicholas and Sibusiso Mamba from Swaziland on that.

SMcC: What would you say is your definition of success?

RK: Success certainly has a lot to do with what I hear from people, especially young people, when something lights up in them because of something I've directed, written, or said. They all work together. Amiri [Baraka] used to say, you can't be black without music, without the blues. There can't be black theatre without music. And there can't be black artists who don't also imagine and talk.

The epitome of success for me would be *Fences*. It's on my mind … . Doing in a theater in South Africa, run mainly by black people. The CEO is a black woman. The lobby is teeming with folks who were involved with all kinds of different shows going on in the building. There's a restaurant there that *we run*. There are rehearsal halls that *we run*, and marketing departments and development all that *we run*. The custodial department and the drivers … . To be able to do a show in an environment, with that level of pride and self-dignity. Then that concept is shared by an audience in the theater who are a part of it is something else. I was asked to speak to a graduating class there and I got to them. They were lit up. But, they were lit from the beginning, before I met them. So,

Figure 14.2 *Fences* by August Wilson, Joburg Theatre, 2023; l. to r.: Lunga Radebe, Tumisho Masha, Khutjo Green, Subsiso Mamba, and Hlomla Dandala. Photo by Masi Losi.

success, for me, is having opportunities and being ready for those opportunities to transcend your current condition and allow you to imagine something new. And then to pass it on.

SMcC: How do you talk to designers, and have you ever sent them back to the drawing board?

RK: [*He laughs.*] Yes, many, many times. I was really not a very good student in architecture. And my God, trying to do those models with these fingers. I was terrible. I was just bad. I do have a sense of spatial reality. I also know that there are times I'm more interested in the negative space than the positive space. Because of that there have been times when I've asked designers to go back.

SMcC: Can you give us an example of "negative space"?

RK: We were doing *Flying West*, by Pearl Cleage for example. The designer came in with this really beautiful set, but it wasn't their space. It wasn't something I imagined a family of black women, traveling on foot from the South to Nicodemus, Kansas, to take advantage of the Homestead Act, and then be able to build on the land and rely on themselves. For me, the walls should not be perfect. If the walls were imperfect and I was able to see through walls, through the cracks, then not only would I get a better sense of where they're living physically, but negative space would allow the possibility of fear to be present. From the outside, there was always this threatening environment. The negative space ... the negative spaces allow in all kinds of dynamics.

CTD: How do you prepare as a director?

RK: I go back to Shirley Prendergast again. She had some relationship with hearing a show, as opposed to looking at it. When I read a play, whether it's something that I'm about to direct or something that I'm considering as an artistic director, I tune into the rhythms of it. I tune into how it sounds in my head. Then I start to hear music. I know the music and how this song connects to that. When I know how sound, music, and rhythm connect to the play, I know how to tell the story.

CTD: What inspires your work as a director?

RK: The characters, absolutely the characters. There is somebody noble in your family lineage, or in your direct path, or in the history books, or on TV in each of those characters. They are heroes. If I can find the hero in each of the characters, then I'm inspired to tell their story.

SMcC: Have you ever had a bad review? Does it affect you?

RK: Yes, I've had bad reviews. It wasn't so much the directing. I find that if a critic does not like a play, especially a new play, most of the time they're going after the writer. Unfortunately it happened with *Black Eagles*. It was great when we did it at Crossroads first. After that we did it at the Ford's Theatre. That went great. Then we brought it to Manhattan Theatre Club. While in rehearsals, the United States sent the first planes to the Gulf. War had begun. At Manhattan Theatre Club, the audience is primarily white. Certainly, all the reviewers were white. The first review was Frank Rich. Killed it. Totally killed it. He didn't talk about anything else other than the writing. Tore Leslie [Lee] up and he never got over that. Leslie was also teaching playwriting at the time at NYU. The second review a few days later was Clive Barnes. He loved it. But for those three days, that bad review was our worst nightmare.

SMcC: But that review focused on the writer.

RK: We were all in the same boat. It's not like we didn't love Leslie Lee. And who else was telling the story of the Tuskegee Airmen?

CTD: In addition to *Shelia's Day* and *Fences* in South Africa, what other international directing experiences have you had?

RK: *Bubbling Brown Sugar* in Port of Spain, Trinidad. *Don't Bother Me I Can't Cope* went to the US Virgin Islands. So did *Ain't Misbehavin'*. I left Crossroads in '99. I lived in Trinidad for a year. I wanted to find a different way into the issues of race in America. I knew that they had a different way. At the same time, I was really discouraged that Actors Equity would not allow us to do more international work. The only reason we were able to do *Sheila's Day* was because I went to Equity and made an appeal to explain that on the basis of education and training black people, black artists are never given the opportunity to learn the works of Mbongeni Ngema, the works of Gibson Kente, and Township Theatre ... those styles. Yet we could get Chekhov whenever we wanted, because there was an exchange between Equity in the US and the Brits, but not Africa. This is an opportunity for us to learn.

I approached Equity as an actor. That's how we were allowed to do it. Do you know what they told me? They said, "We see Joe Papp on your list. We're gonna let you do it until you get to Joe Papp. When you get there we want you to replace the South Africans with American actors." Mandela was still in prison. *Sheila's Day* was part of the protest. South African actors were part of the experience. They told Papp you'd have to pay them Broadway rates then. It was just crazy. We ended up never doing it, and a year later, Papp died.

SMcC: They must have changed that rule because *The Lion King* hires African actors. So did *Sarafina*.

RK: But they are all members of Actors Equity US *and* they now have green cards. There are a lot more South African actors in America who have green cards than before. There was hardly anybody back then. Thuli Dumakude was probably the only one I knew at that time. So, in Trinidad, trying to figure out what to do if I wanted to do international work, I started meeting with Derek Walcott. We discussed creating an international theatre that didn't have anything to do with Actors Equity. If we set it in the islands, in St. Lucia, where he had contacts and where he was born, then no one would have jurisdiction over us. We could hire actors from wherever we wanted. That never happened.

But what did happen was I started the World Theatre Lab, a group of writers based in three different countries. That year was the year of Katrina. I was curious about what it felt like to be a person after Katrina sitting on top of the roof of their house waiting for somebody to save them, wondering, "Where's my country? What does it mean to be a citizen, and yet I can't be saved from this?" Around that same time were the London bombings. In the London bombings, the aftermath of that was "It has to be a Muslim, it's gotta be a Muslim who did this." So, I wondered, what it would be like to be a person who had a name like me, a beard, going to work one day, but then the next day everybody's looking like it's your fault? What did that feel like? In South Africa, the question I had was, "What does it feel like as a black person when the 'you' in 'you did this to me' is now the 'me,' because the power had shifted to black people?"

The lab was essentially eight writers at the Lark Play Development Center in New York, who focused on Katrina. John Eisner was running that. We were there for a week developing plays, short plays, writings about Katrina. But also, we were able to have conversations as writers between each other, which never happens. In London, the lab was at Theatre Royal Stratford East. In South Africa, the lab was at the Market Theatre. I literally went from one lab to the next. When I went to the second lab, I shared the stories from the first. In London, I shared stories from the first two. We created a world bond. We still continue to talk and work. The World Theatre Lab went on for about five years. TCG supported it. Baraka Sele at the New Jersey Performing Arts Center said, "I will do a lab and pay for one writer from each of the labs to come in. Then we could have a fourth lab." We did that. Out of those labs came long-term relationships and commissions to write and develop plays. My desires have moved from just directing to things like that—trying to put in place things that make a difference.

SMcC: How do you express your concepts to designers?

RK: It starts with the set designer. With most of the shows I do now I prefer non-realistic sets. My first conversation with a set designer focuses on why I want to work with them. For me it is really about poetry. It's about their ability to look at a piece and translate it into a space I can work within, as opposed to a space that does it for you. That requires the designer to think about how an audience can imagine what you do not put up there. Imagination is the most interesting thing in theatre. I love working with set designers who are driven by the central metaphor of a play, and how it speaks to a performing space.

SMcC: Do you have any new directing projects?

RK: We are talking about some things that may continue the connection with the Johannesburg theater. John Kani, who's an international star, had to pull out in the middle of *Fences* because of an inner ear infection. It was causing him to lose balance. He's 79 years old and was playing Troy. His son, Atandwa, was playing Cory. I was always curious as to how John was going pull this off, until I realized how much South Africa loves him. Just love him. So, John and I are looking at what next to do together.

Do you know Lonnie Bunch? He was the founding head of the Smithsonian African American Museum. He is now the Secretary of the entire Smithsonian. He and Kinshasha Coleman were the ones who brought me to the museum. I was doing programming for the Oprah Winfrey Theatre, which is in the museum. I got sidetracked into writing and directing plays for them. One of them was the opening night ceremonies of the African American Museum.

I've always wanted to bring the classics of black theatre to the Smithsonian, not so much producing shows, but possibly presenting them in the same way that *"Encores"* does at City Center. You don't need all the sets, all this and that, to make a statement to witness a play that really mattered in the canon of Black Theatre. Maybe it's a staged reading. That's my next big project I'm working on.

SMcC: What is your legacy?

RK: My legacy? I don't know, I'm still working. [*We all laugh.*]

SMcC: Where do you see theatre headed in the future?

RK: It is harder to do theatre nowadays because of COVID. It is harder to produce. It's not just because of money. I think people have started to question certain things that we would never question before about what we do and why. I never imagined that corporate America would one day be deciding whether or not they're going to work in offices. It has affected real estate. It has caused homelessness. You can see all of that in Manhattan. Buildings are not filled anymore. People aren't coming to work the way they used to. It's not that much different with theatre. We know we cannot do theatre by Zoom. We know that. We have to be in a room to do it right, to do it fully. The act of trying to convince people to do theatre is harder, I find.

I just directed a piece called *When Day Comes* that I wrote. It's about COVID and my times during COVID. The central storytellers are Sweet Honey in the Rock. We're going to do that in DC next year. Going to rehearsal, they all had to be masked. How do you sing, masked? How do you convince a group you have respected all your life that we need to do this nowadays? We need to get vaccinated. Vaccination? There are some people who don't want to do it. You can't ask who it is.

All the rules have changed. We can't sit and eat lunch in rehearsal because that means taking your mask down. The cost is incredible to a theater. It's incredible, the testing costs. Having a COVID officer that you're paying full time, often more than the actors. These are the things that our industry is trying to grapple with right now. How do you know who's going to test positive and not be able to make the show that night? If you have understudies, it means that your costs are much higher. That affects everybody. If you don't have understudies and the audience comes, you have to say "bye." They may not come again. The understudies may be kept in quarantine. And yet the cast and understudies will go out after rehearsals to eat and drink with their mask off.

Sets that used to cost $20,000, now cost $60,000 because of the cost of lumber. You can't give artists the experience we were accustomed to giving because you're always fighting the realities of this day. During those years, '20 and '21, we "discovered" Netflix. And all of a sudden, it's so much easier to be home than to go to the theater. It's not just in the US, it's all over the world. What is the role of theatre, live performance, in people's lives? The answer is how we treat and bring the young generation into the theater.

When we were young, we had no choice. There were no roles really for us—opportunities in television and film—the way they are now. Now young people ask, "Theatre, TV, film? Where do I want to go?" And there's the Web. That's the new one, working on the Web—online. "We don't need to go to Hollywood. We could do our own series online now." At one time we looked at live theatre as the only thing we *could* do, our opportunity to communicate and express ourselves. Now, with all of these opportunities, it's harder. As an industry, we need to open new ways of delivering theatre.

CTD: In this post-Floydian era of diversity and change, where do you see theatre going?

RK: I've seen in the regions a hesitancy for audiences, black and white, to come together. When people come to see a show like *Freedom Rider*, they're seeing a show about a shining moment in history, when people crossed racial lines to do amazing things for the sake of other people. I don't know how that speaks to young black and white people who have grown up, not only in a time of George Floyd and Brianna Taylor … the list goes on and on. In school, we had to learn to get under desks in case the Russians were coming, remember that? Now, what do you do in the case of an active shooter? It is a very different world today. A world of fear. When raised in a world of fear, and given the opportunity by technology to communicate with the rest of society via your headphones, or one-on-one with your computer, or your cellphone, what are you going to choose? Only the brave ones will say, "I want to go to a theater." We have to figure that out.

CTD: Do you have a first step in mind for venturing into those new testing grounds?

RK: I started talking with Phylicia Rashad, and Nicole Salter at Howard University. Remember when Crossroads had the African American College Initiative Program—the internship program? I'm interested in creating a bridge between young people in the arts attending historically black colleges to see what's possible when they graduate.

SMcC: If you have the opportunity to start your career over, is there anything you would do differently?

RK: No. I left Crossroads in '99 and I went to live in Trinidad. I started doing more international work.

CTD: Why did you leave?

RK: I left because as an artist, I realized that I had hit a certain ceiling. I needed to find who that Rick was, who would be willing to take risks and be scared of where his next paycheck was coming from.

SMcC: Welcome to my world.

CTD: Mine too.

RK: I also wanted to see what a new leadership at Crossroads could do. I was particularly interested in what a female artistic director from Canada, or London, somewhere outside of America, but who was black, would do? Someone who could bring a different perspective to Crossroads. I was tired of always having the same conversation about race. There needed to be a new language. I was looking for the new language. I knew I didn't have it, at least not then. I left thinking, I would come back and run an international component of Crossroads. I thought that we were going to be okay because we had just won the Tony Award and we had three thousand subscribers. The day I left, with the last plant from my office, Leslie Uggams and Stephanie Mills were on stage doing a matinee of *Play On* directed by André De Shields. I thought, "Okay. It's gonna be okay." But, a year later, Crossroads closed down.

The one thing I would have done differently would have been to be more involved with who my successor was going to be. What I was doing was following the advice of people from white theatres, and people like Peter Zeisler at TCG, who said, "When an artistic director leaves, you should leave it up to your board to form the committees to do this and that, and do the search." And so, I did. I was the president of TCG at the time, too. So, I said, "I'm going to leave you guys alone. Whatever you want to do. The board has to take ownership, not the founders. The board has to. Until they do, the institution will never be strong." What I didn't realize was that *our* institutions were not ready for that yet. We didn't have those kinds of boards yet.

The people whom I think did it right? Woodie King, Jr. Now, Liz Van Dyke runs New Federal Theatre. In the same way, Sade is at National Black Theatre, which was founded by her mother, Barbara Ann Teer. Penumbra is the same. It was passed on. My question is, "What's the better way to do it?" One way seems more organic, more connected culturally to our people—passing it on. Then, there's another approach: "This is an institution. It is supposed to be this, this, and this!"

CTD: Unfortunately, too often that traditional model doesn't work for us.

RK: It doesn't. I did a lot of things based on the traditional model. But that was one thing I regret. I didn't realize we *are* different. It *is* about passing on and *that* legacy. Take the case of Bruce Beach, a very well-to-do coastline area in California. After decades of trying to get their deed back, do you know what happened?

SMcC: They sold it.

RK: Yes. It made me think about Berry Gordy selling Motown. The question becomes who owns legacy? We're not a people, yet, who understand and can appreciate reparations because they haven't happened. The closest to reparations might have been what happened at Bruce Beach, because it was taken from black people by the county for racist reasons. And then they sell it. So, all of a sudden, it's like, wait a minute, where are we? We are a people who still haven't figured out how to pass on wealth. We haven't.

Forbes did a great thing by saying that I'm not going to give my children anything. His job was to give them opportunity. But he's Forbes! We're not there, yet. We are still in the debate and we haven't yet figured it out. We get mad at other ethnic people and companies for opening up bodegas and everything else in our neighborhoods, but we don't open our own. We don't think that the reason they have that bodega is because they passed it down, the family works after school in that place. We don't do that. We say, "Well, I don't need to do that." We have missed something here. And we have to, we have to figure it out.

SMcC: Many of us don't have that generational connection.

RK: I remember, my parents saying "You have a choice as to what college you go to. But you do *not* have a choice to *not go* to college." That's how many of us grew up. We have to discipline ourselves *against* our history to make that change to build wealth.

Once Mbongeni Ngema asked me, "Rick, what does it feel like to be in a country that's not your own?" No one had ever asked me that. I don't know if anybody ever asks African American people that. We don't think that way. We think we earned our right to be here. When you travel to another country and see how they work, how they operate, *and* that country is black run, it's a black country ... you see the country like any other American tourist. That doesn't work, and that doesn't work, and they have electrical problems, and they have this, they have that. But they can say, "Yeah, but it's *mine*." In this country we have yet to say, *"This* is mine." If we really believed "it's mine," then we would own our s**t. We would build our businesses. In 1999, if Crossroads was mine, I would have done something differently.

SMcC. May I ask you one question? What happened between you and Lee Richardson?

RK: Lee always had his demons. He always had things with which he was dealing. We loved each other. But it got to the point where I received a call from the State Arts Council about an incident with Lee. They wanted us to know about it. His wife and I got together and did an intervention. He was good for two years. Clean. Until *The Colored Museum* went to the Public Theatre.

SMcC: **I was in it.**

RK: So, you know.

SMcC: **It felt more like George was directing me.**

RK: People were covering for him. We cover for each other because we love each other. It was a decision the board made. I couldn't get Lee to resign, to do so for the sake of his own health. And he wouldn't. So, he was terminated. We stayed in touch for a long time. And for a long time, we didn't. Until one day, Tico Wells calls.

SMcC: **My "little brother."**

RK: Everybody's little brother. Tico asked, "You have a moment?" I said, "I have a moment for you. What's up?" He said, "I have somebody else on the other line." It was Lee. In Black Theatre, we are very forgiving people anyway. At the end of the day, one of the most beautiful experiences I ever had was when the alums of Crossroads got together and invited us for Founders Day. They created a Founders Day. It was the first time I saw Lee in all those decades. I was able to walk him into the new theater we built. *That* was beautiful. That was a really beautiful thing. That meant more to me than any of those problems we had before.

CTD: **What do you do to relax?**

RK: I live on the river. I've always loved water. But when COVID hit, I didn't have a place to go anymore to write. I had to find my own studio. Here, I have the water, I also have my piano. We just got a dog a year ago, a rescue. If ever I'm really out of it and I need to relax, my dog reminds me to just chill. Chill.

SMcC: **What advice would you give to your younger self?**

RK: I would tell my younger self there's nothing more important than believing in yourself. Put yourself in situations and among people who bring you positive energy. You can always deal with people who have negative energy if you root yourself in the positive. Then go from there. I would tell my younger self, stay rooted in your ancestors and how you were raised and the gifts you have to be different from everybody else. Have the courage that is necessary to see it through, and the love that allows you to appreciate the God that's inside you as well as the gifts you have for as long as you live. That's what I would tell younger people now. Unfortunately, they're not being taught this nowadays. You have to say, "It's okay to be who you are. It's okay."

SMcC: That said, how would you describe yourself in one word?

RK: What? One word? [*He laughs.*] I could tell you that I aspire to be in the moment. But one word would be Grateful.

CTD: Grateful is a good choice.

SMcC: I have always wanted to ask, what was the "aha" moment that made you say, "Crossroads"?

RK: Our stage manager was painting a wall. Looking out the window, he saw these roads being built. He was a white stage manager, who said, "What about Crossroads?" As soon as he said it, it made so much sense. We grew up with Amiri Baraka, the Negro Ensemble Company, and the National Black Theatre. There was a clear sense of the black theatre movement. We wanted black theatre to also be appreciated by *everybody*, by *all* people. It was about the coming together of people from different backgrounds to appreciate black culture, black life, and black art. *That's* Crossroads … .

Final Thoughts

Figure Final Thoughts 1 Screen shot of Zoom Meeting.

Saundra McClain in California, and **Clinton Turner Davis** in New York

> **CTD:** Saundra, this has been a very interesting and compelling experience and collaborating with you on *Pushing Boundaries*. The interviews have provided greater insights into *all* of the directors, many of whom are good friends. I am fascinated to find that our career paths are so similar.
>
> **SMcC:** I agree. Having worked with so many of them previously as an actor, I found it most illuminating and inspiring to hear them discuss their creative processes, and how their life experiences, having grown up during turbulent times, affected their work.

CTD: So many of our mothers played a vital role in our development. They introduced us to the arts.

SMcC: My mother took me to dance classes, but it was my father who bought us a piano and took me to all types of entertainment venues and would come see me perform.

CTD: Growing up in DC, my father wanted me to come home and get a good job in the government.

SMcC: Things were different then. There weren't many opportunities for black artists in the business, let alone directors. But things are different today. There's a whole new generation of artists today who have different marching orders than we did "back in the day."

CTD: In this post-Floydian era, with the rapidly changing artistic landscape, combined with increased attention to diversity, equity, and inclusion, what are the experiences of younger directors?

SMcC: That sounds like another book … .

CTD: *Pushing Boundaries II*: this time it's personal. [*We both laugh.*]

SMcC: But seriously, we should consider a series of books about African American artists—designers, choreographers, and playwrights.

CTD: *Pushing Boundaries*: the complete collection.

SMcC: Sounds good to me. Clinton, you never mentioned why you decided to be a director.

CTD: Because I wasn't going to be a neurosurgeon or concert pianist.

SMcC: I was going to be an astronaut, but I was afraid of heights. Almost every artist I know once envisioned a career in the sciences—left-side, right-side of the brain.

CTD: Seriously, I began directing because I could combine my interests in acting, dancing, singing, puppetry, music, dance, choreography, literature, research, storytelling, stage-managing, technical theatre and design into one job description.

SMcC: So, when asked … "What do you do?"

CTD: Oh, that's easy.

CTD/SMcC: I'm a DIRECTOR … .

Biographies

SAUNDRA McCLAIN (Co-author), over four decades ago, joined the staff of *Johnny Carson's Tonight Show*. As an actor/director, she has worked in all levels of the theatre discipline, internationally and receiving critical acclaim for numerous Broadway and off-Broadway productions at such theatres as the Kennedy Center, the Shakespeare Theater in Washington, DC, Shakespeare Santa Cruz, Alliance Theater, Alley Theater, Philadelphia Drama Guild, Two River Theater, Musical Theater West, Syracuse Stage, McCarter Theatre, A.R.T., Spoleto Festival, New York Shakespeare Theatre, 2nd Stage, N.E.C., New Federal Theatre, Classic Theatre Company, Hudson Guild, Billie Holiday Theatre, Coconut Grove, A Noise Within, Ensemble Theatre Company, Colony Theatre, Virginia Stage, International Theatre Company, Antaeus Theatre Company, guest-starring and recurring on TV and film. She was awarded three CIBA Awards, nominated for three Ovation awards, two NAACP Theatre Awards, and the Los Angeles Drama Critics Circle Award for Best Lead Actor. She was co-founder of Troupe NY, and its artistic director for seven years. Presently, she is developing three new musicals, a children's book and film series, *Peepo & the Magic Talisman*. As an adjunct, she directed at Queens College, California Lutheran University, AMDA, AADA, Pomona College and California State University-Fullerton where she received her MFA in Directing. She is extremely honored to have been inducted into West Catholic High School's Hall of Fame in Philadelphia. Ms. McClain is an ensemble member of Antaeus Repertory Theater and a lifetime member of the Actors Studio. www.saundramcclain.com

OZ SCOTT is an accomplished and award-winning television, theatrical, and motion picture director. In his four decades plus years, he has directed hundreds of television episodes along with dozens of stage productions, made-for-TV movies, and motion pictures. Mr. Scott believes being well rounded is essential to achieving longevity. His versatility has allowed him to maintain his presence in the theater. In the midst of his success in New York, Norman Lear and Universal called Scott to come out to Hollywood. No stranger to success, Oz's directorial talents enhanced the success of many popular prime-time skeins. He directed the first of Disney Channel's musical franchises, *The Cheetah Girls*, for which he received a DGA Award Nomination for Outstanding Directorial Achievement. Besides the entertainment business, he is very involved in the Los Angeles Community. For seven years, he was a commissioner for Los Angeles Cultural Heritage Commission. For more than ten years, Oz was on the Board of the Charles Drew University of Medicine and Science. Oz Scott has been on the Advisory Board for Cal State Northridge College of Arts, Media, and Communication and has been very active in both of his unions, the Stage Directors and Choreographers Society (SDC) and the Directors Guild of America (DGA).

SHELDON EPPS conceived and directed the Duke Ellington musical *Play On!* which received three Tony Award nominations, and the highly acclaimed musical revue, *Blues in the Night*, also nominated for a Tony Award for Best Musical of the Year and two Laurence Olivier Awards. As artistic director of the renowned Pasadena Playhouse for two decades, he is widely credited with the rejuvenation and rebirth of that respected theatre company. During his tenure, several productions successfully transferred to Broadway, off Broadway and numerous theatres all over the country. In recognition of his work in television, he was invited to be the Pankey Chair/Filmmaker in Residence at Chapman University. Among his many honors, the NAACP Community Service Award and the prestigious James Irvine Foundation Leadership Award. He also served as Artistic Advisor for Theatre Under The Stars in Houston, Texas and is currently a Guest Lecturer at the Yale School of Drama. Mr. Epps received the coveted Alumni Achievement Award from his alma mater Carnegie-Mellon University, is a long-time member of the Executive Board of the Stage Directors and Choreographers Society

(SDC) and served as Chair of the SDC Foundation Board of Trustees. Recently he was appointed senior artistic advisor at Ford's Theater in Washington, DC.

SHIRLEY JO FINNEY (1949–2023) is an award-winning international director and actress. She has worn her director's hat in some of the most respected regional theater houses across the country. Ms. Finney has received many prestigious awards over the years for her special talent and eye for storytelling and for creating exciting ensembles. Her awards include the LA Stage Alliance Ovation Award, the Los Angeles Drama Critics Award, LA Weekly Award, the NAACP and the Santa Barbara Independent awards for her directing work. Ms. Finney is also an established television and film director. She was honored with the UCLA Department of Stage Film and Television Distinguished Alumni Award, the Black Alumni Association's Dr. Beverly Robinson Award for Excellence in the Arts, and the African American Film Marketplace Award of Achievement for Outstanding Performance and Achievement and leader in Entertainment. Ms. Finney is an alumnus of the American Film Institute's Director Workshop for Women and holds an MFA degree from UCLA. www.shirleyjofinney.com

CLINTON TURNER DAVIS (Co-author) is a director, playwright, dramaturg, production supervisor, educator, and arts consultant who has directed productions off-Broadway, and at numerous regional theaters, and universities in the United States and abroad. A noted interpreter of August Wilson, his productions have received multiple awards, including a citation from the US Senate. A recipient of the Lloyd Richards Directing Award from the National Black Theatre Festival, Mr. Davis held residencies at the University of Wisconsin, and three years at the Taipei Artist Village, and New Dramatists, among others. He was an associate professor at Colorado College for 17 years and has been a guest lecturer at numerous universities. Davis was a member of two United States delegations to the ITI World Congress and a board member of the SDC and its Foundation, AEA, ASSITEJ, New Federal Theatre, the National Black Arts Festival, and the Tony, Obie, and Drama Desk Award-winning Alliance for Inclusion in the Arts/Non-Traditional Casting Project, which he co-founded. He has worked on

Broadway, nationally and internationally as a production supervisor. A member of the Negro Ensemble Company for 16 seasons, he was associate artistic director, literary manager, casting director, dramaturg, and director. A consultant to foundations, ministries of culture, state arts agencies, and the NEA, he is a PEW/TCG National Theatre Artist and a NEA/TCG Director and Theatre Fellow.

CHUCK SMITH is a member of Goodman Theater's Board of Trustees and is Goodman Theater's resident director. His Goodman credits include the world premieres of *By the Music of the Spheres*, *The Gift Horse*, and *Objects in the Mirror*; the Chicago premieres of *Pullman Porter Blues, Race, Having Our Say, The Good Negro, Proof, The Story*, and *By the Way, Meet Vera Stark*; he directed James Baldwin's *The Amen Corner*, which transferred to Boston's Huntington Theatre Company where it won the Independent Reviewers of New England (IRNE) Award for Best Direction. He served as dramaturg for the Goodman's 2003 world-premiere production of August Wilson's *Gem of the Ocean*. He is an associate member of the American Blues Theatre Company. He won a Chicago Emmy Award as associate producer/theatrical director for the NBC teleplay *Crime of Innocence* and was theatrical director for the Emmy-winning *Fast Break to Glory* and the Emmy-nominated *The Martin Luther King Suite*. He was a founding member of the Chicago Theatre Company, where he served as artistic director for four seasons.

SERET SCOTT is a theatre director, playwright, and actress. Her directing credits include productions off-Broadway, and in regional and university theaters across the country. In 2020, Ms. Scott was honored to receive the Gordon Davidson Directing Award for Lifetime Achievement in Regional Theatre. She performed on Broadway in *For Colored Girls* and *My Sister, My Sister*, for which she received a Drama Desk Award. In 1969, Seret was a member of the Free Southern Theater, a civil rights theatre group that performed throughout rural and urban Louisiana and Mississippi addressing human and voting rights, school desegregation and income inequity. Ms. Scott was honored to shape the tribute program for the Martin Luther King, Jr. Statue on the National Mall. As a teaching artist, Ms. Scott is invited to universities and theatre forums to read from her extensive acting-directing journals.

A. DEAN IRBY is a New York City-based director, actor, and educator. In his distinguished career, which spans more than three decades, he has acted and directed on Broadway and off-Broadway, for the New York Shakespeare Festival, Negro Ensemble Company, Arena Stage, New Federal Theater, and Crossroads Theater, and at numerous regional and university theaters. He is the recipient of two AUDELCO Awards for his direction of the original production of *Home* for the Negro Ensemble Company and *Boogie Woogie and Booker T.* for the New Federal Theatre. Irby is also the former acting coach for *The Cosby Show* and has appeared in more than thirty television commercials. Mr. Irby is Associate Professor of Acting at State University of New York at Purchase.

MICHELE SHAY has 47 years of experience as an award-winning actress who also develops, directs, and produces events for education and entertainment. She has twenty years' research in the transformational aspects of acting through the study of the human energy system via various disciplines and healing modalities, and fifteen years' coaching and facilitation experience in performance preparedness and public identity design for business clients and professional artists. Known for providing artistic insight career counseling and direction to artists, script writers, major funding, and service organizations, she pursues an ongoing exploration of humanity, through ontological studies in cutting-edge philosophical, biological, and linguistic breakthroughs in understanding the role language and cognition play in generating physical and emotional experience. www.micheleshay.com

ELIZABETH VAN DYKE is an award-winning actress, director, and producer. She has received an AUDELCO Nomination for Best Director, an ONYX Award for Best Director at Kuntu Repertory Theatre, a Giorgee Award for Best Director at the Ensemble Theatre, and a Superior Award for her direction and production at Seminole State University. Ms. Van Dyke is a member of EST, a Usual Suspect at New York Theatre Workshop, and a member of the League of Professional Women in Theatre, the National Theatre Conference, the Actors' Center, the Dramatist Guild and the SDC. Elizabeth is currently the producing artistic director of Woodie King, Jr.'s New Federal Theatre, the 2021 Tony Award honoree for Excellence in Theatre. Elizabeth received a Lifetime Achievement Award for Excellence in Black Theatre from AUDELCO in 2020. www.elizabethvandyke.me

GREGG T. DANIEL most recently directed *End of the Line* by Peppur Chambers (Antaeus, Zip Code Plays, Season 2), The Road Theatre Company's season premiere of Harrison Davis Rivers, *This Bitter Earth* (recorded on multiple cameras). Other credits include August Wilson's *Gem of the Ocean* at A Noise Within theatre (2020 Ovation Nominee-Best Production of a Play), Lanie Robertson's *Lady Day at Emerson's Bar & Grill*, and Katori Hall's *The Mountaintop* at the Garry Marshall Theater, West Coast premieres of Mfoniso Udofia's *Her Portmanteau* (Boston Court Theatre), and Tearrance Arvelle Chisolm's *Br'er Cotton* (Lower Depth Theatre). With Rogue Machine, Gregg has directed Lorraine Hansberry's *Les Blancs* (Ovation-nominated, Best Director), the Los Angeles premiere of Greg Kalleres' *Honky* (nominated Best Director, Comedy), Lorraine Hansberry's *A Raisin in the Sun* at A Noise Within (Ovation nominated, Best Director) and a revival of Alice Childress' *Wedding Band: A Love/Hate Story in Black and White* with the Antaeus Company (Winner Stage Raw Award–Best Revival, Best Ensemble). Gregg is the artistic director/founding member of Lower Depth Theater (Lower-Depth.com). He is married to the actress, Veralyn Jones.

RUBEN SANTIAGO-HUDSON is a Tony Award-winning actor, and a WGA, Emmy and Golden Globe-nominated writer. As a director, Ruben has been awarded the Drama Desk, Outer Critics Circle, Lucille Lortel, Drama League, a Tony Award nomination and three Obie awards. Ruben penned the screenplay for his autobiographical film *Lackawanna Blues* for HBO, receiving numerous accolades including an NAACP Image Award and National Board Of Reviews honors, along with the Humanitas Prize and a Christopher Award. Ruben most recently penned the screenplay of August Wilson's *Ma Rainey's Black Bottom*, directed by George C. Wolfe. Ruben made his Broadway acting debut in *Jelly's Last Jam* and originated the role of Canewell in August Wilson's *Seven Guitars*, which earned him a Tony Award. Ruben directed August Wilson's *Jitney* which won the Tony for Best Revival of a play. Most recently on Broadway, Ruben directed Dominique Morriseau's *Skeleton Crew* which received four Tony nominations. In that same season, he directed his autobiographical play *Lackawanna Blues* becoming the first person in the history of Broadway to write, direct, and star in a play. Ruben received a Tony nomination for Lead Actor, as well as Outer Critics and Drama Desk Awards.

GEORGE C. WOLFE, renowned director and playwright of theatre and film, five-time Tony Award winner, has firmly established himself as one of America's most important and influential cultural voices. Wolfe most recently directed the highly anticipated, award-winning feature film adaptation of August Wilson's play *Ma Rainey's Black Bottom*, starring Viola Davis and Chadwick Boseman for Netflix. A master storyteller, Wolfe first gained critical acclaim in 1986 for his penning of the off-Broadway production of *The Colored Museum*, a series of vignettes exploring different aspects of the African American experience that electrified audiences and established him as a bold new voice in the American theatre. In 1990, Wolfe's adaptation and direction of *Spunk*, based on three short stories from Pulitzer Prize-winning author Zora Neale Hurston, garnered him an Obie Award for Best Off-Broadway Director and cemented his position as one of Broadway's visionary writer/directors. In 1991, he directed the musical, *Jelly's Last Jam*, which resulted in eleven Tony nominations, Best Book of a Musical and Best Direction of a Musical, and a Drama Desk Award. In 1993, he helmed the Pulitzer Prize-winning *Angels In America—Millennium Approaches*, for which he would win his first of five Tony Awards, and its follow-up production *Angels in America: Perestroika*. In 1996, Wolfe garnered his second Tony Award for *Bring In 'da Noise, Bring in 'da Funk*, a musical which he conceived, produced, and directed.

RICARDO KHAN, director, writer, educator, and Tony Award-winning artistic director, co-founded the Crossroads Theatre Company, one of history's few African American theatres to ever rise to both national and international prominence as a major professional arts institution. For two decades, Khan nurtured and guided the creation of well over a hundred new works that have forever enriched the American theatre canon, while launching countless artistic careers. In 1999, he accepted the Tony Award for Outstanding Regional Theatre in America, making Crossroads the first black theatre company in history to ever receive that honor. Khan himself pursued and founded the World Theatre Lab, a multi-national writers' collective based simultaneously in Johannesburg, London, and New York, which is still active to this day. Khan's plays, *FLY* and *Satchel Paige and the Kansas City Swing*, have also received critical acclaim over the years. One of Ricardo Khan's most high-profile achievements was in service to the Smithsonian's new National Museum of African American History and Culture, where in 2013 he began a multi-year appointment, first as creative consultant, and then as the producer and director for the museum's highly acclaimed opening night gala ceremonies that were held in multiple venues on the National Mall in Washington, DC.

Glossary and Works Cited

Glossary

Actors Equity Association / AEA / EQUITY
Equity, or AEA, was founded in 1913. With over 51,000 members, including actors, dancers, singers, and stage managers, Equity advances the careers of its members by negotiating wages, improving working conditions, and providing a wide range of benefits, including health and pension plans.
https://www.actorsequity.org/

ASSITEJ
The International Association of Theatre for Children and Young People is dedicated to the artistic, cultural, and educational rights of children and young people around the world. ASSITEJ shares information and knowledge to enhance the practice of theatre, create new opportunities for individual artists, theatres, and organizations regardless of nationality, cultural identity, ability, gender, sexual orientation, ethnicity, or religion.
https://www.assitej-international.org/en/

AUDELCO
Founded in 1993 AUDELCO (Audience Development Committee, Inc.) acknowledges and honors black artists in New York City and stimulates interest in and support of performing arts in black communities. AUDELCO offers many services to its members by creating and supporting relationships with individuals, local groups,

churches, and other organizations to introduce new audiences to non-profit performing arts.

www.audelco.org

Black Theatre Festival

The National Black Theatre Festival (NBTF) presents a week of performances by national and international theatre artists and companies bi-yearly in Winston Salem, NC. Through full productions, workshops, films, colloquia, and other programming, the NBTF showcases the exceptional talent s of performers, designers, directors, technicians, and producers from across the country and abroad. Founded in 1989 and hosted by the North Carolina Black Repertory Company, the NBTF is the largest festival of black theatre in the country.

ncblackrep.org/about-nbtf/

CESD

Cunningham-Escott-Slevin-Doherty, a talent agency based in Los Angeles, was founded by Bill Cunningham.

CETA Program

The Comprehensive Employment and Training Act was a US Federal law enacted by the Congress 1973 to train workers and provide them with jobs in the public service. The program offered work to the long-term unemployed and people with low incomes, as well as summer jobs to low-income high school students. Through CETA, participants developed marketable skills that would help them make the transition to unsubsidized jobs. The program was an extension of the Works Progress Administration programs of the 1930s.

DGA

Representing the creative and economic rights of directors and members of directorial teams working in film, television, and commercials, the Directors Guild of America is a labor organization that through the collective voice of more than 19,000 protects its members' legal and artistic rights, contends for their creative freedom, and strengthens their ability to develop and sustain meaningful and credible careers.

https://www.dga.org/

Glossary and Works Cited

Dundun

A dundun is an hourglass-shaped, rope-tuned cylindrical drum with a rawhide drumskin of cow or goat. The drum is played with a stick with the drum held against one's side as the arm squeezes and releases the ropes of the drum. By playing the "talking drum," the drummer imitates spoken language's intonations and rhythms. The drum is frequently used in African rituals.

Eshu

Often called Elegba or Legba, Eshu is the trickster *orisha*, or god of the Yoruba people of Nigeria and often present in Afro-Caribbean culture. A benevolent, protective unpredictable spirit who is fond of pranks, Eshu is often cruel and disruptive. Possessing knowledge of all languages spoken on earth, Eshu is the messenger between heaven and earth.

HBCU

Historically Black Colleges and Universities are institutions of higher learning established prior to the Civil Rights Act of 1964, primarily serving African Americans. Most of these colleges and universities were founded during the Reconstruction era in the United States.

Juba

A lively dance characterized by rhythmic hand clapping, body and thigh slapping, and stomping, Juba came from dances in Africa (where it was called Giouba) and Haiti (known as Djouba), and developed by African Americans enslaved on Southern plantations in the nineteenth century.

The Links

Established in 1946, The Links is a not-for-profit, international volunteer service organization committed to sustaining and ensuring the culture and economic survival of African Americans and people of African ancestry.
https://linksinc.org/

LORT Theaters

League of Resident Theatres is the largest professional theatre association in the United States. Its member theatres issue more Equity contracts to actors than Broadway and commercial tours combined. LORT is a forum for sharing information regarding all aspects of theatre. LORT's by-laws provide a succinct overview of its mission which includes promoting the general welfare of resident theatres,

establishing and maintaining stable and equitable labor relations between its members and unions representing employees of its members, and providing guidance and assistance to its members in administering collective bargaining agreements.
https://lort.org/

NEA

The National Endowment for the Arts, an independent federal agency authorized and funded by Congress, promotes, funds, and strengthens the creative capacity of communities throughout the country and provides diverse opportunities for arts participation.
https://www.arts.gov/

NEH

The National Endowment for the Humanities is an independent federal agency authorized and funded by Congress, promotes excellence in the humanities through funding of cultural institutions such as museums, archives, libraries, colleges, universities, public television and radio stations, and individual scholars.
https://www.neh.gov/

O'Neill Playwrights Conference

The O'Neill Theatre Center, founded in 1964 by George C. White, is the country's preeminent organization dedicated to the development of new works and new voices for the stage. Through its many programs including National Puppetry Conference, National Musical Theatre Conference, National Playwrights Conference, Cabaret and Performance Conference, National Critics Institute, Young Playwrights Festival, and Residences, the O'Neill Theatre Center, is often referred to as "the Launchpad of American Theater."
www.theoneill.org

Obie Awards

Created by the *Village Voice* newspaper in 1955, the Obie Awards give recognition to the work of off-Broadway and off-off Broadway theatre artists and companies.
https://www.obieawards.com/

SAG-AFTRA

Through a merger of the Screen Actors Guild and the American Federation of Television and Radio Artists, SAG-AFTRA was created to represent media professionals throughout the country.

Its members work to secure the strongest protections for media artists by negotiating the best wages, working conditions, health and pension benefits, and vigorously to enforce contracts. The union also protects its members against unauthorized use of their work throughout all media distribution platforms.

https://www.sagaftra.org/

SDC

The Stage Directors and Choreographers Society, formerly called the SSDC-Society of Stage Directors and Choreographers is a theatrical society that secures and protects the interests of professional stage directors and choreographers by negotiating and enforcing employment agreements across a range of jurisdictions including Broadway, off-Broadway, National Tours, LORT, Non-Profit Theatre in New York City, Resident Stock Theatres, Dinner Theatre, Regional Music Theatre, Outdoor Musical Theatre, and through its Special Contract agreement, theatrical presentations not covered in its other contractual areas.

https://sdcweb.org/

SDC Foundation

The Foundation is the professional educational extension of the SDC and provides opportunities to practice the crafts of directing and choreography, promotes emerging artists and provides a forum for the exchange of knowledge about the craft.

https://sdcfoundation.org/

Works cited

Beyond Tradition: Transcripts of the First National Symposium on Non-Traditional Casting, edited by Clinton Turner Davis and Harry Newman. Non-Traditional Casting Project. 1988. ISBN: 0927340003.

The Drama of Nommo: Black Theatre in the African Continuum by Paul Carter Harrison.

In this seminal work, Harrison explores the concept of *Nommo*, an aesthetic for theatre, daily life and literature that is grounded in a black world view and strengthens the authentic expressions of African cultural expressions throughout the diaspora. Grove Press, 1973. ISBN 0394177770.

My Own Directions: A Black Man's Journey in the American Theatre **by Sheldon Epps**

Sheldon Epps' highly personal memoir of how he changed the trajectory of the Pasadena Playhouse by making diversity throughout the institution an essential component of the theatre's mission. Epps' memoir provides a distinctive voice on the realities that ethnic artists often encounter in the American theatre. McFarland & Company, 2022. ISBN: 9781476688589.

Seven Black Plays: The Theodore Ward Prize for African American Playwriting, **edited by Chuck Smith**

A collection of Theodore Ward Prize award-winning African American plays produced by the theatre department of Columbia College. Northwestern University Press, 2004. ISBN: 0810120453.

Viewpoints **by Anne Bogart**

Viewpoints is a text that explores and creates a language of improvisation techniques adapted from the world of postmodern dance; it examines the relationship and use of space and time by actors and directors to create moving theatrical work. Theatre Communications Group, 2004. ISBN: 0873388283.

Index

Abercrombie Apocalypse: Clinton Turner Davis director 67–68; Paul Carter Harrison writer 67–68
Actors Equity Association (AEA) 29, 70, 72, 208, 213
Africans in America 5
Ain't Misbehavin': Ricardo Khan director 193
Ain't Supposed to Die a Natural Death: Melvin Van Peebles actor 180; Shirley Jo Finney actor 52
Aladdin 154
Alice in Wonderland 51, 91
Alley Theater 208
Alliance Theatre 85, 208
Amen Corner, The: Chuck Smith director 208; James Baldwin writer 208
American Blues Theatre 90
American Blues Theatre Company 208
American Place Theatre 93
American Society of Composers, Authors, and Publishers (ASCAP) 5
Androcles and the Lion 156
Angels in America: George C. Wolfe director 174–175, 211
Anna: Charles Dumas writer 93; Seret Smith director 93
ANTA Theatre 16
Antaeus Theatre Company 146, 205
Antigone: Seret Smith director 97
ASCAP *see* American Society of Composers, Authors, and Publishers
ASSITEJ (International Association of Theatre for Children and Young People) 213
AUDELCO (Audience Development Committee, Inc.) 213; awards A. Dean Irby 206; awards Michele Shay 125;

nominations Eliabeth Van Dyke 207

Bacchae, The: A. Dean Irby director 111
Bachelor of Fine Arts (BFA), Clinton Turner Davis 66
Back Alley Theatre 17
Ballad for Bimshire: Loften Mitchell writer 156
Ballad of Emmett Till: Ifa Bayeza 25
Battle Creek Civic Theatre 159
Bee-luther-hatchee: Saundra McClain director 11
Beyond Tradition: Transcripts of the First National Symposium on Non-Traditional Casting 72, 215
BFA *see* Bachelor of Fine Arts
Billie Holiday Theatre 4, 125
Billy Rose Theatre 172
BIPOC (Black, Indigenous, and people of color): Elizabeth Van Dyke 136; Greg Daniel 150; Ruben Santiago-Hudson 169
Bitter Earth, The: Gregg T. Daniel director 210
Black American Theatre 66
Black Eagles: Ricardo Khan director 188, 192
Black Girl: Clinton Turner Davis 65; J. E. Franklin 1, 3–4; Saundra McClain director 1
Black Picture Show, The: Oz Scott stage manager 20
Black Theatre Workshop 7, 184
Blue Stockings: Jessica Swale writer 116–117, 125; Michele Shay actor 116–117; Michele Shay director 123, 125–126
Blues for an Alabama Sky: Michele Shay actor 121; Pearl Cleage writer 121
Blues for Mr. Charlie, A. Dean Irby actor 105
Blues in the Night: Sheldon Epps director 38, 206
BMI Musical Theatre Workshop 5
Boesman and Lena: Elizabeth Van Dyke actor 133
Boogie Woogie and Booker T: A. Dean Irby director 209
Boston Court Theatre 210
Br'er Cotton: Gregg T. Daniel actor 210; Tearrance Arvelle Chisolm writer 210
Bring in 'da Noise, Bring in 'da Funk: George Wolfe director 172, 211
Bubbling Brown Sugar: Loften Mitchell writer 156; Ricardo Khan director 193
Busting Loose: Oz Scott stage manager 20; Oz Scott writer 22
But I Was Cool: A. Dean Irby actor 104
By the Music of the Spheres: Chuck Smith director 208
By the Way, Meet Vera Stark: Chuck Smith director 208; Elizabeth Van Dyke director 136; Lynn Nottage writer 136

CAG *see* Community Action Group

Camelot 130
Capital Repertory Theatre 178
Car Wash: Ruben Santiago-Hudson director 165
Career Paths of Eight Contemporary Black Directors, The: Saundra McClain thesis 3, 14
Caribe: Saundra McClain writer 5
Cat on a Hot Tin Roof: James Earl Jones 19
Celebration: Saundra McClain actress 4
Central Avenue: Shirley Jo Finney producer 50
CESD *see* Cunningham-Escott-Slevin-Doherty
CETA (Comprehensive Employment and Training Act) 212; Ricardo Khan 185–186
Chairs, The: Eugène Ionesco writer 156
Chanticleer International Book Awards (CIBA), Saundra McClain 208
Cheetah Girls: Oz Scott director 22, 206
Cherry Lane Theatre 7, 68
Chicago Theatre Company 79, 88; Chuck Smith founder 208
Chorus Line, A: Robin Wagner designer 175
Christmas Carol, A: Chuck Smith director 87
Christmas Party Crashers: Sheldon Epps director 49
CIBA *see* Chanticleer International Book Awards

Cincinnati Playhouse 158
Citizen: Claudia Rankine writer 59; Shirley Jo Finney director 59
Civil War Christmas: Elizabeth Van Dyke director 137; Paula Vogel 137
Classic Theatre Company 205
Clinton: Saundra McClain director 4
Coffee House: A. Dean Irby producer 103
Colony Theatre 8, 208
Colored Museum, The: George C. Wolfe writer 7, 172–174, 176–177, 211; Lee Ricardson 200–201; Ricardo Khan director 200–201
Colored Water: Erika Dickerson-Despenza writer 139
Community Action Group (CAG) 105
Conversations in Exile: Bertolt Brecht writer 154; Ruben Santiago-Hudson actor 154
Coriolanus: Gloria Foster actor 115–116
Cosby Show, The: A. Dean Irby acting coach 209
Crime of Innocence: Chuck Smith director 208
Crossroads Theatre 176, 209
Crossroads Theatre Company 186, 209
CSI New York: Oz Scott director 25–27
Cullud Wattah: Karen D. Jones director 140

Cunningham-Escott-Slevin-Doherty (CESD) talent agency 7, 214

Daily News 107
Dame Lorraine: Chuck Smith director 82
Dance Theatre of Harlem 70
Dancing at Lughnasa: A. Dean Irby director 112
Dancing Lessons: Saundra McClain director 8
Dark of the Moon: Saundra McClain director 4
Dashiki Project Theatre 103
Daubers, The: Chuck Smith director 81; Theodore Ward writer 81
Daughters of the Mock: Judi Ann Mason writer 115
Death of a Salesman: Troupe NY, Inc. (TNY) 6
Denver Center Theatre Company 96
Destiny of Desire: Karen Zacarias writer 161; Ruben Santiago-Hudson director 161, 164–165
Director Prepares, The: Anne Bogart writer 146
Directors Guild of America (DGA) 28–29, 34, 214; award nominations, Oz Scott 203; rules 34
Divine Comedy: Clinton Turner Davis director 67; Owen Dodson writer 67
Don't Bother Me I Can't Cope: Ricardo Khan director 189, 193
Don't See My Bones and Think I am Dead: Saundra McClain producer 10; Saundra McClain writer 5
Down by the River All by Yo'self 139
Drama of Nommo: Paul Carter Harrison 73–74
Dream on Monkey Mountain: Derek Walcott writer 186; Ricardo Khan director 186
Dreamgirls: Robin Wagner designer 175–176
dundun 74, 213
Dutchman: Oz Scott actor/director 16

Ebony Repertory Theatre 113
Echo Theatre Company 144
Echoes of Us: Michele Shay director 120
Eden: Chuck Smith director 81–82; Steve Carter writer 81
El Hajj Malik: N. R. Davidson, Jr. writer 103
Electra, Saundra McClain director 7
Electra, Trojan Women: Seret Smith director 97
Elegba *see* Eshu
Emmet Till: Shirley Jo Finney director 60–61
"Encores" 195
End of the Line: Gregg T. Daniel director 210; Peppur Chambers writer 210
Ensemble Studio Theatre 136, 139
Ensemble Theatre 207

Ensemble Theatre Company 8–9, 209
Equity *see* Actors Equity Association
Eshu 95, 215
ETC *see* European Theatre Convention
European Theatre Convention (ETC) 8
Experimental Theatre 4

Fantasticks, The: Oz Scott actor 16; Saundra McClain director 8
Fast Break to Glory: Chuck Smith director 208
Fault Lines: Clinton Turner Davis developer 76
FCC *see* Federal Communications Commission
Fear Itself: Eugene Lee writer 154; Ruben Santiago-Hudson actor 154
Federal Communications Commission (FCC) 156
Fences: August Wilson writer 191; John Kani 195; Michele Shay director 123; Ricardo Khan director 187–191; Skip Mercier designer 24
Finian's Rainbow 182
First Breeze of Summer, The: Lee Ricardson director 186; Leslie Lee writer 161, 186; Ruben Santiago-Hudson director 161
First Militant Minister, The: Ruben Santiago-Hudson actor 156

Fly: Clinton Turner Davis director 178; Ricardo Khan writer 178, 188–190, 211
Flying West: Pearl Cleage writer 191; Ricardo Khan director 191–192
For Colored Girls Who Have Considered Suicide When the Rainbow Is Enuf: Ntozake Shange 15, 22; Oz Scott director 22, 24, 31–32; Seret Scott actor 98, 206
Ford's Theatre 38, 47, 192, 207
Fountain Theatre 50, 57, 60
Frankie and Johnny in the Clare de Lune: Saundra McClain director 8
Free Southern Theatre 93, 98, 103, 208
Freedom Rider: Ricardo Khan director 189–190, 197
Fundamentals of Play Directing: Lawrence Carra 118–119, 124
Funny Girl: Ricardo Khan actor 181

Garry Marshall Theater 210
Garvin Theatre 10
Geffen Theatre 30
Gem of the Ocean: August Wilson writer 210, 211; Chuck Smith dramaturg 87, 208; Gregg T. Daniel actor 148, 210; Ruben Santiago-Hudson actor 159; Ruben Santiago-Hudson director 160
George Street Playhouse 186

Gift Horse, The: Chuck Smith director 208; Lydia Diamond writer 83
Gloria: Brandon Jacob Jenkins writer 120; Michele Shay director 120
Goin' Thru Changes: Michelle Shay actor 115; Richard Wesley writer 115
Going to the River Festival 139
Golden Leaf Ragtime Blues: Chuck Smith director 90
Gong Lum Legacy: Charles L. White writer 137; Elizabeth Van Dyke director 137–139
Good Negro, The: Chuck Smith director 208
Goodman Theatre 25, 79–80, 84, 86, 208
Graduation Night: Oz Scott director 31
Great Men of Gospel: Elizabeth Van Dyke director 138
Grls (Pt1): Bleu Burrell Beckord writer 136; Elizabeth Van Dyke director 136, 141
Guthrie Theatre 126
Guthrie Theatre Company 124
Guys and Dolls: Saundra McClain actress 3
Gypsy: Arthur Lawrence writer 175

Hair: Seret Smith actor 98
Hamlet: Cleavon Little actor 174; Joe Papp director 174
Hand is on the Gate, A: Roscoe Lee Brown 16
Harriet Returns: Saundra McClain writer 7
Having Our Say: Chuck Smith director 208
HBCU *see* Historically Black Colleges and Universities
HBO *see* Home Box Office
Headhunters: A. Dean Irby director 110; Herbie Hancock writer 110
Hello Dolly 178, 180, 183; Pearl Baily actor 174; Ricardo Khan actor 181
Her Portmanteau: Gregg T. Daniel actor 210; Mfoniso Udofia writer 210
Historically Black Colleges and Universities (HBCU) 213
HMS *Pinafore* 179
Home: A. Dean Irby director 206; Ruben Santiago-Hudson actor 158; Samm Art-Williams writer 115
Home Box Office (HBO) 210
Honky: Gregg Kalleres 210; Gregg T. Daniel director 210
How to Succeed in Business: Ricardo Khan actor 181
Huntington Theatre Company 208

I Hear a Symphony: Diana Ross 182
Immodest Acts: Clinton Turner Davis writer 77
Importance of Being Earnest, The: Gregg Daniel actor 145

Impressions of a Loud Reader: Shirley Jo Finney actor 54
In the Continuum: Saundra McClain director 8
In the Upper Room: Beaufield Barry writer 151; Gregg Daniel actor 151
In White America: Gloria Foster actor 115; Shirley Jo Finney actor 52
In the Wine Time: A. Dean Irby actor 105–106; Ed Bullins writer 105
Independent Reviewers of New England (IRN) 208
Inherit the Wind: Jerome Lawrence and Robert E. Lee writers 82
International City Theatre 8
International Theatre Company 205
International Theatre Institute (ITI) World Congress 207
Intimate Apparel: Saundra McClain director 8; Saundra McClain producer 10; Sheldon Epps 46
Invisible Theatre 135
Ira Aldridge Theatre 65
IRN *see* Independent Reviewers of New England
It Bees That Way: Ruben Santiago-Hudson actor 156

Jamaica 91
Jelly's Last Jam: George Wolfe director 172, 175–176, 209; Robin Wagner designer 175–176; Ruben Santiago-Hudson actor 210
Jesus Christ Lawd T'day: Clinton Turner Davis actor 66
Jitney: August Wilson author 168, 210–211; Ruben Santiago-Hudson director 168, 210
Joburg Theatre 191
Joe Turner's Come and Gone: August Wilson writer 74; Chuck Smith producer 88; Clinton Turner Davis director 74
Johnny Carson's Tonight Show: Saundra McClain actress 3, 205
Juba 75, 215
Jumpers: Tom Stoppard writer 156

Kennedy Center 7
Kennedy Center American College Theatre Festival Awards 9
Kennie Playhouse 88
Kièu: Clinton Turner Davis developer 76
King and I, The 182: Seret Scott actor 92
Kirk Douglas Theatre 59
Ku Klux Klan (KKK) 112
Kuntu Repertory Theatre 209

LA Actors Theatre 55
La Gente: Oz Scott stage manager 19
LA Times, The 54
Lackawanna Blues: Ruben Santiago-Hudson writer/director 164, 210–211

Lady Day at Emerson's Bar and Grill: Gregg T. Daniel actor 147, 210; Lanie Robertson writer 210

Land Beyond the River: Loften Mitchell writer 156

Lark Theatre 7

Last Man, The: Saundra McClain actress 3

League of Resident Theaters (LORT) 72, 215–216; Equity Agreement 72

Legba *see* Eshu

Lena Horne: The Lady and Her Music: Clinton Turner Davis production supervisor 68–69; Veronica Claypool 68

Les Blancs: Gregg T. Daniel director 207

Letters from Freedom Summer: Ricardo Khan director 190

Li'l Abner: Oz Scott actor 16

Links, The, Camden County Trail 183, 215

Lion King The 193

Living Six Feet Apart: Saundra McClain director 9

Long Wharf Theatre 94

LORT *see* League of Resident Theaters

Love to All, Lorraine: Elizabeth Van Dyke actor 134–135

Lower Depth Theatre 143, 207

Lower Depth Theatre Company 149

Lucille Lortel Theatre 65

Ma Rainey's Black Bottom: August Wilson writer 210; Chuck Smith director 85, 87; George C. Wolfe director 211; Ruben Santiago-Hudson writer 210

McCarter Theatre 159, 208

Madame Butterfly: Oz Scott 26

Main Street Playhouse 8

Man of La Mancha 16

Manhattan Theatre Club 26, 192

Marat Sade 16

Mark Twain: Hal Holbrook writer 16

Market Theatre 194

Martin Luther King Suite, The: Chuck Smith director 208

Master of Fine Arts (MFA): A. Dean Irby 105; Clinton Turner Davis 66, 69; George C. Wolfe 173; Ricardo Khan 185; Saundra McClain 8, 208; Shirley Jo Finney 53, 204; students 184

Matrix Theatre 117

Meet Vera Stark: Chuck Smith director 208

Meeting, The: Shirley Jo Finney director 55

Merry Wives of Windsor: Oz Scott stage manager 20

MFA *see* Master of Fine Arts

Middle Passage, The: Avery Brooks director 184–185; Ricardo Khan production stage manager 184–185

Mikado, The: Gilbert and Sullivan 179

Military Occupational Specialty (MOS) 104

Mio: Saundra McClain director 4
Miss Maude: Sheldon Epps director 49
Moesha: Shirley Jo Finney actor 54
Monkey's Paw, The: Skylark Players 79
MOS *see* Military Occupational Specialty
Mountaintop, The: Gregg T. Daniel actor 210; Katori Hall author 210
MPAACT (Ma'at Production Association of Afrikan Centered Theatre) 84
Musical Theatre Workshop 5
My Fair Lady 130; Ricardo Khan actor 181
My Own Directions: A Black Man's Journey in the American Theatre, Sheldon Epps writer 42–43
My Sister, My Sister: Ray Aranha writer 91; Seret Scott actor 91, 98, 206
Mystery of Phyllis Wheatley, The: Ed Bullins writer 135; Elizabeth Van Dyke director 135

National Association for the Advancement of Colored People (NAACP): award Shirley Jo Finney 204; Community Service Award Sheldon Epps 206; Image Award Ruben Santiago-Hudson 210; Theatre Award Saundra McClain 205
National Black Theatre 184, 199, 202; Ricardo Khan 184–185, 199, 202
National Black Theatre Festival (NBTF) 214; Clinton Turner Davis 207
National Broadcasting Company (NBC): Chuck Smith 208; Saundra McClain 3
National Endowment for the Arts (NEA) 216; Clinton Turner Davis 69–70, 207
National Endowment for the Humanities (NEH) 69, 216
Negro Ensemble Company (NEC) 67; A. Dean Irby 106–107; Clinton Turner Davis 67–68; Michele Shay 128; Ruben Santiago-Hudson 157
Nevada Conservatory Theatre 76
Nevis Mountain Dew: Chuck Smith director 82
New Federal Theatre 24, 67, 130, 135, 138, 141, 199, 205
New Theatre of Brooklyn 154
New York Shakespeare Theatre 209
New York Theatre 209
New York Times 59, 170
New York University (NYU): A. Dean Irby 103–106; Elizabeth Van Dyke 131, 133; George C. Wolfe 173–175; Michele Shay 116, 120, 123, 126; Oz Scott 16–17, 19–20, 23–24, 105; Ricardo Khan 192
New Yorker 147

Night Thoreau Spent in Jail, The: Chuck Smith actor 82; Jerome Lawrence and Robert E. Lee writers 82
Noise Within, A 8
Nommo 52–53, 57
Non-Traditional Casting Project, The 72
Nowhere to Run, Nowhere to Hide: A. Dean Irby director 107, 110; Herman Johnson writer 107, 110
NYU *see* New York University

Oak and Ivy: Shirley Jo Finney director 58
Obie Awards 70, 214
Objects in the Mirror: Chuck Smith director 205
Of Ebony Embers: Saundra McClain writer 7
Old Globe Theatre 47, 161
Old Settler, The: Elizabeth Van Dyke director 135; John Henry Redwood 135
Oliver, Ricardo Khan actor 181
O'Neill Playwrights Conference 216; Michele Shay 126; Oz Scott 18, 20–21, 24; Seret Scott 95
ONYX Award for Best Director, Elizabeth Van Dyke 209
Open Theatre 111
Oprah Winfrey Theatre 195
Orisha 74–75
Ornette: A. Dean Irby director 108–110; Clay Goss writer 108
Orpheum Theatre 106
Orpheus Descending: A. Dean Irby director 111–112; Tennessee Williams writer 111
Our Lan': Theodore Ward writer 81, 157

Pasadena Playhouse 38, 40–42, 45, 48, 206
PBS *see* Public Broadcasting Service
Pecong, Steve Carter writer 82
Peepo and the Magic Talisman: Saundra McClain writer 5, 205
Personality: Sheldon Epps director 49
Phonograph, The: Loften Mitchell writer 156
Planet Meatball 34
Play On: André De Shields director 198; Sheldon Epps director 38, 206
Play That Goes Wrong, The: Saundra McClain director 10, 12
Playhouse on the Green 7
Post Black: Regina Taylor writer 139
Prodigal Sister: Saundra McClain actress 4
Proof: Chuck Smith director 208
Public Broadcasting Service (PBS) 5
Public Theatre 5, 19, 27, 66–67, 99, 106, 140, 158, 170, 172, 201
Puerto Rican Traveling Theatre 158

Pulman Porter Blue, Chuck Smith director 208
Puppetplay: Clinton Turner Davis director 67–68; Pearl Cleage writer 67–68, 91; Seret Scott actor 91
Pure Confidence: Carlyle Brown 88; Chuck Smith producer 88
Purlie, Ricardo Khan director 183, 186
Pushing Boundaries, Saundra McClain writer 1, 14

Qualifying list (QL) 29
Quarantine Memoirs, The: Saundra McClain writer 8–9
Queenie Pie: George C. Wolfe writer 7, 172, 174

Race: Chuck Smith director 208
Raisin: Ricardo Khan director 186; Ruben Santiago-Hudson director 159
Raisin in the Sun, A: Elizabeth Van Dyke director 140–141; Gregg Daniel director 144, 210; Lorraine Hansberry writer 210; Robert O'Hara writer 140, 179–180
Real Thing, The: Sheldon Epps director 40; Tom Stoppard writer 40
Reclamation of Madison Hemming, The: Charles Smith 90; Chuck Smith director 90
Reparations: James Sheldon writer 125; Michele Shay director 125

Ride or Die: Chuck Smith director 83; Reggie Lawrence writer 83
River Niger, The: A. Dean Irby actor 106–107; Shirley Jo Finney actor 62
Road Theatre Company 210
Romeo and Juliet, Ricardo Khan actor 184
Royal Hunt of the Sun 16
R.U.R. (Rossumovi Univerzální Roboti), Oz Scott actor 16

Safehouse: Seret Scott writer 99
SAG-AFTRA *see* Screen Actors Guild and the American Federation of Television and Radio Artists
Saint James Theatre 178
Sanford Arms: Teddy Wilson actor 17
Sarafina 193
Satchel Paige and the Kansas City Swing: Ricardo Khan director 211–212
Scoop USA: Sonny Driver entertainments manager 184
Screen Actors Guild and the American Federation of Television and Radio Artists (SAGAFTRA) 27, 216–217
Seven Black Plays: Chuck Smith 83, 87, 218
Seven Guitars: August Wilson writer 115, 210; Michele Shay director 119, 127; Ruben Santiago-Hudson actor 154,

210–211; Ruben Santiago-Hudson director 161
1776: Peter Stone writer 175
Shadow Box, The 156
Shadow, The 35
Sheila's Day: Ricardo Khan director 188, 193
Sidney: Ruben Santiago-Hudson director 161, 165, 167
Sierra Madre Playhouse 8
Sierra Madre Theatre 11
Signature Theatre 161
Signifying Monkey: A. Dean Irby actor 104
60 minutes 27
Sizwe Banzi is Dead: Ricardo Khan actor 185
Skeleton Crew: Dominique Morriseau writer 209; Ruben Santiago-Hudson director 210–211
Skylark Players: *Monkey's Paw, The* 79
Slaughterhouse Play: Clinton Turner Davis actor 66; Richard Voss director 66; Susan Yankowitz writer 66
Slave Ship: Seret Scott actor 93
Socrates: Tim Blake Nelson writer 112
Soldier's Play, A: Clinton Turner Davis stage manager 68; Ruben Santiago-Hudson actor 154, 157–158
Split Second: Michele Shay actor 128
Spring Awakening: Michele Shay director 121; Saundra McClain producer 10

Spunk: George C. Wolfe writer/director 12, 173, 211; Saundra McClain producer 6, 12
Stage Directors and Choreographers (SDC) 7, 27–30, 34, 135, 217; Clinton Turner Davis 207–208; Elizabeth Van Dyke 209–210; Oz Scott 206; Sheldon Epps 206; 217–218
Stage Directors and Choreographers (SDC) Foundation 206, 217
Star of the Morning: Loften Mitchell writer 156
Star Trek 33
State Theatre 174
Storm Warning: Saundra McClain writer 5
Story, The: Chuck Smith director 208
Studio Arena Theatre 154
Stuff: Oz Scott director 31
Sty of the Blind Pig: Clinton Turner Davis actor 67; Philip Hayes Dean writer 67; Shauneille Perry director 67
SWAT: Oz Scott director 22
Sweat: Chuck Smith producer 88; Lynn Nottage writer 88
Sweet Charity: Ricardo Khan actor 181
Syracuse Stage 208

Taiyuan Puppet Theatre 77
Tale of Kiều, The: Nguyễn Du writer 76

TCG *see* Theatre Communications Group
Ten, The: Ruben Santiago-Hudson director 161, 165
Theatre Communications Group (TCG): Clinton Turner Davis 208; Ricardo Khan 194, 199
Theatre De Lys 1, 4, 65
Theatre Four 68, 158
Theatre Royal Stratford East 194
Theatre for Social Change 11
Theatre Under The Stars 204
Thimble of Smoke, A: Gregg Daniel actor 144
Ti-jean and his Brother 132
Tiger, Tiger Burning Bright: A. Dean Irby producer 102
TNY *see* Troupe NY, Inc.
Township Theatre 193
Tribune 88
Troupe NY, Inc. (TNY) 6; *Death of a Salesman* 6; Saundra McClain 6
24th Street Theatre 144–145
Two River Theatre 6–8, 13, 208
Two Trains Running: Michele Shay director 117–118

Ujima Theatre 157
University of California, Santa Barbara (UCSB) 60
University of Southern California (USC) School of Dramatic Arts: Gregg Daniel 145, 152; Michele Shay 121
Urban Youth Theatre 4–5

Victory Gardens Theatre 81–82
Viewpoints, Anne Bogart 122, 146, 218
Village Voice 107
Virginia Stage 208

Wedding Band: A Love/Hate Story in Black and White: Alice Childress writer 119, 124; Awoye Tempo director 141; Gregg T. Daniel director 207; Michele Shay director 119, 124, 126
West Side Story: A. Dean Irby actor 104–105; Arthur Lawrence writer 27, 174–175
WGA *see* Writers Guild of America
What the Winesellers Buy: Ricardo Khan production stage manager 184; Ron Milner writer 184
Whatever Happened to Vera Starks: Chuck Smith director 82
When the Chickens Come Home to Roost: Elizabeth Van Dyke director 134
When Day Comes: Ricardo Khan director 196
Who's Afraid of Virginia Woolf?: Gregg Daniel actor 144
Wilma, Shirley Jo Finney actor 62
Winnie, Shirley Jo Finney director 55
WOKS (radio station) 105
Women of Plums: Dolores Kendrick writer 115; Michele Shay actor 115; Saundra McClain actor 115

Works Progress Administration (WPA) Program 185
World Theatre Lab 194, 212
Writers Guild of America (WGA), Ruben Santiago-Hudson 210–211

You Can't Take It With You: Kaufman and Hart writers 101–102

Zora: Elizabeth Van Dyke actor 134

For Product Safety Concerns and Information please contact our EU
representative GPSR@taylorandfrancis.com
Taylor & Francis Verlag GmbH, Kaufingerstraße 24, 80331 München, Germany

www.ingramcontent.com/pod-product-compliance
Lightning Source LLC
Chambersburg PA
CBHW071825300426
44116CB00009B/1443